T0305261

BROADCASTING MODERNITY

CONSOLE-ING PASSIONS

Television and Cultural Power

Edited by Lynn Spigel

BROADCASTING
MODERNITY

Cuban Commercial Television,

1950–1960

YEIDY M. RIVERO

Duke University Press

Durham and London

2015

Printed in Great Britain by TJ International Ltd, Padstow, Cornwall
Designed by Amy Ruth Buchanan
Typeset in Minion Pro by Copperline

Library of Congress Cataloging-in-Publication Data
Rivero, Yeidy M.
Broadcasting modernity: Cuban commercial television,
1950-1960 / Yeidy M. Rivero.
pages cm—(Console-ing passions)
Includes bibliographical references and index.
ISBN 978-0-8223-5859-6 (hardcover : alk. paper)
ISBN 978-0-8223-5871-8 (pbk. : alk. paper)
1. Television broadcasting—Cuba—History—20th century.
2. Television and state—Cuba—History—20th century.
I. Title. II. Series: Console-ing passions.
HE8700.9.C9R58 2015
384.55097291'09045—dc23
2014036010
ISBN 978-0-8223-7568-5 (e-book)

Cover art: Illustration by Courtney Baker, based on
two images: a promotion for Noticiario Unión Radio and
"En la Televisión se hizo historia," *Bohemia*, July 26, 1959 (both
courtesy of the Cuban Heritage Collection, University of
Miami Libraries, Coral Gables, Florida).

DUKE UNIVERSITY PRESS GRATEFULLY ACKNOWLEDGES
THE UNIVERSITY OF MICHIGAN, COLLEGE OF LITERATURE,
SCIENCE, AND THE ARTS, AND OFFICE OF RESEARCH,
WHICH PROVIDED FUNDS TOWARD THE PUBLICATION
OF THIS BOOK.

To Agustín Rivero Quintero

and

To the witty and gifted coquí *who,*

for more than twenty years,

inspired me

CONTENTS

ACKNOWLEDGMENTS

The idea for this project began in Puerto Rico, while I was conducting research for my book *Tuning Out Blackness*. During the research process, I engaged in numerous formal and informal conversations with several media professionals who had worked in Cuban television before the Cuban Revolution of 1959. While listening to their stories and to the anecdotes of Puerto Rican producers who were familiar with Cuban television, it became clear to me that Cuba had played a pivotal role in the development of the medium in Latin America. My first words of gratitude, then, go to these late Cuban and Puerto Rican producers and creators who, without realizing it, sowed in me the seeds of curiosity.

While my interest began in Puerto Rico, my passion for the project developed at the University of Miami's Cuban Heritage Collection (CHC). It was at the CHC that I had the privilege of meeting and working with one of the most knowledgeable Cuban studies librarians in the United States: Lesbia Orta Varona. Lesbia introduced me to a wide range of sources, was always on the lookout for information that could help my research, and even scanned materials on a tight schedule so I could have all the sources I needed for my analysis. Lesbia also put me in contact with her good friend Dr. Araceli García Carranza, the head librarian at the Biblioteca Nacional José Martí in Havana, Cuba. I am immensely grateful for Lesbia's ongoing support and enthusiasm for this project. I also want to thank the CHC's new director, María Estornio Dooling, and new librarian, Meiyolet Méndez, who digitized many of the images included in this book. A big thanks goes to all members of the CHC's previous and current teams: Esperanza de Varona, Gladys Gómez Rossie, Zoe Blanco-Roca, Annie Sansone-Marínez, and Rosa Monzon-Alvarez. Their helpfulness, friendliness, and daily *cafecitos* made the research at the CHC an enjoyable experience.

In Havana, Dr. Araceli García Carranza offered valuable information for this research and opened the doors to the Centro de Investigaciones del Instituto Cubano de Radio y Televisión. I want to thank her for helping me maneuver some of the bureaucracy in Havana and for welcoming me to the city with open arms. At the Centro, Fabio Fernández Kessel provided access to the invaluable Anales de la CMQ Radio-TV and made sure I had everything I needed for my research. Fabio and all the *compañeros* and *compañeras* there made me feel like part of the family (and, yes, the daily *cafecito* with a *lot* of sugar was also part of the experience). Special thanks go to Horacio Rodríguez, who on many occasions came to the office early and stayed late so I could spend more time conducting my research. In Havana, I also thank Juana García Abás for introducing me to an important figure in the history of Cuban television and Norge Espinosa Mendoza for being on the lookout for information that could be useful for my research. Norge also introduced me to the theater scene in Havana, and in doing so, he brought me back home.

While I was completing the final phase of the book, Philip Hallman at the University of Michigan's Department of Screen Arts and Cultures library and Alex Hofmann at the Paley Center for Media iCollection for Colleges were able to get last-minute materials I needed for my research. I thank them both for their prompt responses to my queries and, in the case of Alex, for digitizing programs I needed for my analysis.

This project greatly benefited from my semester as a scholar in residence at the University of Pennsylvania's Annenberg School for Communication. I am indebted to Barbie Zelizer, whose program provided me not only with time to write but also with the opportunity to share my work with scholars I highly respect and admire. The research support from the University of Michigan was also fundamental to finishing this project. The College of Literature, Science, and the Arts's (LSA) Humanities Award and the Associate Professor Support Funds gave me the time and financial backing to complete this book.

Throughout the years I had opportunities to present parts of this research at a number of venues. Portions of what became the introduction and chapter 2 appeared in different versions in "Broadcasting Modernity: Cuban Commercial Television, 1950–1953," *Cinema Journal*, vol. 46, no. 3. I want to thank my former colleagues Matthew Pratt Guterl and Vivian Nun Halloran for selecting me to participate in the "Variations of Blackness" seminar at Indiana University Bloomington; Patrice Petro for inviting me to present my work at the 2006 Society for Cinema and Media Studies conference plenary session; L. S. Kim for her invitation to speak at the Film and Digital Media Department Spring Colloquia at the University of California, Santa Cruz; Lillian Guerra for the opportunity to present my research at the Council for Latin American and Iberian Studies' Colloquium Lecture Series at Yale University; Karin Wilkins for welcoming me back to my intellectual-institutional home, the Department of Radio-TV-Film at the University of Texas at Austin to share my new project at the "New Agendas in Global Communication and Media" symposium; Susan Douglas for inviting me to present a portion of this research at the University of Michigan's Department of Communication Studies colloquium; and Anna Cristina Pertierra and Graeme Turner for their invitation to the "Locating Television: Zones of Consumption" symposium at the University of Queensland's Centre for Critical and Cultural Studies in Australia. At the aforementioned sites and at the Annenberg School for Communication, I shared my ideas and engaged in fascinating dialogues with colleagues. I want to thank Nancy Morris, Katherine Sender, Patrick Murphy, Elihu Katz, Deborah A. Thomas, John L. Jackson Jr., Devra Moehler, Monroe Price, and Joseph Turow (the Annenberg-Philadelphia crowd); Joseph Straubhaar, Shanti Kumar, Michael Curtin, Michele Hilmes, Aswin Punathambekar, Flor Enghel (the "New Agendas" symposium); Amanda Lotz, Paddy Scannell, Robin Means Coleman, Derek Vaillant, and Shazia Iftkhar (the University of Michigan's Department of Communication Studies); and John Sinclair, Tania Lewis, Jack Qiu, Zala Volcic, Jostein Grupsrud, Mark Andrejevic, Sukhamani Khorana, Jonathan Corpus Ong, Tom O'Regan, and Jinna Tay (the "Locating Television" symposium). Last and definitely not least important is Marwan Kraidy, a colleague who has been part of several academic adventures; I am fortunate to have shared my work with someone who is not only brilliant but also a great human being.

Intellectual dialogues with César Salgado, Cristina Venegas, Anna Cristina Pertierra, Luisela Alvaray, Richard Bauman, Licia Fiol, Gilberto Blasini, Victoria Johnson, Ariana Hernández Reguant, Tasha Oren, Arlene Dávila, Brenda Weber, and Naomi Warren enriched this research. Special thanks go to Stephen Berrey, who provided instrumental feedback during various stages of this project. Additionally, I thank two extraordinary anonymous reviewers who took time to carefully read this manuscript and offer helpful suggestions. It is also a pleasure to join the Duke University Press team once again and to work with Ken Wissoker as my editor. Thanks to Ken, Elizabeth Ault, and Sara Leone for their support and editorial assistance in the birth of this book.

I had originally planned to finish this project in 2012, but life took me down an unexpected path. I was fortunate to have colleagues, staff, and graduate students at the University of Michigan's Department of American Culture and Department of Screen Arts and Cultures who offered support and help during that difficult year. I am especially indebted to Evelyn Alsultany, Daniel Ramírez, Penny Von Eschen, Silvia Pedraza, Gregory Dowd, Judy Gray, and Mary Freiman in the Department of American Culture and to Richard Abel (and Barbara Hodgdon), Caryl Flinn, Giorgio Bertellini, Markus Nornes, Daniel Herbert, Philip Hallman, Matthew Solomon, Marga Schuhwerk-Hampel, Mary Lou Chilipala, Carrie Moore, Erin Hanna, Katy Ralko, and Courtney Ritter in the Department of Screen Arts and Cultures. I am also grateful for the love, care, and unconditional support of my selected family: Gilberto Blasini, Deborah Carthy-Deu, Axel Cintrón, Marithelma Costa, Yinan Estrada, Sallie Hughes, Harry Nadal, Shirley Santos, Rochelly Serrano, Eva Cristina Vázques, and my numerous aunts, uncles, and cousins.

This book is dedicated to two *boricuas* who, while they never realized it, made a significant impact on the professional person I am today.

INTRODUCTION

Broadcasting Modernity, Spectacles, and Television

The building that holds the Yara Cinema in the Havana neighborhood of El Vedado is considered one of the best examples of Cuba's modern architecture. Built in the 1940s, the structure was part of an architectural renaissance in the early to mid-twentieth century that aesthetically positioned the island alongside economically developed countries.[1] Yet, the building generally known today as *el Yara* (in reference to the 1868 battle that initiated Cuba's movement for independence from Spain) is not the only modern feature associated with the structure. Originally called Radiocentro, it served as the headquarters for CMQ-TV, the most important television network in 1950s Cuba (see fig. I.1). Emanating from a period when many Latin American media professionals saw Cuban television as the most advanced system in the region, CMQ-TV, like the building itself, was a symbol of Cuba's progress. Nonetheless, if Radiocentro/*el Yara* became a modern icon the moment it was completed, the relationship between television and Cuban modernity was, in the 1950s, much more of a work in progress.

Throughout the approximately ten years that television functioned as a commercial media outlet (1950–60), the medium became directly and indirectly entangled with Cuba's politics and society. As the *country* changed, *television* changed circuitously, particularly in terms of its uses and the attention paid to it by Cuba's elite (Havana-based, educated, middle- and upper-class individuals) and people in power (e.g., government officials). Television critics, owners, media creators, government officials, regulators, audiences, and nonaudiences (people who did not have access to television) assigned different meanings to the technology based on their economic, cultural, political, and social positions and interests. However, underlying these

FIGURE I.1. Radiocentro, CMQ Radio-TV. Courtesy of the Cuban Heritage Collection, William González Photograph Collection, University of Miami Libraries, Coral Gables, Florida.

multiple and shifting significations of television was the notion of broadcasting modernity. Regardless of the convoluted state of Cuba's political, economic, and social structures, television—the ultimate media innovation in the post–World War II era—would showcase Cuba's modernity to its citizens and the world. Television became a metonymy for Cuban modernity, and thus the medium was continually being reinvented technologically, culturally, and discursively to conceal any signs that belied Cuba's image as a modern nation-state.

"Broadcasting modernity" refers to the technological, legal, business, production, cultural, geographic, and narrative efforts to employ television as a stage to represent Cuba as a developed nation. First and foremost, broadcasting modernity was about representation and perception. It operated by "reflecting, selecting, and deflecting," aspects of Cuba's society, culture, politics, people, and television.[2] This was done by multiple actors through a range of scenes. By highlighting Cuban television's innovations, international successes, production quality, high-culture performances, and morally appropriate programming (read, Catholic and sexually contained); by attempting to repress or censor particular acts, genres, people, and voices of dissent; and by exalting the progress of the new revolutionary Cuban nation via programming strategies, television owners, regulatory entities, critics, and the state selected and interpreted Cuban modernity for television.

Delineating how to broadcast modernity was a complex process. Questions regarding what aspects of Cuban culture should be depicted, what entities should regulate the transmissions, what segments of the Cuban population television should serve, and what labor conditions should prevail, among other issues, were important factors in determining how to represent modern Cuba. That said, historical circumstances that were shaping the nation during the 1950s became a major source of signal interference. Between the introduction and development of television in Cuba, the nation-state moved from a democracy to a dictatorship (by way of Fulgencio Batista's military coup of March 10, 1952), from having relative economic prosperity to financial decline, from a general sense of societal stability to a growing feeling of insecurity, and from a revolutionary struggle to a state of rejoicing over a revolutionary victory. These rapid and unexpected transformations continued until 1960, when the revolution, initially intended to return the nation-state to its democratic-constitutional principles, began to change its course, showing signs of socialist doctrine. Cuban television was born in a democracy, matured during a dictatorship and a revolutionary struggle, and was born again when the nation-state began to adopt a socialist perspective. The broadcasting of modernity, then, materialized and responded to the particularities of Cuba's contemporaneity while also appropriating and reformulating external influences.

Historical legacies, time, and place played diverse and substantial roles in the broadcasting of modernity. The imaginings and structuring of television in Cuba incorporated U.S. ideologies regarding technological progress, capitalistic expansion, the division of labor, work ethics, and mass consumption. As a legally regulated technology, television was also initially influenced by the U.S. broadcasting system in terms of its commercial structure and democratic rules. Nonetheless, with changes in the political sphere, the technology went through various legal redefinitions, distancing itself from the principles of cultural protection and democratic dialogue that had been part of the Cuban broadcasting system since its first legal provisions in the 1930s. Television's visual and aural presence in the living rooms of well-off and middle-class families' homes was, to a certain extent, imprinted with

Cuba's social, class, and racial marginalities. The Eurocentric cultural, gendered, and racial stratifications that defined what it meant to be civilized and uncivilized permeated Cuba's television, particularly regarding its cultural performances.

Parts constituting the broadcasting of modernity had their origins in colonial and neocolonial encounters. Cuban discourses of socioeconomic modernization were intertwined with, and to a certain extent responded, to Cubans' view of the United States as the most progressive country in the world.[3] This narrativization of the United States as the location of modernity had its roots in historically based economic and political convergences. Cuba's incorporation into the U.S. economic system before the Spanish-American War of 1898 and its total immersion into the U.S. market economy and consumer culture during the early twentieth century propagated a complicated notion of Cuban modernity. Even though Cubans created a sense of "self and consciousness," a Cuban national culture and identity, the United States was a dominant force in the foundation of Cuban modernity.[4] As historian Louis A. Pérez writes, "It was [to] the North Americans that Cubans compared themselves."[5] Cubans imagined themselves in the vanguard of the Latin American path to modernization, as a close second to the United States.

Still, in terms of social norms and racial hierarchies, Europe was also a foundation of modernity and, as such, a constant impediment to representing Cuba as Western and modern. Michel-Rolph Trouillot reminds us that modernity "always require[s] an Other and an Elsewhere."[6] The ideology, symbolism, and rhetoric of modernization attached to U.S. capitalistic culture was part of Cuban modernity, framing the way Cubans saw themselves and their geographic neighbors. Nonetheless, at the same time that the Other was placed elsewhere (in terms of socioeconomic modernization), the Other not-modern element (as defined by the legacy of European colonialism) was an undeniable part of Cuba's national self. Within a nation composed of whites, blacks, and *mulatos*, and that since the late nineteenth century had been represented as a mestiza "Cuban race" (racially mixed), the ideologies of *Cubanness* appeared in contrast to notions of Western modernity.[7] However, despite the national culture's inscription of equality, interwoven factors around gender, sexuality, and class informed Cuba's marginalities.[8] Either by culturally foregrounding the *mulata* as a highly visible icon that "contrast[ed] sharply with [nonwhite women's] social invisibility" or by ethnographically recounting what was defined as the hypersexual, criminal, and infantilized practices of Cuban black males, the Cuban *mulataje/mestizaje* functioned through what literary scholar Jossianna Arroyo calls *travestismos culturales* (cultural transvestisms).[9] For Arroyo, this represents the theories and writing strategies that Cuban intellectuals developed to appease racial difference in the discourses of a racially mixed nation, while also objectifying and sexualizing the black gendered Other.[10] Thus, the ideology of Cuban homogeneity and equality operated in a discursive conjunction of heterogeneity and difference that allowed intellectuals and elites, as several scholars have argued, to reposition themselves as modern, Western people.[11]

Considering how colonialism and neocolonialism pervaded aspects of the discourse of Cuban modernity, one could say that components of the broadcasting of modernity were influenced by what Aníbal Quijano labels the "coloniality of power," that is, "the transhistoric expansion of colonial domination and the perpetuation of its effects in contemporary times."[12] The broadcasting of modernity retained the ideology, symbolism, and rhetoric of modernization attached to U.S. capitalistic culture while at the same time embracing class-based and racially inscribed cultural practices associated with a European high-culture tradition.

Nevertheless, modernity, as several scholars contend, "is not one but many," and it is imbued with pastiches of historical, political, social, economic, cultural, collective, and individual processes and elements from the past and the present.[13] While manifestations of modernity differ from one nation to another, the incorporation, perception, and experiences of modernity and modernization can also vary within a particular nation. These national-internal disparities function through the redefinition, conciliation, or ambivalent acceptance of non-Western and Western cultural discourses, respond to colonial and/or neocolonial economic-capitalistic expansion into particular geographic areas, and are influenced by internal and external political processes. Consequently, the ways in which people see themselves as modern, conceptualize modernity, or assess modernization are not identical in culturally akin regions, nor are they performed in the same way within national borders.

In the case of Cuba, while the United States and Europe represented the basis for what it meant to be modern, the precarious political, economic, and social conditions of the 1950s led some citizens to question their position in and path toward modernization. As Pérez writes regarding the uncertainty that wrought this decade, "At the heart of the deepening crisis was the collapse of the central formulations by which a people had come to define themselves. This was far more complex than a political conflict. It was a crisis of individual identity and inevitably a crisis of nationality."[14] This crisis of nationality that Pérez describes informed the debates about television in the 1950s.

Media scholars Marita Sturken and Douglas Thomas observe that "technological development is one of the primary sites through which we can chart the desires and concerns of a given social context and the preoccupation of particular moments in history."[15] For Cuban commercial television in the 1950s, the more unstable Cuba's political, economic, and social structures became, the more rigorously television was monitored, the more palpable were the debates regarding the function and uses of television, and the more numerous were the questions about what it meant for the medium to be and remain Cuban. Thus, while the main objective of the broadcasting of modernity was to represent Cuba as a Western nation-state, the discussions and debates that surfaced regarding Cuban television's uses, functions, programming, working conditions, and reach reveal challenges to the representation of a Western-inspired Cuban modernity on television. These dialogues about the medium interrogated how the industry and government officials (and some reviewers and audience members) were crafting the representation of Cuban modernity, thus pluralizing its meanings. Hence, I argue that the broadcasting of modernity operated as a series of spectacles, representations in which the industry, the government, and some reviewers utilized mediated images, language, signal distribution, technology, transmission, and laws to convey Cuban progress, democracy, economic abundance, high culture, education, morality, and decency. However, as staged productions, they faced the criticism of unsatisfied audience members and creators who questioned these representations.

Certainly, on some occasions the particular political moment established limits to people's interrogations of the broadcasting of modernity and its spectacles. With the intensification of the revolutionary movement in the late 1950s, Batista's censorship tactics made it impossible for the national media to discuss the "lawful" and "unlawful" repression of dissent that took place across the island.[16] On the other hand, the furor invoked by the Cuban Revolution made it difficult to express critical views of the government and its leaders. Nonetheless, what I want to foreground is that even as there were moments when public dissent was out of the question, the technology, regulations, programming, and the apparatus itself became sites and tools that constituted a particular view of modernity that was then ideologically dismantled by television professionals, reviewers, audiences, and nonaudiences. Television was used to both stage and contest Cuba's modernity.

In using the word "spectacle," I draw on Guy Debord's conceptualization of the term. In *Society of the Spectacle*, Debord defines spectacle as "not a collection of images, but a social relation among people, mediated by images," a worldview that "has become actual, materially translated."[17] According to Debord, the power of the spectacle resides in its representation and its capacity to convey positive outcomes for citizens and society at large. Debord's theorization positions citizens as passive entities immersed in and blinded by the spectacles—an inertia that does not completely apply to Cuba in the 1950s, given the emergence of a revolutionary movement. In borrowing his term, then, I am more interested in examining how the broadcasting of modernity articulated an appearance of progress, sustained Eurocentric racial and class norms, and positioned democracy as the state's primary goal during a period of political, economic, and social chaos. In other words if, as Jonathan Crary writes, spectacle is "not an optics of power but an architecture," then how did the broadcasting of modernity and its spectacles serve as building blocks in Cuba's architecture of power?[18] In which ways did television's regulations, technology, and prime-time programming become barometers of larger sociopolitical and cultural processes? Last, but not least important, what do the debates surrounding the Cuban medium in the 1950s reveal about the role of television and popular culture in transitional societies?

These questions guide my analysis of the broadcasting of modernity and its *spectacles* of *progress, decency, democracy*, and *revolution*. While I explain each thematically focused spectacle separately in subsequent chapters, I want to stress that all were interconnected and constantly evolving based on the specific political, social, and economic conditions of the period. Furthermore and closely related, even though each chapter chronologically analyzes moments within which discussions about progress, decency, democracy, and revolution took center stage, it should be clear that these concepts had been part of Cuba's broadcasting laws and dialogues about broadcasting since the 1930s. Therefore, it is possible to argue that the broadcasting of modernity in Cuba began with the institutionalization of radio on the island in 1922.

Nonetheless, even though modernity became intertwined with radio before the arrival of television, it was the medium of television that constituted the broadcasting of modernity. By way of laws, signals, images, transmission, reach, buildings, studios, technology, antennas, and the actual sets, television offered the literal and symbolic possibilities of *screening*—that is, examining, disguising, and broadcasting—Cuba's development, progress, and democracy. As Anna Cristina Pertierra and Graeme Turner write, "There would be some justice to claim that since television is, in a sense, an instrument of modernity, what television does within any one system is related to the formation of modernity it serves."[19] In Cuba, the broadcasting of modernity originated with television.

The 1950s—when the rhetoric of modernization signified economic and technological developments *à la the American way*, and Cuba ranked as one of the top economically developed nation-states in the region—serve as discursive background for the spectacles of progress.[20] Technology and the mastery of it were indispensable to these representations. The prominence of being the first Latin American country to establish a television network, the second country in the world to incorporate color television, and the first country to use an airplane as a relay antenna to transmit a live event (the 1954 World Series of baseball) were some examples that television owners, media professionals, and critics cited to demonstrate Cuba's television superiority. Television owners and media professionals viewed themselves as front-runners in the race to innovate the medium, so they tried to keep up-to-date with the latest gadgets, production processes, and business initiatives. Staying a close second in relation to the technological advances of the United States or pioneering particular aspects of television production was critical to the spectacles of progress.

The incorporation and development of television on the island reaffirmed Cubans' image of themselves as progressive and technologically, economically, and culturally advanced in comparison to the rest of Latin America, and as keeping apace with the United States. In many ways, the descriptions of television successes functioned through what Pérez categorizes as the "narrative on nationality," that is, an "imagery of self representation: a mixture of pride and self-esteem, of conceit and confidence."[21] Television owners and some critics employed terms such as "progressive," "advanced," "civilized," and "modern" to explain Cuba's television and its media professionals' accomplishments on and off the island. These television achievements, along with the language and narrative used to describe them, constituted the spectacles of progress. In these spectacles, Havana was cast as a protagonist in the global television world, and every aspect of television was supposed to match or surpass each technological, business, and production triumph.

The spectacles of decency addressed cultural representations on television and implied not only performances but also an audience who, according to some media producers and reviewers, would have preferred a televised culture defined by high-culture artifacts and morally appropriate programming. The main objective of these spectacles was to conceal aspects of Cuba's popular culture that challenged the perception of Cubans as white, Europe-oriented, Catholic, and sexually constrained people. Television critics used words such as "uncultured," "indecent," "uncivilized," and "vulgar" to describe performances, genres, and people that defied the image of Cuba as European modern.

In some ways similar to Latin American early cinema and its mediated modernities, the broadcasting of modernity—particularly the spectacles of progress and the spectacles of decency—operated within a process of "neocolonial dependency typical of Latin America's position in the global capital system."[22] In Cuba, however, this neocolonial economic condition was exclusively interrelated with the United States and its well-established political and economic hegemony. As well, and different from the responses emerging around early cinema in the region, the Cuban "elites" did not have a "civilizing desire [to] ignore the 'barbarism' of the national 'others.'"[23] Quite the opposite. Some members of this Havana-based, educated, and somewhat class-differentiated group strongly advocated eliminating elements they deemed uncivilized, vulgar, and barbarous. Navigating between Western ideals of culture and Cuban vernacular cultures, commercial imperatives, and increased governmental censorship, these "elites" attempted to implement a national television project with a "civilizing," Eurocentric imprint. The main goal of the spectacles of decency was to reposition Cubans as modern, European-like people.

But the process of repositioning Cuba as modern was ongoing and complicated, given the circumstances on the island in the 1950s. On the one hand, class discrepancies, illiteracy, and the rural-urban divide served as reminders of the nation's "discontinuous" path toward socioeconomic modernization, wherein colonial and neocolonial political and economic factors shaped national and regional routes to development.[24] On the other hand, the presence of a dictatorial regime functioned as a shadow in the broadcasting of modernity. Fulgencio Batista's route to power destroyed the liberal-democratic government instituted by the 1940 constitution and, with his dictatorship, the foundation and hopes for a democratic present and future.[25] Even as his form of government kept some elements of democratic participation and dialogue in an attempt to, as political science scholar Jorge I. Domínguez observes, garner support from the United States, a repressive environment took over as soon as he perceived discontent and uprising.[26] Batista's recurrent and somewhat erratic imposition and then lifting of media censorship, his legalization of censorship in 1957 and 1958, and his attempts to create a series of legislative proposals to preserve the illusion of democracy formed the spectacles of democracy.

Although one can trace the beginning of these spectacles to 1952, when democracy collapsed and the first instances of media censorship occurred, I pay particular attention to the performance of democracy in the late 1950s to foreground the theatricality of the spectacles. First and foremost, the spectacles of democracy were produced for a U.S. audience. As a result, by focusing on a period during which the U.S. media disclosed that rebel Fidel Castro and his soldiers were fighting in the mountains of Sierra Maestra to reinstate Cuba's constitutional democracy, we can see Batista's contradictory efforts to appear committed to freedom and civil liberties. The legal stipulations enacted in the late 1950s decorated the final scene on the theatrical stage that Batista constructed to maintain the fantasy of democracy.

If in the spectacles of democracy the United States was seen as the primary audience, in the spectacles of revolution the United States was the creator of a preamble to the spectacles. Herbert L. Matthews's *New York Times* articles on Fidel Castro and the 26th of July Movement, published in February 1957, and the U.S. media's focus on and fascination with Castro prior to the Cuban Revolution's victory promoted a series of images and themes that influenced the spectacles of revolution. Although the spectacles of revolution refer to the government's political use of television in combination with the programming and structural changes that occurred during 1959 and 1960, the iconography that defined the spectacles began to take shape in the United States. The *barbudos* (bearded ones) were invited first into U.S. homes (via newspapers and television), and then, after 1959, entered the home of Cubans via television. Equally important, the fact that

Cuban television was technologically developed and that Cuban producers and technical staff were highly experienced media professionals greatly facilitated Castro's political use of the medium. Thanks to the U.S.-inspired spectacles of progress, the spectacles of revolution and its creator and protagonist, Fidel Castro, successfully marketed the revolution to the Cuban people.

While the spectacles of revolution, similar to the other spectacles, operated via a commercial system, a new conceptualization of modernity began to take shape during 1959, emerging from changing ideas about progress, morality, and democracy. As historian Lillian Guerra writes, "Starting in January 1959, the mutual interplay of the media, citizen activism, and mass rallies launched the Revolution's story of national redemption and posited Fidel Castro's guerrilla as its primary authors. . . . By the late fall of 1959, citizen-based efforts to redeem the poor, defend national sovereignty, connect to the *campo* [countryside] and cleanse consumer culture of its imperialist habits continued apace."[27] The broadcasting of modernity became the broadcasting of the Cuban Revolution, which progressively symbolized a break with a neocolonial past and present. Feeding themselves with the fast-paced transformations taking place in Cuban society, and incorporating new ideals of progress, decency, and democracy derived from the Revolution, the spectacles of revolution absorbed the spectacles of progress, the spectacles of decency, and the spectacles of democracy. In the liminal stage of 1959–60, the spectacles of revolution were the only ones guiding the broadcasting of modernity, foreshadowing some of the ways in which the state would use television in the early 1960s.

Yet even as, via television programming, the spectacles of revolution integrated alternative ideas of what it meant to be Cuban and modern, these spectacles could not subsist in socialist Cuba. They contained traces of a political, economic, and cultural system that the Cuban Revolution aimed to dismantle and erase from the annals of Cuban history.[28] Aspects related to television genres, production processes, and commercial television's conceptualization of the audience, among other things, were linked to U.S. imperialism and capitalistic exploitation. To use Debord's words, the spectacles of revolution came from a "society without a community."[29] As a result, the state pushed those spectacles and the broadcasting industry that created them off the national stage by the end of 1960.

With the nation's rebirth, television was born again, and in the process of ideological and structural transformation, the state assigned new uses and functions to the medium. While in early socialist Cuba, television continued to broadcast a style of modernity formed by new notions of citizenry, politics, culture, and temporalities, its primary function was to help construct the island's socialist modernity. In other words, by utilizing the medium to support literacy campaigns, by incorporating propaganda-oriented programming, and by providing the television audience with access to "high culture," television helped build socialism in Cuba while also reinforcing the advances and, thus, the benefits of the Cuban Revolution. In building socialist modernity, television was concomitantly broadcasting modernity.

As historian David E. Nye observes, "A technology is not merely a system of machines with certain functions; rather, it is an expression of a social world. Electricity, the telephone, the radio, television, the computer, and the Internet are not implacable forces moving through history, but social processes that vary from one time period to another and from one culture to another."[30] Following Nye's argument, one could say that, in Cuba, the revolution was televised not only because television broadcast the revolutionary victory but also because some of the causes of discontent and the impetus behind the revolutionary struggle permeated different aspects of television. In this regard, the spectacles of progress, decency, democracy, and revolution serve as reminders that the radicalization of the Cuban Revolution might not have been a deus ex machina developed by powerful Cold War conspirators but, instead, a domestic drama a long time in the making. *Broadcasting Modernity*, then, tells the story of how this drama unfolded via the various aspects associated with the most powerful media outlet of the time: television.

This book analyzes the debates, meanings, purposes, and readings assigned to television in Cuba from 1950 to 1960, when the medium operated as a commercial enterprise. By focusing on the industry's business practices, its regulations, and its entertainment programming, as well as the state's and Cuban citizens' responses to the medium, the chapters examine how Cuban television was understood as a technology, a cultural artifact, a regulated space, and a political place. This broad view also reveals how transformations on the national stage affected the industry. *Broadcasting Modernity* is about television, 1950s Cuba, modernity, and change. This book is also about the past and, as such, it is a selection and reconstruction of particular moments that occurred in another time period. As historian Keith Jenkins writes, "The world/the past comes to us always already as stories and . . . we cannot get out of these stories (narratives) to check if they correspond to the real world/past, because these always already narratives constitute reality."[31] As I explain below, several factors and narratives came into play in selecting the subject and in reconstructing the Cuban commercial television past that animates the pages of this book.

Cuban Commercial Television: Sources and Narrations

Recuperating a key missing link in the history of Latin American television was one of the primary motivations behind this research. Although the last decade has seen numerous studies published in the English language that focus on Latin American and U.S. Spanish-language television, most of the research has dealt with contemporary television flows, powerful media conglomerates, and the popularity of *telenovelas* (soap operas) around the world. Television systems and countries that are not global business players *today* have been left out of the scholarly spectrum. Thus, by focusing on Cuban television in the 1950s, I am calling attention to the importance of temporal, geographic, cultural, and social specificity in the studies of television across the region. Not only do television owners, the professionals, the government, the critics, the audiences, and the nonaudience present diverse perspectives on the medium, but these sometimes intertwined, sometimes disconnected "sites" are constantly being transformed by a variety of competing forces. In both the Latin American and the Spanish Caribbean television "past" and "present," multiple political, economic, cultural, and legal circumstances and people define and redefine the medium. To eliminate a particular television system either because it ceased to exist or because it is not one of today's television exporters is to erase a portion of television history and of the social actors that were and are part of that history. However, even though I would argue that the business of television has defined most of the scholarship on the medium and, thus, the erasure of Cuba in the Latin American television literature, the lack of research on Cuban television might be a product of other factors as well.

In her seminal essay, "Greater Cuba," film scholar Ana López takes up the task of examining the creative trajectory and artistic production of Cuban exiles and Cuban American filmmakers beginning in the 1970s and evolving up to the 1990s. Early in the piece she posits an intriguing question: Why is it that when cinema scholars analyze exile cinema, the studies unavoidably focus on the production of exiles escaping conservative and murderous regimes, leaving aside the creators who have left socialist states such as Cuba? As López writes regarding the marginalization of Cuban exile filmmakers, "Although buttressed by official U.S. policies and actions against Cuba since 1961, Cuban exile film- and video-makers have, paradoxically, had a difficult time articulating their arguments and being heard. Within artistic circles, their exile has, in general, not been a privileged position from which to speak."[32] While López convincingly explains the relevance and ideological diversity of the Cuban exiles' cinematic productions, the fact that she needs to justify her analysis or clarify that not all Cuban exiles are reactionary rich people who want to see the system collapse reveals some of the issues facing those who research nonrevolutionary Cuban media.

Cold War politics still frame academic discussions and silences about Cuba. Dealing with nonrevolutionary Cuban culture invariably comes with left-wing and right-wing baggage that affects what is and is not being researched and what is or is not said about an object of analysis.[33] And, in many cases, what is said immediately puts the scholar on one side of the ideological spectrum, where in-between positions are usually missed not necessarily by those speaking but by those listening. Probably because of this baggage, open dialogue and criticism of the revolution are mostly absent in U.S. and Latin American academic discussions outside of Cubanist circles.[34]

Of course, this black-and-white dichotomy that is part of academia is performed differently in the nonacademic world. As historian Lillian Guerra writes in the first pages of her pathbreaking book, *Visions of Power in Cuba: Revolution, Redemption, and Resistance, 1959–1971*, when recounting one of her visits to family on the island, even her hard-core revolutionary family members criticize the system while also recognizing the legacy of colonialism that defined the prerevolutionary past. As a result of the fall of the Soviet Union, Guerra explains, the "historically rooted story of national redemption was undoubtedly disintegrating, but it also served as the common anchor of a society left adrift in rough political seas. Long accustomed to defining *cubanidad* according to positions of allegiance or opposition to this narrative, Cubans experienced disorientation with the end of the Cold War."[35] Whereas at the Centro de Investigaciones del Instituto Cubano de

Radio y Televisión, one of the two main places where I conducted my research, no one openly criticized the government, those *compañeros* who became friends did not hesitate to complain about the Castro brothers' regime in private conversations. Yet, this private/public division and the additional pressure of focusing on the contributions of the Cuban Revolution when talking in public (and particularly in front of a foreigner such as myself), influenced one of my projected research methodologies.

Early in the project I had planned to interview people who were involved in the development of Cuban commercial television and its transitional period. In Havana, I had the opportunity to talk to a woman who not only began to work in the industry in the mid-1950s but also was on camera narrating the entrance of Fidel Castro and his caravan into the city of Havana on January 8, 1959. Every time I asked her to explain the transitional period of 1959–60 in relation to programming genres and themes, she invariably talked about "the great Fidel" and "our revolution," never answering my questions. She sounded as if she was giving me a memorized speech that she had probably presented on camera to mark every anniversary of the Cuban Revolution. The politics of the revolution and the fear of possible repercussions—perhaps related to my tape recorder, which was not turned on—defined my conversations with her as well as my dialogue with another potential interviewee in Havana.

In Miami, in contrast, an antirevolutionary passion permeated many of my conversations. At the University of Miami's Cuban Heritage Collection (CHC), the second location where I conducted most of my research, I had the opportunity to meet many elderly Cuban exiles who frequented the collection, usually to do some research to satisfy a personal curiosity. Similar to the people I met in Havana, they were all interested in my research and wanted to help by introducing me to friends who had worked on TV in the 1950s (the friendliness and sense of humor that define Cubans transcend generations of political differences and geographic distance). In Miami my problem was not finding people who would talk about Cuban commercial television; the issue arose once we reached the year 1959, when "todo se fue al piso" (everything went downhill). For the exiles I talked to, nothing positive came after 1959, and there was no way to transcend this rhetoric. Thus, because of the exiles' antirevolutionary politics and what I would describe as the "walking-on-eggshells" encounters in Havana, I decided to abandon interviews as a research methodology. Even though this work has been enriched by the interviews with television professionals included in the documentary *Hasta el último aliento* (Until the last breath, 1995), in a thesis written by a University of Havana student, and in the CHC's Luis J. Botiffol Oral History Project, the bulk of the research came from archives.

Although I conducted research at the State Historical Society of Wisconsin (where I looked specifically at the papers of Martin Codel, a former journalist, editor, and media consultant for U.S. media corporations invested in Latin America), most of the sources utilized in this project, as I have noted, were found in two locations: Miami and Havana. At the University of Miami's CHC, I gathered information from the magazines *Bohemia*, *Carteles*, *Gente de la Semana*, and *Show*, as well as the newspapers *Diario de la Marina* and *El Mundo*. In addition, all the broadcasting laws analyzed in the book were obtained from *La Gaceta Oficial de la República de Cuba*, also available at the CHC. In Havana, as mentioned previously, my research was conducted at the Centro de Investigaciones del Instituto Cubano de Radio y Televisión, which holds the Anales de la CMQ Radio-TV, a collection of newspaper and magazine clippings related to CMQ and the broadcasting business in general. The Anales included clippings from the magazines and newspapers just mentioned, in addition to television- and broadcasting-related stories published in newspapers such as *Alerta*, *Ataja*, *Avance*, *El Crisol*, *Diario Nacional*, *El País*, *Prensa Libre*, *Pueblo*, *Información*, *Vocero Occidental*, *Revolución* (1959), and *Noticias de Hoy* (1959) and the magazine *Cinema*. I looked at the Anales from 1949 to 1959, all of which included volumes for all twelve months of each year. Unpublished materials regarding commercial radio, television surveys, and audiences were also found at the Centro.

The newspapers and magazines I utilized for this research came from a broad ideological spectrum. For example, I read television reviews and stories published in the highly conservative *Diario de la Marina*; in the government-influenced *Alerta* (owned by Ramón Vasconcelos, minister of communication during Fulgencio Batista's regime) and *Pueblo*; in the politically moderate and intellectually engaged *Bohemia*; in the politically moderate and popular-culture-oriented *Carteles* and *Gente de la Semana*; and in the entertainment magazine *Show*. While most of the voices present throughout the chapters come from television reviews, commentaries, and letters published in the *Diario de la Marina*, *Bohemia*, *Carteles*, and *Gente de la Semana* (all of which had established television sections and respected television reviewers), the history narrated in this book was also informed by politically liberal sources (e.g., *Cinema* and *Prensa Libre*).[36] Television-related pieces published in the communist newspaper *Noticias de Hoy* and the government-run newspaper *Revolución* and *INRA* magazine helped me analyze the period after the triumph of the Cuban Revolution.

While in Cuba, I obtained a few clips from television shows broadcast during the 1950s, segments that were part of *Hasta el último aliento*, a program devoted to the history of Cuban television. As documentary segments, the clips were already literally and figuratively reframed through montage and voice-over. They, to use Bill Nichols's theorization of documentary filmmaking, "reference[d] . . . a 'reality'" that articulated a particular point of view.[37] In this case, the narrations of reality positioned the revolution as the beginning of a new nation and as the producer of the one and only reality. The television past was recounted with a mixture of factual data, omission of positive outcomes, and sporadic criticism of the commercial period. For example, when discussing the transitional phase of 1959–60, the voice-over indicates that "the process of the television intervention was gradual and circumstantial. Nineteen sixty was a defining moment for the country and for television. . . . Television began to palpitate together with the Cuban people."[38] Even though *Hasta el último aliento* represented Fidel Castro's participation on commercial television as an important use of the medium by the leader, the official narrative, or what has become the history of the new post–1959 Cuban nation, erased commercial television's role in 1959 as a major promoter of the Cuban Revolution. The fact that *Hasta el último aliento* did not consider commercial television's sponsorship of the revolution and of Fidel Castro is certainly not surprising. "Collective memories," as Barbie Zelizer writes, "allow for the fabrication, rearrangement, elaboration, and omission of details about the past, often pushing aside accuracy and authenticity to accommodate broader issues of identity formation, power and authority, and political affiliation."[39] In socialist Cuba, the official narrations of the nation are made to accommodate the binary construction of Cold War political rhetoric.

With the intention of analyzing some of the television shows depicted in the documentary, in 2008 I met with the writer and director of *Hasta el último aliento*, the late Vicente González-Castro. During our conversation he indicated that almost nothing was available. The extremely difficult economic phase of the Special Period (the economic crisis of 1990 through the 2000s), the lack of technological equipment to transfer the material for preservation, and, last but not least, the fact that until very recently television was not seen as part of Cuba's cultural patrimony influenced the deterioration of the material and thus, the limited programming available. *Hasta el último aliento* has been digitized and is now the primary source for those interested in studying television on the island.

In Miami, I was able to find various websites that sold a few episodes and clips of 1950s Cuban television. While it is not clear to me how those selling the shows obtained the material, the nostalgia for a prerevolutionary Cuban past that still defines the Miami exile culture (a culture that, given the age of the 1960s exiles, might disappear with the generation that developed it) has created commercial ventures designed for those who want to reproduce a temporarily static and idyllic 1950s Cuba.[40] In addition, YouTube had some visual material, although, contrary to the "collectibles" sold in Miami, many of the videos were ephemeral—subject to removal from one day to the next. Still, all of these disjointed fragments of programming served as background information for analyzing the broadcasting of modernity and its spectacles. The sophistication of Cuban television scenery, the inclusion of high-culture performances on variety shows, the participation of black Cuban singers on television, and the theatricality of Fidel Castro's televised persona were present in the fragmented programming, providing a visual and aural reference to the accounts included in newspaper and magazine articles.

Regarding the written sources utilized for this research, I would like to point out that even as they provided multiple views of the business and culture of Cuban television, they were not equally distributed across the class spectrum. Television reviewers and the people who sent letters to magazines and newspapers came from the middle class, upper-middle class, and upper class. References to international travel and professional affiliations listed in some of the letters provided hints regarding the class position and cultural capital of the reviewers and those who wrote letters. This suggests that the racially heterogeneous and geographically dispersed working class was not involved in the national dialogues and debates about television. While economically disadvantaged Cubans residing in Havana and some of the eastern provinces probably had the opportunity to watch television, either in other people's homes or through store windows in the 1950s, it is not until the end of the decade that their viewing patterns were recorded via surveys.

Hence, although the Cuban working class was directly and indirectly implied in the discourses of television, its voices were absent.

In addition to the class dynamic, there were different levels of power behind those who discussed the medium of television and those who exercised changes in the industry, even as, on many occasions, these categories intersected. At the top of the power hierarchy was the state. In different moments, presidents, ministers of communication, and legislators tried to control the medium primarily via laws and censorship tactics. At the end of the decade, of course, the main exercise of power came with the nationalization of the industry.

The industry followed the power of the state. This broad categorization included television owners and advertisers at the top of the pyramid, followed by producers, directors, writers, performers, and technical staff. Whereas performers and technical staff were the least powerful individuals within the industry, on some occasions they freed themselves from power constraints and momentarily impacted the culture being televised. Additionally, though with less power than the state, television owners, and advertisers, entities such as labor unions and private organizations also influenced industry practices when it came to television morality. And, mediating all these interests were the television reviewers. Passing judgment within the ideological boundaries of the newspaper or magazine that employed them and providing factual information, television reviewers were powerful individuals. Their power resided not in legislation or economic maneuvers but in how their words demarcated the discourses about television.

The last aspect I want to address regarding the narration of Cuban commercial television's past is my relationship to the object of study. As a non-Cuban, I did not grow up listening to visceral rampages about Fidel Castro or romantic accounts about the wonders of the pre-Castro era. Certainly, the topics were not foreign to me given that some of my best childhood friends were Cuban and that the theme of Castro and the Cuban Revolution was all over television in Puerto Rico, where I was raised. Still, an obsession with destroying the ideology that informed the revolution and a longing to return to Cuba, while familiar topics, were not part of my familial interactions. Thus, my interest in the subject was personal only in the sense that I consider Cuban commercial television an important component of the region's history; as such, I believed it had to be studied. Needless to say, what I present here is only one approach to that history.

In Cuba, researchers such as Raúl Garcés, Reynaldo González, Oscar Luis López, Mayra Sierra Cúe, and a new generation affiliated with the Centro de Investigaciones del Instituto Cubano de Radio y Televisión and the magazine *En Vivo* have embarked on analyzing different aspects of Cuba's broadcasting. I see my work as complementing those studies, examining facets of the history of television in Cuba and the place of television during a limited period of Cuban history.

My narration begins before the arrival of television in Cuba. Chapter 1, "Prelude to the Spectacles: Constituting a Modern Broadcasting System through the Law, 1923–1950," analyzes the legislation that regulated Cuba's broadcasting prior to the launching of television. By exploring how national and transnational circumstances influenced legislation and its conceptualization of broadcasting, the chapter traces the ways in which notions of modernity began to infiltrate the legal and regulatory imaginings of Cuban media. In addition, this chapter draws attention to the development of Havana as an important radio center in Cuba and Latin America. The prestige of Havana-based media industries across the region, a reputation that began in the 1940s, became one of the narratives of the spectacles of progress, the focus of my second chapter.

Chapter 2, "Spectacles of Progress: Technology, Expansion, and the Law," examines how narratives about Cuban television's technology, business, and production accomplishments during the early years of television's establishment on the island were used to highlight Cuba's progress. Whereas these narrations promoted an understanding of Cuban modernity aligned with a U.S. conceptualization of socioeconomic and political development, the uneven processes of geographic modernization, the destitution of a democratic government, and the decline in economic growth began to reveal the artifice behind the spectacles. Audiences and nonaudiences became important players in dismantling the spectacles of progress, calling attention to the stagings created by media owners, some television critics, and the government. Chapter 2 also examines the television law of 1953, legislation that drastically altered the conceptualization of Cuba's broadcasting, particularly regarding television programming, media creators, and audiences.

Chapter 3, "Spectacles of Decency: Morality as a Matter of the Industry and the State," centers on the ways in which television reviewers, private entities, some audience members, and the state conceptualized morality for television, from the incorporation of the medium in Cuba to the 1955–56 period, when the government began to intervene in entertainment programming. While initial discussions about morality and decency on television intersected with ideals of education, high culture, and bourgeois norms of conduct, increasingly debates about morality became a way for the government to blame those in charge of media industries for the island's social decay. As a result, morality on television turned out to be more than a commentary on the performances of the body; it became an excuse to avoid addressing the performance of the state.

The legalization of media censorship at the end of the decade and the government's transformative interpretation of morality and decency in entertainment programming are the subject of chapter 4, "Spectacles of Democracy and a Prelude to the Spectacles of Revolution." As the chapter demonstrates, for the government, morality not only related to the topic of sex on television but it also entailed themes that could convey transgressive behaviors about law and order. Whereas the government proclaimed that all regulatory changes enacted during the 1957–58 period were designed to protect Cuba from communist threats, the U.S. media had already been dismantling the spectacles of democracy by reporting on Fidel Castro and the 26th of July Movement soldiers. This U.S.-mediated imagining of the rebellion was prominent in the CBS documentary *Rebels of the Sierra Maestra: The Story of Cuba's Jungle Fighters* (1957), the first television program devoted to Cuban revolutionaries. Even as the documentary attempted to adhere to the norms of objective reporting that defined U.S. journalism in the late 1950s, the Hollywood-style shots and themes served as a preamble to some of the narratives that formed the spectacles of revolution.

Chapter 5, "Spectacles of Revolution: A Rebirth of Cubanness," centers on the first year of the Cuban Revolution and examines how the revolution's political, cultural, and social transformations and the citizens' enthusiasm for the revolutionary victory shaped television. My analysis of the production of fiction and nonfiction programming about the revolution, Fidel Castro's ongoing appearances on television, and changes in commercial television's programming flow demonstrates how the commercial medium promoted the revolution and how the government utilized it for political gain. During 1959, television was revolutionized, and in this process of transformation, it began to merge with the government.

The last chapter, "From Broadcasting Modernity to Constructing Modernity," explores the state's top-down restructuring of television. Beginning with the nationalization of all television industries, new station names, high-culture-oriented programming, and a new broadcasting law, the state created a new television system. Absent of commercial interferences and U.S. influence, the socialist revolution was televised.

CHAPTER 1

Prelude to the Spectacles

*Constituting a Modern Broadcasting System
through the Law, 1923–1950*

> And today we are pleased to report that a law that will set
> radio down a path guided by norms of equity and cul-
> ture has been fully approved.—Alberto Giró, "La Ley de
> Radio," *Diario de la Marina*, April 22, 1934

Since early April 1934, Alberto Giró, radio critic for the conservative newspaper *Diario de la Marina*, had been devoting several columns to the soon-
to-be enacted Ley de Radio, the first legislation dedicated entirely to radio.
Even though the medium had launched in Cuba in 1922, several earlier legal
stipulations regulating channel distribution and advertising had ignored the
topics of culture, education, and commercialism. Giró thus had high hopes
for the first radio law and its potential consideration of the "radio listener's
rights," which he related to cultural enrichment, educational programming,
and the reduction of advertising.

Giró's opinions regarding the rights of the radio listener were not unusual
on the island. Many radio critics and even government officials held similar
views about the new medium. During the years leading up to the incorporation of television on the island, legislation paid considerable attention to
radio listeners and producers. This was the case despite the Cuban government's move to institute a commercial system that followed the U.S. model
favoring privatization and commercialism. But even as commercialism became part of the legal conceptualization of Cuba's broadcasting system, it
was not the sole or central force. Cuban broadcasting laws in the pretelevision years were ideological footprints that, through introductory paragraphs

and articles, ushered in a broadcasting system that put Cuban citizens and the state at the center of legislation that highlighted education, democratic participation, professionalism, and technological rigor.

This chapter analyzes the laws that regulated Cuba's broadcast system prior to the launching of television. In addition to commercial imperatives, I look at the other factors that went into pretelevision legislation and how these elements influenced the broadcasting of Cuban modernity. The "writing and articulation of the law," as Steven Classen observes, "is always political, involving the construction of a particular frame or point of view through which reality, life and human behavior are viewed."[1] Cuba's pretelevision laws reflect the ongoing negotiations that were taking place in the island's public sphere regarding the institutionalization of a commercial rather than a public broadcasting system. The laws also reveal how different views of broadcasting intersected with aspects associated with Western modernity.

Echoing the discussions taking place in Cuban magazines and newspapers, the laws embraced idealism in relation to new technologies, activating what David E. Nye describes as a "utopian narrative" through the "anticipation of a technological breakthrough that allows people to create a society of ease and abundance."[2] In Cuba, the utopian narrative revolved around the uses of radio and television for education and democratic participation. The pedagogical function of broadcasting combined learning about universal themes with all aspects related to Cuban culture. Moreover, calls to create an open arena for political dialogue on radio responded to perceived local and global threats to democracy. The fact that the first radio law (the 1934 "Decreto-Ley Radio") was enacted during the birth of Cuba's second republic and that, in the global arena, fascism had gradually moved from being a distant regional menace to a global threat had an impact on broadcasting regulations.

While the laws sparked a discourse on modernity linked to cultural and educational enrichment and democracy, they also created a countermodernity defined by aural, thematic, and spatial excesses: incorrect uses of the Spanish language, discussions about "improper" topics (usually defined as sex), and technological deficiencies. Within the legal conceptualization of modernity and its alterity, culture and technology operated on two planes: one that promoted European norms of bourgeois conduct, and another that encouraged technological development, precision, and a business code of professionalism more attuned to a U.S. notion of progress.[3] Directly and indirectly, Cuban broadcasting laws were symbolic spaces that contained residual patterns of colonialism and neocolonialism.[4] Nonetheless, the pretelevision laws also formulated spaces of difference, legal dispositions that complicate historical narratives about colonial and neocolonial influences. For instance, the nationalistic sentiment that emerged during Cuba's second republic in 1933 and the discussions about racial discrimination that took place during the early 1940s in Cuba's public sphere informed the broadcasting laws of 1934 and 1942, respectively.

It is in these spaces of difference that the particularities of the historical moments emerge, defying some scholars' generalizations about a carbon-copy appropriation of U.S. cultural and technological parameters through the law.[5] Even though some Cuban legislation was enacted during the same years as major U.S. regulations, the Cuban laws responded to the particularities of Cuba's broadcasting and to national and global political, economic, and cultural factors. The citation and differentiation present in the pretelevision laws and in public discussions about radio and television, together with the specific political, economic, and cultural conditions that shaped the legislation, provide a foundation for understanding the early years of Cuban television and the objectives and hopes that different sectors of the population had for the medium.

My analysis of Cuba's broadcasting regulations is divided into two main parts, beginning with a focus on legislation that pushed for the establishment of public broadcasting. I first discuss the 1923 law, which was dedicated to telephony and telegraphy but included a few articles on radio. This discussion then provides background for understanding the beginning of Cuban radio and the circumstances that shaped the Cuban "Decreto-Ley Radio" of 1934, which I argue reflected the revolutionary sentiment of the period. The chapter then moves to the 1939 decree ("Comunicaciones"), its emphasis on Cuban culture, and how this legislation began interweaving broadcasting with Cuban modernity.

The second section centers on the 1942 and 1950 laws that solidified the commercial broadcasting system in Cuba. The emergence of Havana as the hub of radio production in Cuba serves as the preamble for the 1942 radio law, the first legislative piece to include the word "commercial" in its title ("Reglamento general de radiodifusiones comerciales"). The chapter ends by analyzing the ways in which journalists envisioned the impending introduction of television and how the state conceptualized the medium through the law (the 1950 "Reglamento para el servicio de Radio-Televisión"), marking a gradual movement to commercialism. This provides a backdrop for the transformations that took place in 1953, when President Fulgencio Batista implemented new broadcasting regulations. As I will discuss in the following chapter, it was only after 1953 that Cuban broadcasting laws fomented a capitalistic media environment that privileged private corporations. Prior to the institutionalization of television, as we shall see, the laws performed a balancing act between the public, the private sector, and the state, yet they still privileged the Cuban public in the legal conceptualization of radio and television.

Negotiating Public and Commercial Broadcasting

The first mention of radio in Cuba's legal sphere appeared a year after the technology was introduced in Cuba. In 1923, the Cuban government crafted a law devoted to telegraphy and telephony that, in its thirty-two articles, referred to radio only when addressing the establishment of new license classifications.[6] Reproducing in some ways the U.S. categorizations established in 1922, the Cuban regulation instituted two types of licenses: Class A for radio aficionados and Class B for educational institutions. However, contrary to the United States, where Class B licenses were reserved exclusively for stations with live programming and were designed to limit frequency access to private corporations, the Cuban license classifications avoided market-driven hierarchies.[7] This legal negation of commercialism also included advertising, which was prohibited by law.[8] Accordingly, while in the United States the 1920s marked the period during which, as Thomas Streeter observes, broadcasting was "defined in strictly business terms," in Cuba the law deemed broadcasting to be a "public service."[9]

The not-for-profit focus of the 1923 Cuban decree responded to both the government's limited knowledge of the technology and the industry's amateur quality. Identified by Oscar Luis López as the "artisanal period," the Cuban radio industry of the 1920s was defined by improvisation, limited hours of transmission, and imported music.[10] For example, by 1925, even though there were forty-nine broadcasting stations in Cuba and "about 20,000 receiving sets," radio transmissions began at 5:00 PM, and only one station could broadcast between 8:00 PM and 11:00 PM.[11] It was not until the early 1930s, during what López classifies as the "commercial period," that scheduled programming began to air on Cuban radio stations.[12] The proliferation of programming and of an unsupervised broker system (in which individuals rented radio hours), the abundance of advertisements (though illegal), and the ongoing channel interference (from Cuban and U.S. radio stations) forced the government to devise a legal structure for radio. As the radio critic from the Cuban newspaper *Diario de la Marina* observed regarding the lack of regulation, "Each radio station has been doing whatever is most convenient for their interests."[13] To tame what had become an unofficial, commercially driven medium, the Cuban government institutionalized the "Decreto-Ley Radio" in 1934.[14]

Scholars consider Cuba's 1934 radio law to be the first legal step toward the institutionalization of a commercial system modeled on the U.S. broadcasting industry. For example, according to journalism scholar Michael Salwen, the Cuban government followed the U.S. model "by setting power standards and assigning frequencies. But it imposed minimal control over program content."[15] While it is difficult to assess how the commercial stations followed all the stipulations of the legislation, the Cuban radio law of 1934 included three elements that distinguished it from the U.S. communication laws at that time: the legal description of broadcasting as a public service, the Cuban state's goal to launch a public-service radio station, and the focus on Cuban-run and Cuba-centered programming. Rhetorically, the Cuban legislation conceptualized broadcasting as both a commercial and a public-service industry whose main objective was to serve the Cuban citizen. Legally, this hybridized conceptualization of broadcasting differed from the system established in the United States.

As scholars have documented, in the 1920s and early 1930s, broadcasting was solidified as a commercial enterprise in the United States. The government granted licenses to broadcasters who agreed to safeguard the "public interest," a broad term that, as Streeter writes, "allowed different groups with different interests to read it as consistent with their own point of view."[16] Throughout the early 1930s, labor and educational organizations advocated for a public-service broadcasting system similar to the British model. Nonetheless, lobbying by broadcasters, along with the Great Depression, led the government to quash that possibility.[17] Even though, as David Goodman's research demonstrates, there were more nuances to how the "public interest" stipulation influenced the radio programming practices of the 1930s, the Communication Act of 1934 provided the legal framework that would define the U.S. commercial broadcasting system for years to come.[18]

In Cuba, similar to other parts of the world, the Great Depression intensified the economic problems that had afflicted the island since the end of World War I. Additionally, political repression, a decline in sugar production, and labor strikes influenced Cuba's financial volatility during the early 1930s. The economic downfall shaped the still-nascent Cuban radio industry. The need to fill the airwaves with some type of programming forced radio owners to rent time to brokers, who began to include advertisements in their shows in order to make a profit.[19] This became the only way for radio owners to sustain the industry. The business and programming practices occurring in radio led the Cuban government to create a series of regulations for the still-developing medium. Aside from industry particularities, the revolutionary sentiment that overtook the island's cultural and political spheres during 1933, and the notion of a national rebirth, also played important roles in how radio was governed. Cuba's political revolution became the main ideological force behind the first radio legislation.

The year 1933 marks the birth of what is known as Cuba's second republic. Three major political transformations characterize this era: the change in political power with the overthrow of President Gerardo Machado's corrupt government, the establishment of socially progressive legislation, and the eradication of the Platt Amendment, an agreement that gave the United States the right to intervene in Cuba's political and economic affairs. Under the political doctrine of "Cuba for Cubans," the new government of Ramón Grau San Martín "committed itself to economic reconstruction, social reform, and political reorganization."[20] New laws improved the labor conditions of workers (including an eight-hour workday, paid vacation, and minimum wage), instituted women's suffrage, and protected the hiring of Cuban nationals.[21]

This rebirth also encompassed Cuba's national culture. With Cuba defined as a country composed of whites, blacks, and *mulatos*, the nation's identity centered on its racial and cultural mixing (*mulataje/mestizaje*). By creating a unified cultural front, intellectuals reconceptualized *cubanidad* (Cubanness) to "minimize social and racial differences internally so as to challenge the U.S. racist stereotypes that depicted all Cubans as biologically inferior and politically unfit."[22] The idea behind embracing "primitive" elements (blackness and racial mixing) came from the anti-U.S. sentiment that was prevalent at the time. Writers and artists exalted the blackness of the "Cuban race" through their literary and artistic productions, while musicians included Afro-Cuban rhythms in their compositions, introducing African-derived styles to mainstream culture.[23] Cultural syncretism, national sovereignty, and democracy became the anthems of the new Cuba. These revolutionary elements infiltrated the 1934 radio law even though the legislation was enacted three months after President Grau San Martín left office. Defining radio as a "public service" under the protection of the state, the first radio legislation promoted education, cultural enrichment, and all things Cuban.[24]

The central position of the state in the development of Cuban broadcasting framed the seven chapters and 119 articles of the 1934 radio law. As the introduction to the law indicates, "Radiotelegraphy, Radiotelephony, Broadcast, Television, Energy Transmission, Experimentation, and all communication media are a public service and, as a result, the Government of the Republic will maintain official control of them."[25] Through this law, the state defined commercial and aficionado stations, the types of licenses it would distribute, the frequencies allocated for each license type, and the professional requirements for radio operators. The state also drafted the basic rationale for a public station in addition to setting the initial parameters for commercial stations' programming.

The government's goal to launch a public radio station was included early in the legislation. Chapter 2, Article 10, announces the intention to acquire radio equipment and outlines the type of programming the public station would broadcast. According to the law, the station would serve both as a laboratory for the study of radio and as an educational venue for Cuba's poor. "The Secretary of Communication will buy or rent a transmission plant for the transmission of artistic programs with cultural, scientific, and educational themes. . . . The objective [is to] foment the study of the technical aspect of radio and provide a broad education to those people and social classes who cannot attend educational centers."[26] The egalitarian component of the 1934 law coincided with the other legal transformations that, as previously discussed, were enacted in Cuba months earlier. Furthermore, the first radio law echoed the aims of some Cuban intellectuals who saw radio as a means to educate all Cubans regardless of class, race, gender, or region.[27] Hence, we should consider the emphasis on using radio to help the country's underprivileged citizens to be another component in the legal and cultural conceptualization of the new Cuban nation.

An interesting aspect of the legal imagining of the public station was its programming. According to the law, the station's programming would feature commercial radio genres in addition to educational and culturally oriented shows. Science, local and national news, opera, classical music, comedies, dramas, and sports all would constitute the public station's programming. By combining different genres, the station was designed to educate and entertain the audience, avoiding the perception that this new medium was an exclusive repository for high or low culture. In terms of finances, money from the state and from independent business negotiations developed by the secretary of communication would support the station. Some of these business arrangements included renting spaces to showcase for-profit theatrical and cinematographic productions and signing agreements with commercial stations to rebroadcast some of their shows.

Commercial stations, similar to the public radio station, were also required to combine educational and entertainment programming. Centering on radio's potential influence in Cuban society, the 1934 radio law dictated that commercial broadcasters (all of whom had to be Cuban citizens) were expected to produce culturally oriented shows. Of the eighteen hours of daily transmission (from 6:00 AM to midnight), four were required to focus on "programs with literary topics . . . in the form of declamation, poetry, comedy, and educational conferences."[28] These culturally oriented shows were expected to address Cuban themes and incorporate Cuban people. The parameters of Cuban topics also covered live musical shows, all of which needed to present Cuban performers and constitute at least four hours of daily programming. Commercial stations had to limit advertisements to a maximum of 20 percent of programming per week.

The legal stipulation to include live shows and culturally oriented programs influenced the commercial radio stations' programming during the 1930s. As Oscar Luis López writes, whereas the small stations relied on recorded music, live programs filled the schedules of the most powerful radio stations. Additionally, the programming on commercial stations included a mixture of high-culture music and shows (zarzuelas, dramas, and classical music), popular-culture programs (comedy, music, and sports), news, and politically oriented shows.[29] Thus, rather than reproducing U.S. communication laws, the first Cuban legislation for commercial radio attempted to protect the interests of Cuba's cultural workers and citizens. By placing a strong emphasis on education and social equality, promoting Cuban culture, protecting local jobs, and defining radio as a "public service," the law envisioned radio as an instrument critical to the rebirth of the Cuban nation.

The depiction of radio in relation to culture and education, as well as the state's custodial function over the medium, also defined the broadcasting decree of 1939. Describing radio as a "public service produced under the vigilance and governance of the State," the 1939 rules were, for the most part, concerned with radio's cultural influence on Cuban society.[30] As the introduction to the regulations establishes, "Via the medium of radio, uncultured, bad customs, and other perturbations that are far from promoting improvement and education, can be introduced to the core of the Cuban family."[31] According to the decree, radio had the potential to educate Cuban citizens; conversely, it also had the capacity to be culturally and morally injurious. As a result, the majority of the twenty-three articles included in the decree were devoted to establishing some type of regulations for what was transmitted on radio. Furthermore, the focus on radio's diverse potential was connected to the definition of the medium as "an eloquent manifestation of each country's degree of progress and civilization."[32] The 1939 decree narrated radio as a symbol of modernity. With this new conceptualization, elements of how Cuban modernity and its alterity were broadcast began to take shape.

To be sure, radio had already been linked to modernity not only because of the technology's perceived sophistication but also because the medium created a sense of integration among geographically dispersed populations. As Anthony Giddens observes, one of the characteristics of modernity was the separation of space and place, where social relations were not necessarily bound to a geographic place. Thus, radio helped establish a national community between "absent others."[33] In addition, within the terrain of Latin American popular culture, radio programs such as *radionovelas* and adventure series represented a new kind of entertainment offering that, somewhat similar to Hollywood movies, articulated a "vernacular" and historically specific experience of modernity.[34] However, what I want to emphasize here is that while different aspects of modernity were already intertwined with radio's technology and programming, the laws began to set particular standards for what would be deemed culturally, politically, and technologically appropriate for conveying Cuban modernity.

The broadcasting of Cuban modernity and the delineation of a modern broadcasting industry through the law underscored three main areas: cultural norms, technology, and power. In the realm of culture, radio laws emphasized civility and good customs, practices associated with bourgeois norms of behavior. These expectations, inherited from Spanish colonialism, were developed to mold "responsible citizens, self-restrained individuals, and educated consumers" who would help build modern society.[35] Being this type of citizen also related to sex. In the context of Europe and its colonies, as Ann Laura Stoler has brilliantly argued, sexual behavior was a "fundamental class and racial marker implicated in a wider set of relations of power."[36] Whereas the 1939 decree did not cover the topic of sex, throughout the 1940s and 1950s a series of new regulations brought the interconnectedness of gender, sexuality, race, and class to the forefront, as discussed later in this chapter and in chapter 3.

The United States, international treaties, and global events influenced technological standards and modernity. In 1938, by means of the Regional Conference of Radio Broadcasting held in Havana a year earlier, the Cuban government signed a decree to institute the National Radio Commission. The main objective of this governmental body was to keep track of radio frequencies and to evaluate renewals and requests for radio licenses. In addition, the commission began to map the international dimensions of broadcasting and the magnitude of radio as a modern communication outlet. As the preamble to the 1938 decree establishes, "The great universal importance that radio-communication has acquired, and its increased progress and development . . . mandated the government to dictate proper measures."[37] Radio was reconstituted as a national and international communication tool that needed "special vigilance and ordering."[38] The regional forces of Nazism and fascism, the power of these movements' leaders, and their use of radio for political purposes contributed to the new perception of the medium. To control broadcasting was to govern the nodes of political power.

But technology was woven into politics, the United States, and modernity in other ways. Given the proximity of the island to the United States and the fact that, after the annulment of the Platt Amendment, the United States retained control of the Guantanamo Bay Naval Base (which was originally part of the Platt agreement), Cuban radio signals had to be constantly monitored to avoid interference with U.S. signals, especially those from the Guantanamo base radio station. This issue of technological rigor became more prevalent during World War II, when minimal interference was seen as a serious threat to military communications. For example, in 1942 the Cuban minister of communication suspended the transmissions of two commercial stations for interfering with the Guantanamo base radio station.[39] Hence, the power of radio and the building of a modern broadcasting system resided in the ability to transmit messages through unobstructed channels. The over-flow of signals signified the inability (or unwillingness) to commit to U.S. technological standards, thus posing a challenge to the institution of surveil-lance, one of the dimensions of modernity that, as Giddens observes, cen-ters on the "control of information and social supervision."[40] Technological standards and the technology itself became key aspects in the broadcasting of Cuban modernity.

The symbiosis between technology and modernity also controlled what was transmitted not only in terms of politics but also in the area of cul-ture. Broadcasting what were considered improper (antimodern) cultural representations (which in the case of radio were limited to verbal perfor-mances), posed questions about Cuba's membership in the modern (Eu-ropean and U.S.) Western world. Thus, given that the 1939 decree centered on radio's connection to modernity and culture, the articles included in this legal document focused on improving Cuban radio's professionalism and programming.

Some of the new legal requirements instituted by the 1939 law included radio owners' obligation to monitor programming and advertising texts; radio hosts' responsibility to prevent performers' improvisation between acts; radio owners' need to receive authorization from the Office of Radio to rent space to independent brokers; and radio owners' requirement to in-terrupt programming for state activities, electoral processes, and patriotic celebrations. The decree also created four categories of programming (infor-mative, cultural, artistic, and variety), and each category, although minimal, had its own stipulations.[41] Additionally, echoing the radio law of 1934, the 1939 decree clarified the government's investment in protecting jobs for local media professionals and its desire to use radio as a space for promoting Cuban culture. Specific percentages were set to delimit broadcasting time for national talent and non-Cuban artists residing on the island.[42]

But, even as the 1939 decree, consistent with the 1934 radio law, described broadcasting as a "public service," some stipulations included in the legisla-tion signaled the movement to a commercial system void of public broadcasting. The expansion of the percentage of advertisements per programming hour (from 20 to 25 percent) and the absence of articles addressing public-service stations signaled the state's intention to promote a commercial system more attuned to the one the United States established. Three years later, the government congealed the commercial broadcasting system through the legal sphere. The economic, social, cultural, and political changes in Cuba during the early 1940s, together with new industrial and legal implementations, made Havana a major center of commercial radio production for the Latin American region. In the 1940s, Havana became, to use Michael Curtin's term, a media capital, a center of commercial radio production and exportation.[43]

Constituting a Commercial Broadcasting System

The 1940s in Cuba were a decade of democratic hope, relative economic stability, and intellectual and cultural effervescence. What has been described as a "remarkably progressive constitution" was established in 1940, offering Cubans, among other things, the aspirations of political and civil liberties.[44] The Cuban economy, which, as in previous decades, relied primarily on the sugarcane industry and was constrained by the nation's economic dependency on the United States, expanded during and after World War II, positioning the island as one of the most economically developed countries in Latin America.[45] Changes also occurred in Cuba's cultural terrain. For example, a new group of literary figures emerged and formed what would later be called the "second republican generation"; the number of formally trained musicians coming from different sectors of the population increased; popular musical groups flourished locally and internationally; and, beginning in the early 1940s, theater aficionados could get a formal education at the Drama Conservatory and the University of Havana.[46] Because of newly established educational venues and a variety of professional possibilities, which included changes in the commercial radio industry, the city of Havana became the nation's popular-culture capital.

At the same time that the 1940s suggested a new political, social, economic, and cultural moment in Cuban history, political corruption, perceptions of moral decay, and a sense of uncertainty began to dominate the first years of Cuba's democracy. As historian Louis Pérez writes, "Politics passed under the control of party thugs, and a new word entered the Cuban political lexicon: gangsterismo."[47] While violence, terror, and corruption spread across the entire country, Havana became the epicenter of decadence. This referred not only to political abuses of power but also to illegal activities associated with U.S. mobsters' investments (particularly in the casino industry), the expansion of sex and drug trafficking, and an increase in criminal activity, all of which exploded during the 1950s.[48]

Havana of the 1940s thus embodied both the promise of utopia and the threat of dystopia. During this decade, some imagined and experienced the city as a site of democracy, economic abundance, sociocultural modernization, and creative vision. Concomitantly, others felt that it was a node of corruption, organized crime, poverty, and excess. It is precisely within this contradictory temporal place that Havana surfaced as a media capital. The fusion of creative talent, the city's economic wealth, and the existence of a financially solvent middle- and upper-class audience influenced the development of Cuban commercial radio. In addition, the experience of Cubans in the advertisement industry and the creation of national radio networks were instrumental in cementing Cuba's status as a center of radio production.

Cubans gained expertise in advertising from the U.S. agencies that operated on the island in the early twentieth century. This U.S. incursion, as Pérez notes, intertwined consumption practices with ideologies of modernity and civilization.[49] Besides incorporating the "American way of (consumer) life" into Cuban society, U.S. advertising agencies created a cadre of advertisers who, by studying in the United States or at Havana's Escuela de publicidad (School of Advertising), or by working for U.S.-Cuban advertising affiliates or local independent agencies, were trained to adapt U.S. advertising strategies to the Cuban and Latin American economic and cultural milieu.[50]

The formal education of advertisers that began in the 1940s coincided with industrial changes in Cuban commercial radio. During this decade, Havana-based radio networks displaced small stations across the country,[51] and Cuban radio obtained a high level of professionalism. According to Oscar Luis López, radio reached this professional phase by combining music, fiction, and news shows in daily programming; hiring the most established and promising talent (such as actors, musicians, and scriptwriters); and clearly defining administrative jobs by title and salary.[52] In López's view, "The most advanced methods of the North American commercial radio system were applied in Cuba with necessary variations that adjusted for an economically reduced medium."[53] Thus, during this period, Cubans began to indigenize U.S. production practices and broadcasting models by adapting them to Cuba's economic, technical, and cultural realities.

The last contributing piece to the modernization of radio emerged from the legal sphere. In 1942, the Cuban government crafted new regulations for the technical, commercial, and cultural components of radio broadcasting.[54] Representing radio as "the voice of every country," a voice that "travels beyond frontiers," the "Reglamento general de radiodifusiones comerciales" had two primary functions: (1) to create the legal parameters for a radio culture that would promote Cuba as a modern nation-state, and (2) to legally solidify Cuba's commercial broadcasting structure. By connecting democracy, capitalism, and professionalism, the 1942 law aimed to create a structured and advanced broadcasting system that, through technological developments and professional programming, would position Cuba among the world's modern nations. As the introduction to the legislation indicates, radio should be used to sponsor Cuba's "economy and collective life, its artistic manifestations and literary production" so that "the public from the exterior could learn about Cubans' civility and personality."[55] Education, civility, and professionalism in commercial radio were rhetorically established as the principal standards for broadcasting Cuban modernity.

Enthusiasm around the formation of a constitutional democracy in 1940 and the threats posed by World War II were the ideological inspirations for the radio law. According to the legislation, the mission of the state in "democratic and liberal countries" such as Cuba was to expand the education of its citizens and to elevate the moral and aesthetic tone of radio programming without discriminating against or censoring diverse opinions. However, even as the law characterizes Cuban radio as a space for entertainment, education, culture, information, and political debate, the war and the "enemies of democracy's" use of radio for "political manipulation, espionage, and indoctrination" served as incentives for the Cuban government to keep a close eye on the medium's programming. Some of the new standards instituted by the 1942 law included requiring radio owners to submit their entire programming schedule to the government's radio office at least five days in advance of its transmission date and establishing that only accredited journalistic organizations could be in charge of informative programming. These prerequisites served a double function. They allowed the Cuban government to have some control over radio content, and they fomented a structured, and thus professional, radio culture.

The legislation's title, "General Regulations for Commercial Radio," addressed the legal parameters for an exclusively commercial broadcasting system. Whereas the preamble stressed the importance of utilizing radio for educational purposes, and while the articles emphasized the government's role in setting standards for broadcasters to create ads with "art, distinction, and elegance," the legislation eliminated the possibility of instituting a public station.[56] Contrary to previous laws, the 1942 legislation did not mention state funding for public broadcasting or define radio as "public service." Instead, to appease the demands of "different sectors of public opinion" for more educational, cultural, and closely regulated radio, the government transformed programming categories by including educational and children's programming. In addition, the legislation specified who could participate in radio shows (defined by professional training) and indicated the amount of advertising that could be incorporated into national networks and regional stations on a weekly basis. Also, following a trend established in previous legislation, the 1942 law required radio owners to include a minimum of 50 percent of Cuban talent in live programming.

The 1942 radio law paved the way for state intervention without compromising the privatized, advertiser-run system. Equally important, through the consolidation of networks in Havana, the introduction of new U.S.-imprinted production practices, the formal training of advertisers, and the establishment of laws that demarcated the commercial system, the 1940s solidified U.S.-style broadcasting in Cuba. Collectively, the aforementioned processes formed what López categorizes as radio's "monopolistic period."[57] In this phase Cuban radio reached a level of maturity in terms of production and artistic practices, but at the same time, the broadcasting industries' connection with U.S. corporations increased, particularly in the area of advertising. Companies such as Procter and Gamble and Colgate-Palmolive created alliances with Havana-based businesses, thereby bolstering Cuba's position as one of the most important centers of radio scriptwriting for Latin America. While not all Cuban agencies were affiliated with U.S. industries, those that were became part of transnational business and creative networks. In other instances, Cuban advertisers foresaw the emergence of opportunities, expanded their business to other countries, and then affiliated with major U.S. advertising agencies. Although during the middle to late 1940s the U.S.-Havana teams mostly exported scripts and advertisers, other creative personnel such as radio directors, scriptwriters, and artists were also part of the business and creative spheres.[58]

The appropriation of the U.S. commercial model of radio not only had an impact in Cuba but also influenced other parts of Latin America. By exporting scripts, advertisers, scriptwriters, producers, and technical staff, Cuban cultural artifacts and people became key pieces and players in the creation of a trans–Latin American commercial cultural space of production and consumption.[59] Furthermore, as discussed in the next chapter, the indigenization of the U.S. broadcasting model became an important component in the connection of Cuban television with symbols of U.S. modernity. Nonetheless, while the transnational prestige of Cuban radio began to showcase the advancement of the island's radio culture in terms of production practices, the content of several radio shows challenged, according to some radio critics, the notion of Cuba as a culturally advanced nation. In an attempt to decrease "immoral" cultural performances, the radio industry formed the Commission on Radio Ethics (CRE).

Instituted in 1947, the CRE was a self-regulatory private organization composed of delegates from the Advertisers Association, the Federation of Cuban Radio Broadcasters, the Cuban Association of Authors, and the Ministry of Communication. Each of these entities selected its own representative as a way both to safeguard its particular business interests and to maintain a close channel of communication between its industry and the CRE.[60] For the most part, the CRE focused on issues of "morality and decency" in entertainment programming; however, to protect the names of sponsors and radio owners, the organization also addressed citizens' complaints. While the CRE did not have the authority to cancel broadcasting licenses, it did have the power to suspend both artists and programs.[61]

The main document that guided the CRE's judgment of radio programming was the "Code of Radio Ethics," a series of regulatory norms that delineated things the organization deemed immoral and indecent. Even though the code addressed violence in entertainment programming, its norms were mostly concerned with the theme of sex. As the document indicates, "Under the general principle [we] regulate the treatment of the following themes in radio programing: religion, matrimony and home, sensuality, sexual themes, dramatization of yellow press events, seduction, prostitution and sexual perversion, death, physical defects, and language."[62]

The fines and suspensions delivered by the CRE during its first years of existence confirmed that the organization mostly targeted songs believed to contain sexual innuendo. For example, in a 1947 report, the CRE listed the titles of forty-two songs that were banned from radio, all of which made indirect reference to sexual intercourse and/or to different sexual parts of the male or female body.[63]

With the arrival of television, as chapter 3 details, the CRE and the critics' ideals of morality and civility highlighted hegemonic notions of civilized and uncivilized cultures that directly related to a European colonial regime. The visual component of the new medium and the CRE's and critics' judgment of "improper" performances revealed that, in many instances, race delimited what was deemed primitive, immoral, and uncivilized. Throughout the 1950s, the CRE's main job was to police cultural performances on television that defied representations of Cubans as modern, white, and sexually contained people. But, before racially sexualized dancers, cross-dressers, and lovers' kisses began to threaten the perception of Cubans as "civilized" (according to some critics, the CRE, and, later, the government), radio critics and the Cuban government pondered the impending Cuban medium. The discussions that took place before the arrival of television on the island, together with the 1950 television law, reveal the contestations around the goals and functions of television in Cuban society, in addition to shedding light on how the state imagined the medium through the lens of the law. Far from being a means to promote consumption, television was viewed as an apparatus of technological sophistication that would be integral to the cultural and intellectual advancement of Cuban society.

Defining Cuban Television before Its Arrival

Extensive discussions about television began to unfold in the radio and entertainment sections of Cuban newspapers and magazines in the year leading up to October 14, 1950, the day Unión Radio-TV became the first television station to broadcast in Havana. Radio critics from the newspaper *Diario de la Marina* and the magazines *Carteles*, and *Gente de la Semana* in many cases dedicated weekly columns to U.S. television programs, technological advances, and educational experiments. It should be noted that the topic of television had been broached years earlier. For example, news about television experiments done in Uruguay in 1944 and stories about the technical aspects of the medium were published prior to 1949.[64] The main differences between previous stories and those that appeared just before television's introduction to the island related to their specific focus on the United States. Whereas critics kept readers informed about early plans to establish television stations in Brazil, Mexico, Puerto Rico, and Venezuela, and devoted some attention to the British public-service television system, the vast majority of stories centered on the U.S. medium. For Cuban critics, U.S. television conveyed artistic, cultural, and technological excellence, a model of television that Cubans should emulate and perfect. In the eyes of the critics, U.S. television was television itself.

The emphasis on U.S. television was a progression from the radio era. As discussed earlier, the model of U.S. broadcasting—which ranged from production practices and advertisements to laws that demarcated the commercial system—was solidified in Cuba in the 1940s. Furthermore, throughout that decade, the "Radio y Electricidad" section of *Diario de la Marina* featured weekly commentaries about U.S. radio shows, particularly those that covered classical music, theater pieces, and important composers. Nonetheless, what is particularly relevant about the pretelevision discussions of Cuban television and their focus on the United States is their redefinition of the U.S. broadcasting model, namely, in the areas of commercialism and entertainment. Although some stories indicated that vaudeville acts, comedies, and dramas were audience favorites, press coverage focused on U.S. networks' (specifically NBC's) broadcast of "high-culture" programming such as classical music, opera, and theater; the utilization of television in educational institutions; and the medium's capacity to keep the U.S. population informed about important national and international events.[65] Little attention was paid to the central role of commercial sponsorship in producing television shows or to the U.S. medium's endorsement of mass consumption. In an attempt to delineate the future functions of television in Cuba and the types of programs that should be televised, Cuban critics reconstructed U.S. television as a media outlet that promoted education, values associated with high culture, and information. Hence, by downplaying the commercial and entertainment elements of the U.S. television system, critics advocated for the emulation of it in such a way that the medium's primary purpose in Cuba would be the enhancement of the "high-culture" education of the Cuban citizen.

Yet, culture and education were not the only aspects that Cuban critics wrote about in their pretelevision stories. Television's technology and the mastery of it played an important role in the critics' discussions. As a result, what was discursively (re)conceptualized as U.S. television would become "Cuban" not only by representing elements of the nation's culture and educating the audience about "high-culture" performances and local and international events but also by the Cuban media professionals' skillful knowledge of the mechanics of the medium. Technological superiority would define Cuban television.

Within approximately one year, the critics' projections of what would soon be Cuban television shifted from wistful comments such as "We ask ourselves, when will we be able to enjoy all the educational advantages of television?" to more critical perspectives such as "In the North [the United States], a good one-hour television program requires the collaboration of 150 people (for example, 'El gran teatro Lucky Strike'). Are we going to be able to do something like that in Cuba . . . or are we going to correct the masters? And if we correct them, how would the newborn be?"[66] Despite this last critic's implicit doubts regarding Cuban media professionals' ability to improve on U.S. television expertise, the notion of Cuban progress generally informed the critics' imaginings of the future of television in Cuba.

In the late 1940s, technological progress was still couched in terms of the nation's previous economic wealth. Although Cuba's economy (sustained through the sugarcane industry) would be in crisis by the mid-1950s, the nation's prior market prosperity and the middle and upper classes' massive consumption and high living standards informed Cuban elites' understanding of their modern selves in relation to the modern world.[67] Thus, while the fragmented elements of Cuba's socioeconomic modernization would become evident in the years to come, in 1949 many Cubans (particularly those with economic means) operated under the assumption that their country, as one of the most economically developed nation-states in Latin America, would excel in the television enterprise. The Cuban state also shared these expectations.

In preparation for the medium's launch, in January 1950 the government published new television regulations. In its twelve chapters and forty-five articles, the "Reglamento para el servicio de Radio-Televisión" addressed issues of technology, ownership, and licenses but devoted little space to the topic of programming. The first ten chapters of the legislation included detailed explanations of how to construct transmission plants, install and test equipment, and distribute permissions and frequencies. They also touched on issues regarding transmission and the location of offices. While only the last two chapters focused on television programming, the text introducing the law placed a strong emphasis on culture and education. As the preamble indicates, "The enthusiasm that the science of television has experienced and the possibility of its implementation in Cuba . . . made it necessary to dictate regulatory norms . . . to foment the most loyal fulfillment of [television's] high cultural mission."[68] Through law, television's technology merged with its cultural potential.

Echoing the larger discussions taking place in newspapers and magazines, the law defined television—and radio—as a technology whose primary objective was to educate the Cuban people. Yet, despite this focus, there was no elaboration of the types of programming that would promote television's cultural and pedagogical functions. The legislation's programming classifications reproduced the parameters established in the 1942 "Reglamento general de radiodifusiones comerciales" (informative, educational, variety, aficionados, and children's programs) and presented genres in a general way: "Television stations may transmit programs on music, poetry, theater, movies, dialogues, conferences, sports events, art, science, literature, religion, politics, sports, and news, as well as advertisements; in general, everything that interests the public as long as it follows the requirements established by the law."[69] Such requirements included hiring personnel who had the training or education for the jobs they were going to perform.[70] In terms of content, the law prohibited challenges to the "social order," mainly referring to topics of morality and sexuality in television shows, thus coinciding with the parameters established by the CRE three years earlier.

While the sections on programming were similar to the ones in the 1942 law, the television law featured two main differences: the percentage of shows that had to be locally produced and the stipulation of who was allowed to enter the studios. Regarding local productions, the new law allocated 70 percent of programming to live shows and allowed 30 percent of programming to be "reproduced mechanically," meaning imported movies and/ or television programs. These percentages altered the numbers established in the 1942 law, which stipulated that only 15 percent of the programming on national networks could be "Mechanical Programs." The new percentages changed the proportion of local talent from 50 to 30 percent, a number that, as discussed later, changed again with the 1953 television law. These new percentages reflected that television was a more elaborate and expensive business enterprise than radio.

The second stipulation specified that all studios should be open to the public without distinction of "race, religion, or ideology." Whereas the 1942 "Reglamento general de radiodifusiones comerciales" included an article on free entrance to studios, it did not incorporate any language regarding discrimination. The clause of "race, religion, or ideology" responded to broader debates taking place in Cuba's public sphere. As historian Alejandro de la Fuente discusses, since the formation of Cuba's second republic, Afro-Cuban organizations and Communist labor leaders had brought the topic of racism in Cuba to the forefront of public debates. Fully aware that the discourse of unity that informed Cuba's national culture did not alter the daily experiences of black and mulatto individuals, Afro-Cuban and Communist leaders (two groups that, in many cases, were interconnected) understood that the best way to protect Cuba's black communities against discrimination was through the law. "The constitutional convention [discussions about the 1940 constitution] was seen as an opportunity—if not the opportunity—to legislate effective equal rights for blacks, turn racial discrimination into a punishable crime, and effectively eliminate racism from the island," de la Fuente writes.[71] He explains that, while the Afro-Cuban organizations did not get all of their demands met, they were successful in introducing the theme of racial discrimination into Cuba's public sphere.[72] Thus, the clause about free entrance into television studios regardless of "race, religion, or ideology" could be seen as part of the larger sociopolitical context that characterized 1940s Cuba.

As with previous broadcasting legislation, the television law was influenced by the peculiarities of its historical moment. Whereas the radio laws were a product of the drastic transformations taking place in the local and global spheres, the first television legislation concentrated on internal technological and cultural processes, some of which connected to national debates. One could say that radio critics and the Cuban state (through the law) embarked on a process of "telespeculations" (to borrow Tasha Oren's term) in which they imagined different aspects associated with the medium, in an attempt to ease its future technological, social, cultural, political, and economic functionality.[73]

Conclusion

From 1934 to 1950, the Cuban state articulated numerous conceptualizations of broadcasting in the law—ranging from a hybrid public-commercial system to a commercial system—that responded to local, regional, and global imperatives. The Cuban revolutionary movement of 1933 and its anti-U.S. sentiment; the emergence of a new notion of Cuban identity; the birth and popularity of fascism across Europe; international treaties that addressed the distribution and monitoring of signals; and the beginning of World War II were all factors that influenced Cuba's radio legislation. Radio laws addressed a technology in the "present"; thus the changing circumstances of radio's functionality and its uses affected how the regulations were crafted. The first television law, in contrast, tackled a technology of the "future," a medium that was not yet part of Cuban society. In the legal imaginings of the future medium, television was seen as a technology, a channel, and a place. In other words, it was envisioned as a complex technological apparatus that required absolute precision; as an instrument designed to improve Cuban people's education; and as a place where towers, offices, and studios existed, and all citizens were welcomed. These imaginings of television as a technology, channel, and place infused discussions of the medium during the early 1950s, as discussed in the following chapters. But even as the basic legal structure for television was established, the real conditions of production, and, more important, the changes within Cuba's political and social spheres highlighted ongoing ideological fractures in the conception of modernity that the law articulated. Via the spectacles of progress, depictions of Cuban television's technological advancements and business successes temporarily concealed the crises of failed democracy and economic prosperity that were affecting the Cuban nation.

CHAPTER 2

Spectacles of Progress

Technology, Expansion, and the Law

We have the best technical quality, we possess a team of
experts who, for two years, have dedicated themselves to
researching the new industry, we have plenty of artistic
material, and we will honor the progress of a country like
Cuba, which marches ahead of the most successful and
civilized nations of the world.—Ramiro Gómez Kemp,
CMQ-TV programmer, *Gente de la Semana*, May 28, 1950

From the launching of television in Cuba in 1950 to the crafting of new
broadcasting regulations in 1953, Cuban television's first three years can be
seen as a success story. Although finding sponsors for programs became difficult and the owner of the first television station launched in Cuba (Gaspar
Pumarejo, Unión Radio-TV, channel 4) had to sell his business in less than
one year due to financial losses, Cuban television grew exponentially in
those three years. By 1953, five stations were broadcasting from Havana
(channel 4; CMQ-TV, channel 6; CMBA-TV, channel 2; CMBF-TV, channel
7; and TV Caribe S.A., channel 11), with evening fare that included locally
produced comedies, dramatic programs, theater adaptations, variety shows,
talent shows, sports, panel shows, and news, in addition to imported movies and programs.[1] In less than three years, CMQ-TV, the second station to
transmit from Havana, expanded its transmissions from the capital to the
eastern provinces of Santa Clara, Camaguey, and Santiago. Additionally, as
part of CMQ-TV's business plan, Goar Mestre, the station's owner (together
with his brother, Abel Mestre), invested in the future of the regional televi-

De que los hay...   Por Roseñada

—¿Compraste aparato de televisión?
—No, pero estoy poniendo esto aquí para que la gente crea que lo tengo!.

FIGURE 2.1. "Did you buy a television set?" "No, but I
am placing this here so people think I have one!" *Diario
de la Marina*, October 25, 1950. Courtesy of the Cuban
Heritage Collection, University of Miami Libraries,
Coral Gables, Florida.

sion market by forming the Pan-American Television Corporation, a buyer
and distributor of movies and programming for television.[2]

The industry's growth went hand in hand with television ownership. Between 1950 and 1953, the number of television sets on the island increased
from approximately 6,000 units in 1950 to "over 100,000" in 1953,[3] confirm-
ing Louis A. Pérez's assertion that in Cuba "the idea of modern was itself
associated with material conditions and inevitably involved vast numbers
of Cubans in modern consumer culture."[4] With most television sets located
in Havana (the center of television production and service), middle- and
upper-class Cubans bought TVs (for cash or on credit) that cost between
350 pesos in 1950 and 287 pesos in 1953. Even though many Cubans still
did not own a set, the growth was undeniable. A cartoon published in the
October 25, 1950, issue of *Diario de la Marina* presents a humorous take on

Invasión de vecinos — *Por Roseñada*

—¡No llores, bobilita . . . ! ¡Tú verás que mañana, a lo mejor, lo podemos ver . . . !

FIGURE 2.2. "Don't cry silly . . . ! You will see that tomorrow, perhaps, we will be able to watch . . . !" *Diario de la Marina*, October 26, 1950. Courtesy of the Cuban Heritage Collection, University of Miami Libraries, Coral Gables, Florida.

Cubans' consumption patterns and the class expectations associated with owning a television (see fig. 2.1). As the cartoon suggests, to have a television set was to possess an artifact that symbolized class status, technological innovation, and progress. Even those without sets quickly became familiar with the medium (see fig. 2.2). Television was the media outlet of the decade, and Cubans embraced the new technology.

News about Cuban television expansion and its production and technological accomplishments spread rapidly across Latin America. Although Cuba was the third country in the region to inaugurate television in 1950, media professionals across Latin America considered Cuban advertisers and technical staff to be experts in television production. It became common for Latin American advertising agency owners, television owners, and state representatives to travel to Cuba in search of experienced advertisers and technicians who could help launch television in their own countries.[5] As Goar Mestre, founder of CMQ-TV (the most successful commercial network in Cuba) explained in an interview in the early 1980s, "Cuba was a sort of mecca for the Latin American broadcasting industry. Everyone who wanted to invest in television came to Cuba. We opened our doors, we showed them everything they wanted to see, and that gave me great satisfaction."[6] By adapting the U.S. broadcasting system's production, programming, and advertising practices, Cuban television became the commercial model for the region.

The accelerated development of Cuban television, particularly in comparison to other Latin American countries, was related to a combination of economic, political, and industrial factors. The Cuban economy, which was sustained by the sugarcane industry, boomed after World War II, leading to a higher standard of living for many Cubans into the early 1950s. This economic solvency was instrumental in Havana's popular-culture boom throughout the 1940s and in the development of commercial radio. Even after the end of World War II, when, as Samuel Farber observes, Cuba's competitors had taken steps to restart their sugarcane production, the Korean War and rising sugarcane prices left Cuba with a solid economic outlook in the early 1950s.[7] Although this optimism quickly began to fade by 1954, in the early part of the decade the island enjoyed economic prosperity and confidence.[8]

However, Cuba's wealth was not the only factor to influence the early development of television. After all, Venezuela, Uruguay, and Argentina had higher standards of living than Cuba;[9] still, their television systems, launched after 1950, did not expand as quickly as that on the Caribbean island. The core difference between these countries and Cuba was the United States. As Pérez writes, "By the mid-twentieth century, Cuba operated almost entirely within the framework of the economic system of the U.S."[10] In Cuba, U.S. investments facilitated the training of personnel, influenced programming practices, and affected the distribution of frequencies, which aided Cuba's broadcasting expansion. Consider that during the North American Regional Broadcasting Agreement (NARBA) meeting of 1950, which addressed the dissemination of radio frequencies across the region, the United States authorized thirty-one stations in Havana and reduced the frequencies available to the United States. According to a *New York Times* reader, these "extensive and unnecessary concessions to other North American countries, principally Cuba, would cause great injury to the listening public, particularly under-served listeners who live in rural areas and small towns."[11] The availability of more frequencies in Cuba, instead of in rural U.S. areas with low population percentages, multiplied the number of commercial stations and consumers. This commercial broadcasting expansion was beneficial to U.S. and Cuban corporations (many of which were intertwined), as well as Cuban radio owners.[12]

However, during the post–World War II era, the distribution of signals and the increase of consumers outside the United States had other, more pressing, purposes tied to an emerging Cold War that would revolve around concerns about democracy, capitalism, and national security.[13] Even though the link between broadcasting and security had already permeated regional radio conferences and treaties since the late 1930s, the Cold War intensified the focus on broadcasting as a political tool. The distribution of signals outside the United States was driven to protect/control the region but also to foment capitalistic democracy, both of which were interrelated. As Lizabeth Cohen explains, consumption "stood for an elaborate, integrated ideal of economic abundance and democratic political freedom," thus creating a binary between the United States and communist nation-states.[14] The cornucopia of consumer choices and the act of consumption were viewed as symbols of democracy. In this regard, television played a key role not only because it helped foment the notion of the citizen-consumer as a staple of democracy,[15] but also because the "governing classes," as Anna McCarthy observes, viewed the medium as a tool to mold the citizenry of the post–World War II era.[16] As the principal communication technology of the 1950s, television was conceptualized as an emblem of U.S. democracy, freedom, and progress. The U.S. interest in solidifying the commercial broadcasting system in Cuba (as well as in Latin America) should be viewed, then, not solely as a commercial strategy (even though this intention was most likely behind corporate investments) but also as part of the United States' Cold War foreign policy agenda of "fostering capitalist democracy through marketing American goods."[17]

In Cuba, the merging of commercial broadcasting with ideas about democracy and consumption had already been established through the radio and television laws of 1942 and 1950, even as these legislative pieces were informed by the political conditions of World War II, not the particularities of the Cold War. It was through the 1942 law that Cuba solidified commercial broadcasting, making its system more similar to that of the United States. Additionally, Cuba had been integrated into the U.S. economy and consumer culture since the early twentieth century; consequently, islanders already envisioned the United States as a capitalistic democracy.[18] Thus, television's incorporation into Cuban culture solidified the U.S.-inspired conceptualization of modernity that was ingrained in Cuba's "narrative on nationality" (to use Pérez's term) and, at the same time, reaffirmed Cuba's place as a modern nation-state. Through the incorporation, reconfiguration, and indigenization of television (a technology generally understood as "American"), Cubans reiterated their standing as citizens of a modernized country. As the CMQ-TV programmer expressed in the quote that opens this chapter, "We will honor the progress of a country like Cuba, which marches ahead of the most successful and civilized nations of the world." The acquisition of the latest television equipment, the technical staff's mastery of that equipment, and the medium's expansion symbolized Cuban progress à la the American way. Still, while the incorporation of television and its immediate technological and commercial success reaffirmed the narrative of Cuba's socioeconomic progress, the country's tumultuous politics unsettled its claims to modernity.

On March 10, 1952, military leader Fulgencio Batista led a coup that destroyed the liberal-democratic government instituted by the 1940 constitution, a document spearheaded during his first term as president of the Cuban republic (1940–44). Publicly, Batista defended the military occupation as an attempt to establish order and end years of corruption, a claim some Cubans believed at first, given his promise of future elections.[19] Nonetheless, even as there might have been potential to reestablish Cuba's constitutional democracy in the first few years following Batista's coup, his appropriation of power dismantled Cubans' perceptions of their country as a modernized nation. Batista's undemocratic political processes fragmented Cubans' discourses of modernity. While the stories about television's technology, business, and production accomplishments aligned Cuban modernity with U.S. modernity, the uneven processes of geographic modernization, the lack of a democratic government, and the decline in economic growth that began to take place after 1954 revealed the artifice associated with the broadcasting of Cuban modernity. Increasingly, the spectacles of progress and their focus on technological and business accomplishments were not enough to mask the gradual decline in social and economic stability in 1950s Cuban society.

FIGURE 2.3. Front cover, "Casting Room Television," *Carteles*,
October 1, 1950. Courtesy of the Cuban Heritage Collection,
University of Miami Libraries, Coral Gables, Florida.

Mastering the Technology

Towers, cameras, and broadcasting trucks. People in front of store windows looking at television sets. "Television in Havana!" headlines. Magazine and newspaper sections that incorporated the word "television" into their titles.[20] For those without the technology, nothing demonstrated the existence of television in Cuba more than the photos and stories about the medium. For those who owned a set, being able to watch their radio "stars," their favorite baseball team, and important national figures most likely accounted for the immediate fascination with television. Even if the first "test pattern" (on October 19, 1950) was unannounced (people discovered it by word of mouth) and technologically limited (a single camera shot), people in Havana were mesmerized by the technology.[21] And it was precisely the technological aspects of television that first caught the attention of journalists and audiences alike. When the official inauguration of television took place at the presidential palace on October 24, 1950, the parameters of what would define Cuban television, technologically speaking, began to take shape. "The technical crew of Union Radio Television triumphed yesterday, by realizing its first remote-controlled transmission," a journalist observed.[22] Cuban television was officially turned on via remote control, demonstrating the importance of technological mastery for Cuban owners and critics. Technology was the initial conduit for exhibiting Cuba's modernity.

The fascination with television's technology can be traced back to the discussions about the medium that took place before its arrival in Cuba, when radio critics devoted attention to both the cultural and the technological components of U.S. television. Cuban magazines and newspapers included translated stories from the United States and local coverage of U.S. technological advancements.[23] By explaining either the nuts and bolts of a television transmission from image to sound or the possibilities of "phonovision," that is, sending television signals via phone lines, journalists interpreted television's technology for the readers.[24] Given this pretelevision trend, radio and self-defined television critics became the first group of citizens to publicly evaluate the medium. And, because the island's television began its programming transmission with the Cuban baseball series (a challenge in itself due to the use of remote control), the critics were able to assess the technological promises of the medium fairly quickly. Described as a "clear success" and a "pleasant surprise," the baseball broadcast demon-

FIGURE 2.4. Front cover, *Carteles*, January 21, 1951. Courtesy of the Cuban Heritage Collection, University of Miami Libraries, Coral Gables, Florida.

strated that Cuban television professionals (particularly those from Unión Radio-TV) were quick students in matters of technology.[25] The next task for the television owners, then, was to extend those skills to entertainment programming. Alternatively, for the critics, their next assignment was to assess the programming of the two existing stations: Unión Radio-TV (channel 4) and CMQ-TV (channel 6).

As soon as what was described as "the first program" began to air in November 1950 (the comedy *Los cuatro grandes*, which originated as a radio show), critics paid close attention to Unión Radio-TV's, and later CMQ-TV's, comedies, dramatic programs, theater adaptations, variety shows, talent shows, and panel shows—the first entertainment genres developed for prime-time Cuban television. Critics began to write detailed reviews that addressed acting, scripts, scenic direction, sets, lighting, scheduling, and technology. Perhaps because they held high expectations for the medium in Cuba, the critics showed no mercy when evaluating the production and artistic value of early shows.

For example, after attending a CMQ-TV "video rehearsal," the *Carteles* critic wrote, "During the week of video rehearsal offered by CMQ, we noticed huge technological flaws. The cameras did not always follow the artists' movements and there were times when the apparatus continued in the same angle even when the artist had stood up from a chair."[26] Other reviews centered on the importance of rehearsing and scheduling and criticized producers for stopping at the end of the half hour or the hour, even though the narrative clearly had no conclusion.[27] In other instances, their columns amounted to lectures on the differences between theater, radio, film, and television, making it clear that television, although influenced by other media, "has its own personality, it prefers the 'close-up', in other words, the intimate."[28] Still, despite stressing the differences among all media, some critics noted the importance of keeping the viewer entertained, thus suggesting film as a primary model for television producers. One critic observed that the one-hour television dramas needed to incorporate "multiple sets and a variety of shots" and have "cinematic rhythm, quality, and good cinematography."[29] Hence, even as critics understood that television had "its own personality," it was difficult for them to avoid comparing it with other media such as film and radio. Furthermore, the media interconnectivity was almost impossible to escape given that most of the first television programs, similar to those in the United States, came directly from radio. In this regard, there was a general consensus that not every radio show could be adapted to television and that, at a minimum, radio programs needed major restructuring before entering the new medium.

This was the case for the *telenovela*, a program that emerged on Cuban television in 1952 as part of the afternoon schedule.[30] In reference to the first Cuban telenovela, *Senderos de amor*, a critic observed, "Yesterday we stayed at home to watch the first episode of 'The Novel on Television.' Luckily for us, it will be impossible to keep watching it because it is scheduled at 1:30 p.m."[31] Similar to other radio genres adapted to television, the telenovela kept most of the radio structure—in this particular case, a narrator who carried the episodes' action. Despite the fact that, a month later, the same critic (*Diario de la Marina*'s Alberto Giró) predicted that "novels on television, if developed correctly, would be a monopolizing program" (a prediction that became a reality and remains true today across the geolinguistic region), he was still critical of the telenovela actors, writer, director, and technical staff.[32] It became common for Giró and the television critics from *Bohemia*, *Carteles*, and *Gente de la Semana* to use words such as "boring," "tedious," and "stupid" to describe some of the early television shows that had been adapted from radio.[33] Critics even panned the radio performers who participated in early television shows. For example, in reference to an actor who participated on a televised zarzuela, the *Gente de la Semana* critic observed, "Evidently, he has a good voice but we can appreciate that on radio, when we do not have to see him. But, on television? All his difficulty, lack of rehearsal, and artistic inability made him look stiff and petrified."[34] Sometimes the reviews were so abrasive and thus taken so hard by television professionals that some critics were compelled to explain that their main objective was not to harm the industry but to help improve the quality of Cuban television.[35]

While the reviews were harsh, they also praised the accomplishments of Unión Radio-TV and CMQ-TV. Remarks like "The media professionals' determination may have been the reason why a fair amount of programs could compete with those produced in North America" and "The wonderful program, 'Estudio 15' assures us of the future of television in our land" applauded the stations' technological and artistic successes.[36] Perceiving television as a barometer of the nation's progress, the critics demanded no less than perfection, which itself was defined by U.S. television standards yet still had to be unmistakably Cuban. Through their reviews, critics created a symbolic map that fused the programs' conceptualizations, representations, and the behind-the-scenes television environment with Cuban nationalism.

The issue of Cubanness was directly and indirectly present in all of the critics' reviews and, *in some cases*, this discursive representation of *cubanidad* operated in opposition to potential U.S. television cultural influences. In an April 1951 article entitled "Con artistas cubanos, ¿por qué no?" (With Cuban artists, why not?), the *Carteles* critic addressed CMQ-TV's broadcast of *Super circo*, a U.S. children's spectacle that, according to the reviewer, could be defined as a Broadway-style variety show. While the critic regarded *Super circo* as a show of "optimum quality," he understood that this type of variety show could and should be produced locally. As he observed, "But 'Super circo' is a video program conceptualized in the United States, filmed in the United States, with artists from the United States. . . . We believe that something similar could be produced in Cuba with Cuban artists."[37] Both the title and the review brought to the forefront the Cubanness that was missing from *Super circo*, and many critics believed this Cubanness should be part of all broadcast programming. Similarly, when CMQ-TV initiated its morning schedule in July 1951, the *Bohemia* reviewer complained that channel 6's morning schedule copied Unión Radio-TV's shows, which at the same time were a copycat version of the United States' morning programming on NBC.[38] In this case, the critic questioned the lack of originality and the fact that neither Unión Radio-TV's nor CMQ-TV's morning programming was conceptualized locally.

It is important to note that during the early period, it was rare for reviewers to criticize U.S. programming influences. When critics addressed U.S. television in negative terms, it mostly related to the possibility of saturating the airwaves with imported movies and shows (a threat that became a reality in the late 1950s, as explained in chapter 4) and the appropriation of particular U.S. programs that, according to critics, were culturally unfit for Cuba or simply, not "Cuban enough." For instance, when the Cuban comedy *Mi esposo favorito* (My favorite husband) began to air in 1953, Emma Pérez, the critic of the magazine *Gente de la Semana*, categorized the program as part of a "new modality of shows . . . with undeniable North American influences."[39] The Cuban *Mi esposo favorito* was an unauthorized translation and adaptation of *I Love Lucy*'s scripts, and after a public controversy between Desi Arnaz and the writer of the Cuban version, critics and viewers learned of the Cuban comedy's U.S. origins.[40] Thus, to emphasize the non-

Cubanness of *Mi esposo favorito*, the *Gente de la Semana* reviewer compared it with a series of comedies conceptualized and authored by Cuban writers. The review's last sentence highlights the relevance of the local by stating, "We must say that the experience is made in Cuba and it is Cuban television that scored a hit."[41] The problem with *Mi esposo favorito* did not have to do with the genre or concept but with what the critic called a lack of Cuban authenticity, which was translated to Cuban authorship. The locality of the production and actors was not enough to position this sitcom as Cuban.

Journalistic panel shows also demonstrated genre and concept importation, as well as the importance of cubanidad in issues of production, authorship, and cultural and political representations. One of the most prestigious and respected shows on Cuban commercial television was *Ante la prensa*, an indigenized version of NBC's *Meet the Press*. Similar to its U.S. originator, *Ante la prensa* (debuted in 1951) immediately became the destination for incisive political commentary. The following passage encapsulates how television critics viewed this imported concept: "Every Sunday prominent men of our national life, either politicians, businessmen, or from other areas of public life, are questioned in front of the audience about themes of general interest."[42] For *Ante la prensa*, and all the journalistic panel shows that emerged afterward, neither the critics nor the audiences were concerned about the direct programming connection to U.S. television. Instead, the main problem facing *Ante la prensa* (and other panel shows) stemmed from government censorship after Fulgencio Batista's coup. The political contemporaneity that defined the panel show as a genre became too tangible to sustain these programs without facing some type of censorship.

As these examples illustrate, cubanidad played a central role in specific program reviews, in which the critics continually highlighted that the concept, scriptwriters, actors, directors, and technicians were all Cubans working together to produce "excellent" local shows. If the programs were deficient in terms of technology, sets, acting, or script, or if some elements associated with the production were not "Cuban enough," the reviewers pitilessly tackled what they perceived as the problem in an attempt to make television "Cuban" and "excellent." These conceptualizations of quality and lack thereof in relation to Cubanness and television transcended issues of technology and production, foregrounding aspects of Cuban society that some sectors of the public wanted to wipe from the screen. As explained in chapter 3, some critics sought to downplay matters of sexuality, race (nonwhite), and class (working class) that would threaten the broadcasting of a "civilized" (read European/U.S.) and modern Cuban nation. Still, the question of television's distinction and Cubanness also encompassed other aspects associated with the medium. The structure that supported the expansion of television across the island became fundamental to promoting the narrative of progress that defined the broadcasting of Cuban modernity.

Advertising Progress

"Luxurious" would have not been the word to describe where Cuban television began (Unión Radio-TV) or, for that matter, the equipment that was first used. Unión Radio-TV's one and only studio was located in the dining room of an old mansion, the control was in the kitchen, and all the television equipment of both Unión Radio-TV and CMQ-TV was purchased from specialized secondhand stores in New York City.[43] Whereas this recycling of cameras, light spots, and microphones (among other things) cannot be compared to the cannibalization that defined media production in socialist Cuba, particularly after the Special Period (the economic crisis of 1990 through the 2000s), the facilities of Unión Radio-TV and the used equipment at both stations hint at the "levels of discontinuity" that characterized Cuba's socioeconomic development.[44]

Despite the fact that the post–World War II environment created an economic cushion and prosperity, the unevenness of the nation's development intensified economic, social, and educational differences among geographic regions and citizens. For example, only the cities that went through the process of socioeconomic development had the infrastructure for television. Furthermore, even for a prosperous businessman such as Goar Mestre (owner of the CMQ Circuit, which included a financially strong radio network), television was a costly enterprise. Mestre's speech at an International Advertising Convention luncheon held in New York City in 1951 hints at Latin America's "levels of discontinuity." In addition, and interrelated, as a representative of the Pan American Broadcasting Association, Mestre made it clear that Latin America needed U.S. financial backing to form a successful television industry: "Latin-American countries, which in transportation terms have moved from the age of the burro to that of the airplane without using railroads, will similarly leap from 'bad newspapers' and 'ill-conducted radio stations' to the fullest use of television as an entertainment and advertising medium. . . . Advertising research has proved that television appeals strongly to the illiterate. . . . American companies should consider increasing their budgets in Latin America."[45]

Mestre's tone can only be taken as a patronizing, bad joke to please his U.S. audience. After all, Cuba had railroads before Spain, other countries in the region also had this mode of transportation, and Mestre would not have categorized his own radio network as "ill-conducted." His remarks nonetheless reveal Cuba's (and the region's) fragmented economic development and its impact on education. Whereas a 1953 census indicated that the island had only a 23.6 percent illiteracy rate (one of the lowest in Latin America), a survey conducted between 1956 and 1957 showed that "43 percent of the rural population could not read or write."[46] Thus, even the most developed countries in the region, such as Cuba, suffered from socioeconomic disparities and educational inequalities. In Mestre's speech, this illiteracy was positioned as a benefit to television and the market: via the audiovisual medium, the illiterate would embrace U.S. consumer culture regardless of their socioeconomic status. Television would develop the local markets and would also help to bring the region into the international market economy.

Local media coverage of Mestre's participation at the International Advertising Convention's luncheon did not mention the topics discussed at the event. Nor was the Cuban public aware of the space that Unión Radio-TV broadcast from, or the used equipment at both stations.[47] Whereas the sale of Unión Radio-TV in mid-1951 hinted at the financial stresses associated with running a television station,[48] newspapers and magazines were dedicated to accentuating television as a symbol of Cuba's progress. Furthermore, nothing validated Cuba's socioeconomic development more than the inauguration of CMQ-TV's new building at Radiocentro (the structural complex housing the television studios).[49] This six-story, $350,000 building housed television studios, dressing rooms, an entire floor for a set shop, office space, a restaurant and a cafeteria, a pharmacy, a bank, a theater, a room to showcase cars, and retail space.[50] Advertising it as the "most modern television building in Latin America," Cuban magazines' and newspapers' photographic coverage of the inauguration highlighted the spaciousness and luxury of the new television building. Based on the narrative that the photos created, the modernity of Cuban television not only was present in the complicated equipment, elaborate sets, and sophisticated furniture but also was palpable in the elegance of the people who worked at CMQ-TV's studios. Even the cameramen were stylish.

The symbol of progress linked to CMQ-TV was not only related to the building but also attached to the station's expansion. Whereas in 1951 Unión Radio-TV promised to provide television to all provinces (something the station's owner accomplished rather literally by driving the broadcasting truck across the island and transmitting in closed circuit), it was CMQ-TV that, on March 9, 1952 (a day before Batista's military coup), expanded its transmission throughout different parts of Cuba.[51] CMQ-TV was advertised as "the first television network in Latin America," with its broadcast including direct transmissions from Havana to specific provinces (e.g., Matanzas) and retransmission of CMQ-TV programs via kinescopes (e.g., in Santa Clara). According to one critic, the television expansion across various parts of the island "offered the world the most grandiose demonstration of our degree of culture, civilization, and progress."[52] Yet, the fact that several provinces had access to television did not mean that the system worked. Deficiencies in electric voltage, delays in the delivery of kinescopes, bad reception, and limited coverage characterized the initial years of television outside the capital.[53] If the distribution of films, according to Jeff D. Himpele, "entails an infrastructure that is discursive and material at once," where regions and citizens define the temporal acquisition of films and the newness of print, the successful expansion of television involved more than installing microwaves and acquiring television sets.[54] Television required an infrastructure tied to the region's socioeconomic development and a television network's ability to transmit and deliver television products across the island.

Critics and owners remained mostly silent about the initial problems associated with CMQ-TV's expansion. Instead, the news regarding transmission issues came from those who watched television, and even those who did not. Through letters submitted to *Bohemia*, *Carteles*, and *Gente de la Semana*, viewers and nonviewers criticized television programming and technological flaws, in addition to questioning which segment of the population was the ideal audience-consumer-citizen. These letters functioned as rhetorical asides to the narrative of progress that characterized Cuban television coverage.

Reassessing Progress

Citizen letters addressing television began to appear in Cuban magazines as early as 1952. While most of the letters were still dedicated to radio (which was and would be the principal broadcasting tool throughout Cuba during the 1950s), those devoted to television initiated interesting conversations and debates about the medium. Three main themes dominated the letters' content: programming, reception, and coverage.

The most discussed topic about programming related to the ongoing broadcast of old Spanish-language movies (from Mexico, Spain, and Argentina) and some audiences who wanted to see English-language movies. While these debates reveal interesting information about audience preferences (e.g., comments such as "It is well known that the Cuban public prefers the North American movies" versus "Around thirty people get together in my house to watch movies, but when it is in English, everybody leaves and I just turn off the television and go to bed"), the ongoing repetition of old movies (as well as cartoons) hinted at the limited funding available for programming.[55] During the first couple of years of television, most programs had partial sponsorship. For instance, companies such as Bacardi and General Electric would cover part of the production costs for a specific period. After the contracted period expired, the company would be offered the option to become the program sponsor and thus cover all the production costs. Known as *programas paquetes* (packaged programming), these shows were used as "tests" for companies to assess the impact of sponsorship via television.[56] The *programas paquetes* were a win-win situation for corporations, which advertised their company or product for a minimal investment. Nonetheless, this strategy represented a financial struggle for talent and stations. Scriptwriters, actors, and technical staff had to work for lower salaries than in radio, and even though the Association of Cuban Artists (the union that regulated radio, television, and theater talent) created special tariffs for television, many, while accepting some television jobs, preferred to work in the "old" medium.[57] On the other hand, station owners lacked the capital to purchase new movies to fill up the schedule. Even though the creation of the Pan-American Television Corporation represented a good business strategy for Goar Mestre, the company's initial library consisted of old movies from Argentina and Mexico.[58] Thus, the viewers who complained about the movies were correct in their assessments: CMQ-TV mostly aired old Spanish-language films. But audience dissatisfaction went beyond the retransmission of movies.

After CMQ-TV's expansion, people from provinces that had access to television (via direct transmission and retransmission) began to criticize the service. For instance, one viewer from Camaguey indicated that getting programs late (i.e., the late arrival of kinescopes to retransmission centers) was equivalent to "not having television at all," while another resident (from the same area) indicated that "watching and listening to TV in Camaguey was repulsive" due to the bad transmission and late arrival of programming. Some audience members indicated that they were grateful to CMQ-TV for bringing television "to the small towns in the interior provinces"; nevertheless, most of the letters addressing the coverage outside Havana were filled with criticism.[59]

Goar Mestre and his business partners paid close attention to those letters. In a savvy public relations–style campaign, Mestre sporadically answered some of the citizens' complaints but then moved on to talk about his media accomplishments. For example, in reference to a letter complaining of the absence of television in Santa Clara, Mestre noted that the region would have television soon, then spent the rest of the column talking about his recent visit to Europe and his experiences with European television. He finished the piece by stating, "The truth is that, after North America [the United States], ours is the best television in the world."[60] Still, sectors of the audience constantly questioned Mestre's claims about the advancement of Cuban television. In a letter criticizing one of CMQ-TV's programs, in which the host referred to Jean-Paul Sartre as a "famous surrealist painter," an audience member remarked, "Lucky for the owner of CMQ-TV (this man firmly believes that Cuban TV is ten years ahead of Europe. What an imagination!), his channel does not reach Paris because, if that were the case, the young existentialist would blast the tower on M street [the location CMQ-TV's tower]."[61] Thus, while Mestre continually promoted Cuban television's modernity, audience members questioned his claims of progress.

One critique that seemed to attract the immediate attention of Mestre and his associates was the insinuation of discriminatory practices. For example, when an audience member complained that one of CMQ-TV's panel shows (*Los chicos Sire*) included only rich kids from Havana's private schools, Mestre's advertising partners (Publicidad Mestre Conill & Cia.

R. M. Conill) responded that "the insinuation was absurd," because "of the 138 kids that had been part of the show, 18.56 percent came from public schools in humble areas."[62] Even as the numbers evidenced the preference for upper-class children, the advertising company attempted to present some degree of fairness in its selection. According to the response, Publicidad Mestre Conill and CMQ-TV were companies that included all Cubans regardless of socioeconomic class or geographic region. Nonetheless, another citizen's letter demonstrates that class and socioeconomic modernization were pivotal to television's expansion.

On December 2, 1952, *Bohemia* published a letter written by Dr. Antonio Sobrino, a resident of Pinar del Río, a province located along the island's western coast. In his letter, Sobrino asked Goar Mestre why he had not installed "the necessary facilities" to send a signal from Havana to his province.[63] More specifically, Sobrino could not comprehend why CMQ-TV expanded its transmissions to Camaguey and Santiago (provinces located at the center-east and eastern borders, respectively) when Pinar del Río was geographically closer to Havana. According to this citizen, discrimination was the only reason his province had been ignored. As Sobrino wrote, "Let me insist, Mr. Mestre, that Pinar del Río, the black continent of the colonial period and the Cinderella of the republic, is being discriminated against by CMQ, probably because our region has been negatively depicted due to its poverty. . . . Maybe your discrimination offends us because we suffer from abandonment issues caused by private corporations like the one you own."[64] Although the author praised CMQ-TV's efforts to establish the first national television network, he also demanded an explanation for Mestre's regional neglect and ended his letter stating that the *pinareños* (the citizens of Pinar del Río) "want to be treated as members of the same class of Cubans as those who live in the east of Camaguey."

Sobrino's letter merged region, class, race, history, and television with the nation's geographically fragmented processes of socioeconomic modernization. One of Cuba's poorest provinces due to its tobacco-based economy, Pinar del Río, as the author wrote, had been marginalized by the government and private corporations who invested financial resources in economically developed regions, many of which were sustained by the sugar industry. Allegorically, the tobacco economy racialized Pinar del Río and its residents and prescribed the province's alleged "primitivism." In other words, in contrast to the regions where sugar mills benefited from U.S. and local capital investments that enhanced other areas' technological advancements, Pinar del Río was left untouched by the processes of economic modernization.[65]

In addition to Sobrino's reference to Pinar del Río's poverty and private-public "abandonment," other national, historically constructed factors defined the province's "Cinderella" status. Pinar del Río's inhabitants had been conceptualized as politically disengaged people who had to be "forced" to join the multiple battles of independence against Spain in the late nineteenth century. Consequently, because of the region's economic underdevelopment and the negative stereotypes of the pinareños—poor, intellectually slow "bobos" (idiots) who were politically flaky—that permeated Cuba's national-regional imaginary, Pinar del Río's population, as Sobrino indicated, was not treated in the same way as the Cubans residing in the island's economically modern and politically radical eastern provinces.[66]

Sobrino's letter also highlights important questions about what he perceived as discrimination and the author's own racial identity. Pinar del Río (unlike Santiago or Oriente) was not racially imagined as "black." This does not mean that blacks and mulattos were absent from Pinar del Río, but since the nineteenth century the numeric majority of the province's inhabitants (based on census numbers) was white.[67] Given Pinar del Río's historically constructed "whiteness," one wonders why Sobrino characterized the region as the "black continent of the colonial period," when the province was not imagined this way either during the colonial period or during the republic era. Was Sobrino a black man? Was he attempting to accuse CMQ-TV of promoting both class and racial discrimination? His letter does not answer these questions. Still, while class, rather than race, was the central theme of Sobrino's letter, Goar Mestre decoded both class and race as intertwined elements that defined this citizen's allegations of discriminatory practices at CMQ-TV.

Approximately three weeks after the letter was published, Goar Mestre replied to Sobrino in a *Bohemia* article entitled "Mensaje a los pinareños" (Message to the pinareños).[68] In the article, Mestre's rhetoric combined Cuban nationalism and its discourse of racial, class, and cultural egalitarianism with the ideology of the nation's progress and modernity. Referring to Sobrino's accusation of discrimination as "calumny" and as a "truly evil description that will only damage the accusers," Mestre represented the CMQ Circuit (i.e., radio and TV) as an industry whose main objective was to broadcast to all members of the nation equally. "Our mission is to serve the Cuban people, without classifying or distinguishing between provinces or regions, poor or rich, whites or blacks." Mestre proceeded by highlighting the progress of Cuban television in comparison to Latin America, England, and France ("Cuban television has distinguished itself with its excellent technical quality") and by specifying that even European countries and some cities in the United States did not have television stations. Notwithstanding his use of nationalistic and modernizing rhetoric to underscore CMQ-TV's efforts to produce excellent television for "all Cubans," Mestre admitted that it was not financially viable to expand television to Pinar del Río: "To offer television in Pinar del Río we need to install at least five or six microwave links, which would cost more than one million pesos. Frankly, Doctor Sobrino, bring up this idea to any business owner or advertiser and you will find that in a period of economic insecurity not everyone is willing to invest one million pesos in a region that represents only 4 percent of the nation's consumption."[69] Mestre's message was crystal clear: Pinar del Río would not have television in 1953. His response demonstrates that the narrative that formed the spectacles of progress not only included technological superiority and sophisticated television spaces and equipment but also encompassed audiences who lived in modern cities or regions.

Audiences and nonaudiences judged how Cuban modernity was broadcast, and like the critics, they pushed for television "excellence." They questioned some critics' and television owners' claims about Cuban advancements in television, most likely in an attempt to push for higher-quality TV, in terms of both reception and programming. Their critical view of television, as I elaborate in the following chapters, continued throughout the 1950s, providing divergent understandings of the function of television in Cuban society. Yet, at the same time that critics, owners, viewers, and nonviewers were assessing the medium in an attempt to improve its quality, the state also became involved in the evaluation process. By way of new broadcasting laws, the state reshaped the industry and transformed the goals and objectives of Cuban television.

Redefining Progress through the Law

In a story entitled "El 10 de marzo en radio y TV," the *Carteles* magazine critic briefly explained what happened to radio and television the day of Batista's coup: "To synthesize: all the radio and television stations were occupied by the police force. CMQ-TV and UR-TV canceled all programming and broadcast the 'test pattern.'"[70] Two days after CMQ-TV expanded its transmission to the eastern part of the country, offering, according to one critic, "the most grandiose demonstration of [Cuba's] degree of culture, civilization, and progress," the coup dismantled one of the primary elements that defined Cuba's claim to modernity: its constitutional democracy.[71] The one-day television pause signaled a change in the way broadcasting would function from then on. Though commercial television would continue the flow of programs, advertisements, and schedules, government censorship would frame a new style of television production.[72]

The first censorship move occurred a day after the coup when, as Michael Salwen documents, the minister of information met with all radio and television owners to let them know that they could express their opinions "as long as they did not make their microphones available to private individuals."[73] This space of allegedly free expression quickly changed. In May 1952, Fulgencio Batista initiated his censorship of news and public affairs programs that criticized the government.[74] One of the first television shows to be censored was CMQ-TV's *Ante la prensa*, a program that would go off and on the air for the next seven years. Other radio and television programs and commentators followed the same path. For instance, the same month that Batista began his censorship campaign, sympathizers of his government showed up at the studio where the culturally oriented and politically engaged show *La universidad del aire* was being broadcast and attacked the show's participants and the studio audience. A year later (in May 1953), Batista's censorship of radio, television, and the press extended to cinema newsreels—all of which had to be approved by the government-run Comisión Revisora de Películas.[75] Then, after the attack on Moncada on July 26, 1953, led by Fidel Castro, Batista proclaimed a state of emergency, absorbed all state powers, eliminated civil liberties, and established stricter media censorship. Though the drastic measures ended after three months, the continuing threat of censorship had television owners and critics in a state of alert.[76] In one of his columns, the *Carteles* television reviewer expressed that radio, television, and newspaper censorship went against the principles of democracy.[77] Similarly, in a speech delivered to Canadian broadcasters, Goar Mestre insisted on the importance of keeping a separation between the media and the government, declaring, "We [broadcasters] want legislations to protect us and we want to be distanced as much as possible from our governments' ups and downs."[78] The critics' and media professionals' claims spoke to the notion of a modern democratic government, foregrounding the principles that had shaped Cuba from 1940 to Batista's coup.

In contrast to his censorship practices, Fulgencio Batista's self-proclaimed "revolutionary democracy" (an attempt to link his regime to the 1933 revolution) drafted a new broadcasting law that embraced freedom of expression for all Cubans.[79] As Article 55 of the new Broadcasting Law of 1953 indicates, "Free expression cannot be previously censored outside the legal sphere."[80] Most likely pressured by the press and members of the private sector who called for a law that promoted "the expression of different points of view," the January 26, 1953, law used a democratic discourse that deflected attention from the conditions in which the regulation was created.[81] Consisting of eleven chapters and seventy-five articles, the legislation vastly expanded commercial broadcasting rights while also (and in theory) opening the possibility for public stations to exist.

Based on the regulation, Cuba had two types of stations: state-controlled public stations and commercial stations. Following the European broadcasting system, the main objective of the public stations, according to the law, was to promote educational and culturally oriented programming without any type of commercial intervention. Besides including a definition of public broadcasting, the legislation contained no other references regarding how the government would sustain public stations, nor did it include specific stipulations on programming. Only one article was devoted to public broadcasting. The rest of the legislation was dedicated to commercial broadcasting, and it was in this arena that the regulation had a major impact. The 1953 law dismantled all the existing broadcasting regulations that had promoted culturally oriented programming and protected the jobs of local media professionals.

In terms of programming, the 1953 law reduced the categories from five (as established in the 1950 law) to four and reframed some of the earlier groupings. On the one hand, recreational (similar to the variety and aficionado categories from 1950) became entertainment programs, while informative (news), cultural (educational programming), and civic (political, economic, and social issues) were a variation of the informative and educational categories established in the 1950 law. On the other hand, the children and aficionado programming categories were eliminated, meaning that stations were not required to cater to children or provide spaces for newcomers to the medium. Whereas the elimination of the aficionado category was connected to issues of professionalism, the removal of the children category was probably a product of the conceptualization of the television audience and surveys. While the surveys in Cuba included children as part of the audience, advertising agencies mainly considered gender and class when defining the Cuban television audience.[82] Hence, the new programming categorizations not only hinted at the desired audience but also provided information about which sector of the media industry's professional audience benefited from the law. Interrelated with the previous change, another stipulation eliminated the stations' requirement to produce shows in all four categories. As Article 46 specifies, "Stations could perform one of these categories or limit them to some, as long as other stations in the area covered the remaining categories."[83] This new rule was a departure from previous broadcasting laws, all of which required a diversity of programming per station (see chapter 1). Even as Article 49 stipulates that all station content include "at least 2 percent" educational programming, the law did not require a balance between entertainment, educational, and informative shows. Any program that discussed education or that was conceptualized (for legal purposes) as educational would fit the requirement.

The most dramatic transformation occurred in the regulations pertaining to live and mechanical programming. The new legislation eliminated the percentages and did not require any recorded programs to be locally produced. As chapter 3 of the law establishes, "Broadcasting stations would regulate the time used for recorded programming. . . . The transmissions of recorded programs or movies could not be limited based on where they were produced, the date of production, or the length."[84] Together with a clause that gave commercial stations the leeway to "freely exploit commercial propaganda," the 1953 legislation introduced the possibility for stations to have a schedule completely filled with imported movies and/or shows and multiple commercials.[85] Equally important and interrelated, contrary to previous legislation that established a percentage for local talent, none of the articles included in the 1953 legislation required the hiring of local performers or the promotion of Cuban culture. The broadcasting law was designed for business expansion and thus considered only the interests of owners and private corporations. In this regard, the article on public broadcasting was probably included to validate the state's interest in Cuban culture, education, and the public, particularly in relation to the drastic changes occurring in

FIGURE 2.5. Promotion for Noticiario Unión Radio. Courtesy of the Cuban Heritage Collection, Cuban Photograph Collection, University of Miami Libraries, Coral Gables, Florida.

FIGURE 2.6. CMAB Telemundo station announcement. Courtesy of the Cuban Heritage Collection, Cuban Photograph Collection, University of Miami Libraries, Coral Gables, Florida.

FIGURE 2.7. CMBF Televisión Cadena Nacional station announcement. Courtesy of the Cuban Heritage Collection, Cuban Photograph Collection, University of Miami Libraries, Coral Gables, Florida.

the commercial arena. The 1953 legislation called for an über-capitalistic environment: Cuban television (and radio) was an open terrain available for financial conquest.

And corporations quickly conquered television. In the same year that the law was instituted, three stations were inaugurated in Havana: CMBA-TV Telemundo, channel 2, owned by Amadeo Barletta, who was also the proprietor of the newspaper *El Mundo* and TV Nacional (previously known as Unión Radio-TV); CMBF-TV, channel 7, partially owned by the Mestre brothers; and TV Caribe S.A., channel 11, the only station owned by a U.S. corporation (the Storer Broadcasting Company).[86] Imported shows (via kinescopes) and movies dominated two of the new channels' programming (channel 7 and channel 11), thus taking advantage of the legal stipulation that allowed for unlimited recorded programs. Both the proliferation of stations in Havana and the expansion of television throughout the island (first via CMQ-TV and, after 1952, by way of TV Nacional and Telemundo) were seen as indicative of the nation's modernization. Even the state appropriated the discourse of television's expansion as a sign of Cuban modernity. As the director of the Radio Office observed, "In matters of television . . . Cuba is a pioneer in comparison to other countries in America and Europe. Television's transmissions are constantly improving, and two other new stations will be inaugurated soon."[87] The political aspects that defined Cuban modernity and the threats of Cuba's public sphere were put aside. In the legal arena, the broadcasting of Cuban modernity became exclusively interconnected with capitalist expansion. Nonetheless, although the law facilitated the launching of stations and a new style of programming, transformations taking place in Cuba's economy and the actual broadcasting legislation quickly affected the industry and its media professionals.

In 1954, Cuban television suffered a major crisis with the decline of the international sugar market (which directly affected the island's economy) and the saturation of the television market.[88] As CMQ-TV's Goar Mestre, one of the few television owners to survive the crisis, explained in a magazine article, "To the decline of the nation's economy we need to add a decisive reality: that we do not have enough advertisers or viewers to sustain the five stations that are operating today."[89] In a period of economic uncertainty and increased political instability (particularly after the Moncada attack, the birth of the Cuban Revolution), it became difficult for Cuban television to continue its exponential growth. Industrial transformations and new programming practices emerged after 1954, establishing a television industry that was different from the one that characterized the medium during its first three years. Stations closed and changed ownership while monopolies emerged. An example of this pattern can be seen with Televisión del Caribe, one of the three stations that began operations in 1953 and then closed in 1954. The station was later acquired by Telemundo. This decrease in competition opened the arena for two businessmen—Mestre and Barletta—to control the market. Backed by other investments (in Mestre's case, a radio network and an advertising company, and for Barletta, a newspaper company and Mafia money), CMQ-TV, Telemundo, and Television Nacional networks (partly owned by Mestre) dominated the industry until 1959.[90]

Programming also changed. Several expensive shows (many of which had high ratings) were canceled and replaced with low-budget music and variety shows, talent shows, panel shows, and game shows. In addition, all networks began to include imported U.S. programming on their schedules.[91] While locally produced programming received high ratings throughout the 1950s, the sweeping importation of U.S. movies and shows dubbed in Spanish became a major concern for television professionals and journalists in the year before the revolution. At the same time, the industry restructure caused the job market to shrink. This, together with the political censorship that began to take place after Batista's military coup, instigated a series of migratory waves of Cuban media professionals and talent off the island to destinations throughout Latin America. While the movement of Cuban technical staff, television executives, and talent was in many cases transitory, it expanded the Cuban media connections that had emerged in the 1940s radio era. As I have argued elsewhere, these migrations were instrumental to the relocation of Cuban media professionals and talent in Latin America after the triumph of the Cuban Revolution.[92]

It should be clear that the crisis did not mean that Cuban television stalled in terms of technological development and creativity. Even though many media professionals left Cuba to work in various Latin American countries throughout the mid-1950s, by the end of the decade Havana still had one of the most developed television industries in the region. In fact, one of the most impressive technological achievements in Cuban television occurred in 1954 when CMQ-TV used an airplane with a relay transmitter (an exercise called "stratovision") to broadcast the baseball World Series. As a UNESCO report indicates, this was "the first time that stratovision ha[d] been used successfully for a series of broadcasts for the general public."[93] Furthermore, as discussed later, CMQ-TV, Telemundo, and Television Nacional continued to expand their signals across the island, adding regions and audiences to their industries and thus feeding the narratives that formed the spectacles of progress. This narrativization of progress went hand in hand with the modernizing trend that took place in Havana during the 1950s. Havana, deemed one of the most cosmopolitan and modern cities in the region, attracted international talent that frequently performed in casinos and on radio and television shows. Additionally, the musical, literary, artistic (from ballet to art and theater), and architectural development initiated in the 1940s flourished in the 1950s.[94] Nonetheless, the political, economic, and social conditions that arose after Batista's coup affected television. In a period of corruption, illegal activity, and political uncertainty, television became a somewhat regulated space where members of the Cuban elite, first, and then the state, after 1955, could represent another (albeit problematic) vision of the country. Without eliminating the spectacles of progress, the spectacles of decency took over the national stage.

A New Stage for Cuban Television

During the first four years of television's existence, critics, owners, audiences, nonaudiences, and the state shifted the meaning of Cuban television away from its earlier conceptualizations. While it was still seen as a technology, a channel, and a place, the very definitions of those descriptors changed. New technological requirements, visions of programming, business stipulations, and the law transformed how the medium was understood. Television was seen as a technology that needed to operate with precision not only because it became a symbol of the nation's progress but also because its effective operation was vital to the success of the business enterprise. Without effective programming transmission, audience-consumers could not receive the expected product. Television technology went from being an array of complex cables, towers, monitors, and signals to an artifact that promoted consumerism. Critics and media owners also saw television as a place that, although open to all Cubans, should showcase and attract upwardly mobile people. The new television buildings and the regions where stations/transmitters were erected defined the populations and regions that constituted the ideal Cuban public. Although the class-based conceptualization of the audience changed in the mid-1950s, Cuban television was first seen as a media outlet for the Cuban elite. Critics, audiences, and media professionals viewed television as a channel whose main objective was to represent excellent Cuban programming. While as in pretelevision discussions of the medium, the education of the Cuban public was still an important component in the evaluation of quality (see chapter 3), technological sophistication and program originality were seen as key components of Cuban television. All aspects of production were scrutinized to evaluate the quality and "level of Cubanness" in television's cultural products.

The Cuban state also reconceptualized the medium through new broadcasting laws. The 1953 regulation represented the culmination of years of negotiations regarding the uses and functions of broadcasting in Cuban society. If the 1942 and 1950 legislation attempted to create a balance between serving the needs of the Cuban public and benefiting media industries, the 1953 legislation moved the regulatory barriers exclusively to revamp the private sector. The Cuban public and those who worked in media industries disappeared from the legal sphere. This regulation was the final stage in the appropriation of the liberal ideology that built U.S. broadcasting: with minimal intrusion from the state, media industries would compete, grow, and provide a variety of programming for the public. The key difference between the U.S. and Cuban cases relates to the political conditions, namely, the antidemocratic government, that shaped Cuba's 1953 law. Cuban television promoted a U.S.-style consumer ideology, but the social and political reality that surrounded the medium challenged the freedom linked to capitalistic democracy, the staple of what was disseminated around the world as U.S. democracy. The new function of television in Cuba was to serve the interests of the market and, progressively, the mandates of the state.

CHAPTER 3

Spectacles of Decency

Morality as a Matter of the Industry and the State

From a political, industrial and commercial angle, the goal
[of television] is to idiotize the people.—Emma Pérez,
"Televerdades," *Gente de la Semana,* December 28, 1952

Radio critics began attempting to delineate the medium's role in Cuban society in the pretelevision years, when it was envisioned as an outlet for promoting the education of Cuban citizens. As Alberto Giró, the *Diario de la
Marina* critic, had expressed one month before the incorporation of television on the island, "We hope that Cuba will take advantage of this wonderful
medium to benefit the educational enterprise."[1] In several reviews, critics advocated for what they considered television's educational potential. This did
not necessarily mean using the medium in a classroom setting (even though
some did address this topic as well), but through broadcasting high-culture
programs such as ballet, opera, and theater as well as informative shows.[2]

The merging of high culture and education in discussions about Cuban
media dates back to the 1930s, when the broadcasting regulations of 1934
and 1939 positioned radio as a medium that could uplift the Cuban people via educational and culturally oriented programming. What differen-
tiated the state's view of radio in the 1930s from the critics' assessment of
television in the late 1940s and 1950s was their conception of the audience.
Radio was accessible to people across the nation and regardless of class.
Television, in contrast, and particularly during its early years, was available
only to the middle and upper classes in economically developed regions.
The audience's class status, together with what some reviewers perceived

as television's potential to culturally elevate "the masses" (a perception defined by class), played a key role in theater, opera, drama, and ballet being favored over popular-culture genres such as comedy and variety shows. In this regard, and following Pierre Bourdieu's theory of class distinctions and taste, television became a technological apparatus that, through its cultural representations, could become a "sign of distinction but also of vulgarity."[3] Critics conceptualized television as a medium for the middle and upper classes, as well as a technological tool that could help educate Cuba's general population.

Cuban intellectuals, somewhat similar to television critics, also saw the medium's pedagogical potential. For example, in a July 1952 roundtable conference held at the University of Havana, a group of intellectuals met with television owners and advertisers to discuss the possibility of using television for education.[4] According to a UNESCO survey of television across the globe, the different constituencies "showed themselves willing to work together in this effort," though broadcasters and advertisers indicated that the government and educational institutions needed to be active participants in this endeavor.[5]

The broadcasting industry and the government had already collaborated successfully. Between 1951 and 1953, the Ministry of Education, in association with CMQ-TV, produced *Una hora de arte y cultura*, a culturally oriented program broadcast on Sunday evenings. This eclectic one-hour show presented theater and ballet performances in addition to interviews and conferences focusing on literature and art. Furthermore, before the incorporation of television on the island, CMBZ radio (1932–33) and, later, CMQ radio (1949–60) broadcast *La universidad del aire*, a radio program most likely inspired by the U.S. program *The American School of the Air*, which addressed political, historical, literary, and cultural topics.[6] Despite these two successful cases, some critics and intellectuals realized that it was unlikely television would be utilized exclusively for education. On the one hand, entertainment genres consistently obtained high ratings, thus influencing the production of more variety shows, comedies, and question-and-answer panel shows instead of, for example, zarzuelas. On the other hand, the Broadcasting Law of 1953 dismantled the possibilities of legally forcing television owners to include culturally oriented programming on their schedules (see chapter 2). Because it limited educational requirements to 2 percent of the programming and did not define the parameters of what constituted educational shows, anything that television owners classified as educational counted as such. Thus, as the UNESCO report indicates, along with the culturally oriented show *Una hora de arte y cultura*, "different aspects of the news, operettas and dramatic programs, children's films, and a children's quiz show" were listed as educational.[7] Programming categories were elastic and malleable, making it easy for television owners to fulfill the limited programming requirements.

The absence of programming quotas and definitions did not mean that culturally oriented shows and high-culture acts disappeared from the schedule. Ballet, dramas, zarzuelas, and operas ran throughout the commercial era.[8] For instance, CMQ-TV's *Jueves de Partagás*, a variety show that, together with *Casino de la alegría*, was one of the most successful programs on Cuban commercial television, combined musical acts, dance performances (from rumba to ballroom dances), comedy sketches, and classical ballet (via its own Ballet Partagás) in its repertoire. Additionally, CMQ-TV's *Casino de la alegría* also incorporated ballet into some of its broadcasts, including televised performances of the renowned ballerina Alicia Alonso.[9] But, despite the occasional representation of high-culture acts, popular-culture genres dominated the television schedule. Thus, up until the triumph of the Cuban Revolution, many reviewers focused their criticism on the monopoly of entertainment genres and what they considered an excessive use of advertising. Most critics believed that the public broadcasting system was the best model for Cuba.

The dismissal of entertainment genres coincided with the disdain that a handful of intellectuals held for popular culture. Whereas both high art and popular culture thrived during the 1940s and 1950s, some intellectuals (particularly the older generation) embraced "a more conservative trend," thus rejecting popular music and programming that were not aligned with an educational and informative agenda.[10] For some television critics, however, the traditionalist understanding of culture also came with a Catholic/Christian, bourgeois, and Eurocentric notion of morality that operated through racial, class, and gender hierarchies. In some ways, the critics' racialized understanding of morality coincided with how European settlers saw themselves in relation to those in the colonial territories. As Ann Laura Stoler argues, "What constituted morality vacillated, as did what defined white prestige—and what its defense should entail. No description of European colonial communities fails to note the obsession with white prestige as a basic feature of colonial thinking."[11] In the case of Cuba, the racial, ethnic, and cultural syncretism that defines the island's society was seen as a threat to televised depictions of a culturally modern nation. Modernity, in this regard then, did not correspond to democratic participation in civil society or economic and technological progress but instead was associated with the racial, ethnic, and cultural composition of the nation. To broadcast Cuban modernity, television needed to control any acts that questioned the Spanish/European, Catholic, and sexually constrained elements that defined Cuba's bourgeois culture.

The *Diario de la Marina* critic Alberto Giró and the Commission on Radio Ethics were the first to police morality in entertainment programming. Following the tradition of the radio era, Giró and the self-regulated private organization strongly advocated for eliminating elements they considered uncivilized, vulgar, and barbarous. By way of reviews and CRE rulings, perceptions of the culture and tastes of the middle, upper, and working classes turned out to be more than just comments on culture and education. Eurocentric meanings of race, along with ideologies of gender and sexuality, became the parameters for judging what was moral and immoral.

By the mid-1950s, however, the topic of morality took another turn when the Ministry of Communication joined the battle against immorality on television. Whereas the state agency reproduced some of the CRE's rules, it also focused on new issues regarding gender and sexuality. Notions of femininity and masculinity began to play a part in what was moral and immoral, particularly concerning male performances. Any act that questioned masculinity and heterosexual desire had to be eliminated from Cuban television programming. At a time when various political contingencies were expressing anxiety about Batista's commitment to democracy, when economic disparities between the rich and the poor steadily grew, and when illegal activities dominated daily life in Havana, immorality on entertainment television became an important theme for the government.[12] With the Ministry of Communication's attention to indecency on television, the topic of morality went from being a matter of civil society to a primary focus of the state. The televised body was integrated into the political body, setting the stage for the legalization of media censorship that dominated the last period of Bastista's government.

The discussions and rulings regarding morality on television produced two distinct outcomes: first, the articulation of different understandings of Cuban cultural modernity and, second, the failure of the state to address

Cuba's problems. In other words, debating morality on television not only involved the monitoring, interrogation, celebration, and condemnation of performances that challenged representations of a European-derived cultural modernity (high art, Catholic/Christian morals regarding sexuality, and racial/cultural superiority, among other things), but also created a distraction from talking about the discontent that diverse sectors of Cuban society were feeling. Hence, morality on television was more than a commentary on performances of the body; it became an excuse to avoid addressing the performance of the state.

Television Morality: The Containment of Racialized Sexuality

In a December 5, 1950, article entitled "Peligrosa perspectiva," the *Diario de la Marina* critic Alberto Giró noted that media professionals needed to pay attention to the types of shows and the cultural representations that were being aired on television. As Giró wrote, "Without being pessimistic, we have a dangerous perspective that future variety shows would include nudity, exaggerated rumbas, and other types of performances that could lean towards the low and the vulgar."[13] His concern about the possible moral decadence in future programming was reaffirmed in his last words: "It is then necessary that the owners of the Cuban video industries try to guide television down a route of high morality and education to avoid the intervention of the Commission on Radio and Television Ethics."[14] "Peligrosa perspectiva" was written not for the general public but for television owners and the CRE, to whose name Giró added the word "Television" probably with the belief that the commission would soon monitor the new medium. Still, beyond the article's limited intended audience, what is relevant about this story is the critic's perception of immorality.

The ideology of immorality presented in Giró's article was coded through ideals of Western civility wherein to be modern and civilized the citizen's body needed to be sexually disciplined and contained.[15] Yet, in Giró's words, the idea of Western civility transcended the realm of the exclusively sexual. The black working-class rumba and its gendered sexuality—the male-female erotic dances and the *rumberas-vedettes'* seminude bodies—were not appropriate for the public. While, as Robin Moore notes, "there is no single definition of rumba," this musical, cultural, and dance expression was associated with "Cuba's black underclass, their life styles, attitudes, and culture."[16] Thus, considering the racial, class, and sexual elements that defined the rumba in Cuba's sociocultural imaginary, Giró's comments created "dependent constructs of bourgeois sexuality and racialized sexuality."[17] The *Diario de la Marina* critic's understanding of immorality (and, as a result, morality) rearticulated the racialized, gendered, and classed factors that defined cultural modernity in Cuba. As a symbol of modern Cuba, television had to implement the "education of desire," a moral, civilized order that was laden with racial, gendered, sexual, and class significations.[18]

Giró's preoccupation with television morality became a central component in his television reviews. For instance, on December 15, 1950, just ten days after his first cautionary words regarding rumba and sexuality, he declared, "We pleasantly observe the rapid expansion of video in Cuba but we are a little worried, as we have mentioned on other occasions, about what could happen when the video competition is established and each competitor tries to get the biggest number of *tele-videntes* [televiewers] or spectators."[19] For Giró, television's commercial imperatives and entertainment programming represented a major obstacle to his ideal vision of the medium. As he observed in late January 1951, when Unión Radio-TV and CMQ-TV began their ferocious battle over Havana's audience, "Television should be essentially used as a wonderful medium for education and all programs should be guided to that end. Morality should prevail even in shows that focus on mere entertainment."[20]

Despite Giró's moralistic, racially coded, and culturally elitist views, the variety shows, in which most black and mulatto musicians, rumberas-vedettes, and *mamboletas* (female mambo dancers) performed, became the most successful programs during Cuban commercial television's early years.[21] As the first television survey indicates, in February 1951, 90 percent of the audience watched CMQ-TV's variety show *El gran show de Bacardi*.[22] This audience preference was once again confirmed with the April 1951 survey, which, to the dismay of the *Carteles* critic, demonstrated that audiences preferred variety shows over dramas. Similar results were obtained in the April 1952 and August 1953 surveys, which reported that the majority of the top ten–rated programs were variety shows and comedies (e.g., the by-then famous variety show *Cabaret Regalias*).[23] And, in 1954, the pattern persisted: variety shows and comedies had the highest ratings.[24] Contrary to the critics' expectations, the financially solvent audience-consumers seemed to enjoy the rumba, the mambo, the erotic dances, and the comedies' *choteo* (a Cuban term generally translated as "mockery").

The commercial success of variety shows and comedies did not alter the *Diario de la Marina* critic's racialized and gendered views of what constituted immorality on television. As I explain later, in some of his remarks his connections between immorality, blackness, and uncivilized cultures became blunter. Nonetheless, Giró was not the only voice in Cuba's public sphere to present a racialized and gendered perception of immorality. In 1952 the CRE joined Giró's crusade, expressing its opinion (via newspapers and magazines) of morality in entertainment programming.[25] Whereas the CRE did not publish an official code, it censored sexuality (e.g., romantic kisses and revealing garments on women) and songs that the organization had originally banned from radio (see chapter 1).[26]

The CRE's emphasis on sexuality in general and women's sexuality in particular responded to upper-class norms of conduct that connected family honor to women's sexual behavior. Even though the early twentieth-century women's movement in Cuba and the 1940 constitution expanded women's rights, motherhood and virginity still defined family decency and decorum during the 1950s.[27] Another aspect associated with family decency and sexuality was race. "Whiteness was a key marker of class status . . . and upper-class white Cubans expressed persistent anxieties about racial contamination through mixed marriage."[28] While sexual coupling between upper-class white Cuban males and black and mulata working-class women was common, these relationships occurred, for the most part, outside the confines of marriage. As a result, the CRE's focus on sexuality went beyond bodies and pleasures; it tapped into hegemonic ideas of race, articulating Anne McClintock's argument that "race, gender and class are not distinct realms of experience . . . , they come into existence in and through relation to each other."[29] Television, as a medium targeted to the upper-middle classes, needed to exclude references to sexuality and desexualized performances that could convey (or incite) sexual desire within and outside of racial boundaries. To this end, in May 1953, the CRE formalized its media censorship via the regulation titled *Circular N60*.

According to *Circular N60*, media professionals were not devoting enough attention to television "ethics." And, due to the professionals' unintentional but somewhat irresponsible behavior, the CRE had to design a set of rules to assure "morality, religion, and good customs" on television.[30] As the organization stated, "Since television is a family-oriented spectacle it should be subjected to special considerations. . . . It is for that reason that we have seen the need to implement effective measures to avoid infractions on television programs."[31] Though the CRE document never defined the term "ethics," the full brunt of *Circular N60* focused on the rumba and mambo dances and, more specifically, the female dancers. By calling attention to the camera shots' exclusion or long shots' distancing of a performer's "dances with sensual movements," of "choreographic presentations," and of "gestures, movements, or anatomic details that are against decency or bad taste," the CRE regulations were clearly designed for the rumberas-vedettes and the mamboletas who, together with singers and bands, dominated the musical performances on variety shows.[32]

With *Circular N60*, televisual "indecency and bad taste" became synonymous with the female body, which through sensual movements, contortions, and dance steps allegorically personified the *mulataje* of the nation.[33] As Peter Wade contends, "Any connection between the body, music, dance forms, and sexuality are cultural constructions but it is important that these constructions take place not just *on* but *through* the body."[34] Considering the racialized sexuality associated with the rumba and mambo musical styles and dances, the drums that conveyed the sounds of Afro-Cuban rhythms, and the racial spectrum of the dancers (mostly whites and mulatas), one could argue that the decency decree was designed to repress the racial, cultural, gendered, and sexual mulataje that produced the "Cuban race." By way of their televisual performances, the rumberas-vedettes and the mamboletas symbolically merged and became the iconic mulata, a national figure that in previous decades had embodied the "multifarious anxieties, contradictions and imperfections in the Cuban body politic."[35] In *Circular N60*, the female dancer/mulata was transformed into an immoral national mark, an emblem of "unproductive eroticism," which in a period of political uncertainty threatened the broadcasting of a sexually contained, bourgeois, and modern national self.[36] Hence, while several Cuban films of the early 1950s (coproduced with Mexico) depicted Cuba as an African-influenced nation and culture (through the iconic mulata figure–protagonist), and whereas rumba, rumberas, mambo, and mamboletas were the principal (racially sexualized) attractions in the casino cabaret shows, commercial television was expected to restrain the mulata and the mulataje.[37]

FIGURE 3.1. Mexican singer and movie star Pedro Vargas dancing with two
mamboletas. Gente de la Semana, November 23, 1952. Courtesy of the Cuban
Heritage Collection, University of Miami Libraries, Coral Gables, Florida.

Given that all television programs were broadcast live, self-censorship was in the hands of producers and cameramen who, through camera shots, were in charge of creating a distance between the audience and the dancers. The medium that, according to one critic, preferred the "close-up" and "the intimate" needed to transform itself and become more similar to theatrical representations. If in theater the proscenium stage creates a "fourth wall," a detachment between the audience and the fictional world of the play, in Cuban television the two cameras' long shots had to disconnect the audiences from the spectacle of female-racial-sexual indecency. Technology, as a key sign of modernization, would be the principal tool used to impose moral civility.

Television owners and producers attempted to follow the CRE's code as much as live television allowed. Broadcasting live was a major obstacle for media professionals, who could not predict what an actor would say, improvise, or physically do; what censored songs musical groups would play; or what sudden "improper" move a rumbera or a group of mamboletas would enact. Only two of the commercial stations that were operating on the island used kinescopes; as a result, it was extremely difficult to prove an infraction had occurred.[38] However, despite the burden of dealing with artists' suspensions, television owners did not protest the CRE's regulations. In a time of escalating government and economic instability, owners and producers were struggling to keep their business afloat. The CRE and television's cultural representations were the least important issue for television owners at the time. More important was the distance that the CRE kept between television industries and the government; the stricter the CRE was, the less likely it was that the government would intervene. Even though, as I explain later in this chapter, the severity of the CRE did not prevent the government from getting involved with television, *Circular N60* and other rules developed by the organization in 1954 delayed governmental censorship.

Nonetheless, not all industry-related people welcomed *Circular N60*. For instance, the *Bohemia* television reviewer criticized the CRE's regulations, indicating that "if their [the CRE members'] opinion prevailed someday, the majority of our musical shows and a significant portion of the dramatic and humorous programs would disappear. . . . Our programming would be dominated by tedious panels, classical music, symphony orchestra, and operas."[39] Contrary to the *Diario de la Marina* television critic, who consistently supported the CRE's positions, the *Bohemia* reviewer embraced a different understanding of morality and modernity. From his perspective, entertainment programs should be televisual spaces wherein media professionals would create diverse representations of the nation. For the *Bohemia* television critic, modernity would be broadcast through a series of bodily, verbal, and musical performances that challenged Western racial, sexual, moral, and cultural discourses.

This was not the first time the *Bohemia* critic publicly disagreed with the CRE. Previous clashes between the television critic and the organization prompted the CRE's director to write a letter to *Bohemia* questioning the reviewer's "journalistic impartiality."[40] However, despite the *Bohemia* reviewer's apparent intention to influence the CRE, the organization did not alter its perspective of what constituted morality and immorality. In fact, one year after releasing *Circular N60*, the CRE strengthened its position on television.

Issued in 1954, the CRE's *Circular N82* and *Circular N83* covered four main themes: kissing, clothing, the exposure of body parts, and choreography based on "cults or beliefs against civilization."[41] The topic of morality on television also included the elimination of "obscene, indecent, and profane language," the performance of musical numbers previously banned by the organization, and the broadcasting hours for adult content (after 9:30 PM). In terms of kissing and clothing, the new rules solidified the CRE's pre-1953 position regarding women's sexuality. With language and music, the organization continued to censor songs that included references to sexual intercourse (this topic was originally covered by the CRE during the late 1940s, as noted in chapter 1). What was new about the CRE's 1954 campaign was the reference to religion. Television programs could not broadcast "choreographic representations of cults or beliefs contrary to civilization, good customs, or social order, even if these expressions have a folkloric character."[42] The CRE did not mention Afro-Cuban religious traditions; however, the *Diario de la Marina* reviewer quickly made the connection. In a 1954 review, Alberto Giró observed that he was concerned about shows that were not following the CRE's regulations and presented "ñáñigo numbers," which "go against our [Cubans'] religious customs and against our civilization and culture. The resurgence of acts committed by witches (recently there were two child kidnapping attempts) is, without a doubt, a product of the interest that has been given to some types of African dances and certain songs with incomprehensible lyrics."[43]

Besides situating television as a medium that is capable of inciting violence (i.e., the kidnapping attempts), Giró replicated mainstream society's prejudice toward the African-based and male-only secret society of Abakuá and its music and dance rituals. As music critic Ned Sublette observes, "Rumba was intimately associated in Cuban society with ñáñigos." Thus, Giró's review highlighted the relationship between commercialized rumbas and their black and working-class origins.[44] In addition, his views coincided with those of the Cuban middle and upper classes, which deemed Afro-Cuban culture and folklore "distasteful."[45] Through the CRE's regulations and Giró's reviews, black bodies were not only agents of immoral sexual pleasures and desires but also symbols of heresy.

The CRE's 1954 rules reduced the number of televised performances associated with Afro-Cuban religious and cultural traditions. As Robin D. Moore notes, "Folklore flourished in the black working-class neighborhoods of major cities and in rural towns but did not often appear on the radio or television."[46] Indeed, 1950s popular music was highly influenced by Afro-Cuban vernacular cultures and African-derived religious practices. "For practitioners [of Afro-Cuban religions], the inclusion of African-derived terminology represented the only means by which they could publicly allude to their spiritual beliefs without risking harassment," Moore observes.[47] In addition, many black musicians performed in variety shows.[48] Nevertheless, these Afro-Cuban vernacular practices needed to be sanitized before being televised. Choreographers, television producers, and directors were in charge of restricting African-derived folklore's access to the television screen.

Sexuality, on the other hand, was more difficult to control. Producers could not predict when performers would sing a censored song or engage in an unscripted passionate kiss. Whereas Afro-Cuban musicians and dancers were closely monitored (a tactic that did not completely stop the performance of "folkloric dances," as I explain later), other singers, actors, dancers, and comedians were apparently left alone and thus at risk of committing an "immoral act." In fact, many of them did engage in more risqué behavior; some actors and singers playfully tested the limits of "being immoral." For instance, a singer who had songs censored by the CRE in the late 1940s was again forbidden to sing one of her *guarachas* in the early 1950s because of its "immoral content."[49] In this particular case, the singer welcomed the censorship because it translated into more record sales. Another example occurred when two performers ended a love scene with an unscripted and prolonged

FIGURE 3.2. Scene from *Jueves de Partagás*, CMQ-TV. Santos, photographer. Courtesy of the Cuban Heritage Collection, Rolando Laserie Papers, University of Miami Libraries, Coral Gables, Florida.

kiss. Two days later, two other actors did the same thing but added "more passion" to the scene.[50] After this doubling down, the CRE temporarily suspended kissing on television. It was as if performers were teasing the CRE to see just how far it would go. However, this relationship changed when a new player entered the game: the Ministry of Communication.[51] In 1955, morality became a matter of the state.

Immorality on Television: Containing Gender, Sexuality, and Race via the State

Since Fulgencio Batista's rise to power in 1952, television owners, critics, and political commentators were aware of the state's vigilant eye on news-oriented programming. Even though the Broadcasting Law of 1953 declared Cuba a nation with legally protected freedom of expression, the presence of a disorganized military movement against Batista was enough to encourage the government to increase its attention on media's political content. The temporary "state of emergency" after the Moncada attack and the possibility that the government would institute legal censorship alarmed television owners, who, during Batista's early years, were cautious when addressing political topics (as we saw in chapter 2).

While the government's monitoring of politically oriented programming was thus somewhat anticipated, its supervision of morality in entertainment programming was unusual. As a result, Minister of Communication Ramón Vasconcelos's intent to take full charge of entertainment shows caught television owners, advertisers, and critics by surprise.[52] Furthermore, the potential of having a state-run commission (as proposed by a Cuban legislator) supervise the scripts of telenovelas, comedies, and variety shows was more than alarming for media owners and critics; it also represented a dilemma for several television reviewers who had been advocating for closer government involvement with the business of television.

After the first couple of years of the medium's inception on the island, some critics, aware of the type of shows that would dominate the schedules, expressed their dissatisfaction with television owners' and advertisers' lack of interest in high-culture programming (dramas, ballet, opera, and informative shows). For instance, in 1952 Alberto Giró published a series of articles in *Diario de la Marina* to voice what he described as "the collective disapproval of the tele-spectator for the progressive disappearance of dramatic shows and the excessive proliferation of other types of 'shows.'"[53] From panning the prime-time programming schedule for "creating a harmful monopoly" to praising all the scriptwriters who worked in dramas, Giró forcefully tried to convince television owners, sponsors, and the government to produce more dramas as well as programs like the Ministry of Education's *Una hora de arte y cultura*.[54] In addition, to push for high-culture programming, some reviewers also criticized television's promotion of materialism and consumerism. This was the case for Emma Pérez (editor and television critic of *Gente de la Semana* and a frequent contributor to *Bohemia* magazine), who believed that the main objective of television owners and advertisers was to sell products without any concern for enriching the public's intellect. As she observed in her end-of-the-year programming review for 1952, "Last year it was dramatic programs. This year it is programs in which the public 'wins money.' . . . From a political, industrial and commercial angle, the goal is to idiotize people."[55]

Over the years, the *Gente de la Semana* reviewer became increasingly critical of commercial television, using her columns to condemn television owners (predominantly Goar Mestre and his business partners/brothers, Abel and Augusto Mestre) for their lack of interest in using the medium to improve the lives of Cubans. From saying that Cuban television could be as destructive as the atomic bomb ("would the effects of television become as dangerous and noxious as atomic explosions?") to accusing television magnates of putting their financial interests before those of the nation, Pérez waged a persistent campaign against Cuban commercial television.[56] As someone who viewed television as the most important invention of its time, Pérez understood that the medium's role in society was to help educate Cuba's citizens. Thus, to promote her vision, she devoted some of her columns to explaining the ways in which several governments in Europe invested in the medium. By writing about the public broadcasting systems in Italy, England, and France and the use of television for education in some U.S. cities, Pérez argued for the importance of government participation in programming development.[57]

Indeed, not all critics agreed with Giró's and Pérez's opinions regarding high-culture programming and the need for government involvement with commercial television. For example, Enrique Nuñez Rodríguez, the critic for *Carteles*, believed that television owners and sponsors in Cuba already produced shows with educational content and that, as a result, the government did not need to impose any programming requirements. As he wrote in a 1955 article that discussed how New York City's government used television for education, "In Cuba private sponsors offer shows every day that, without a doubt, are directed to educating the people."[58] The *Bohemia* critic was also more accommodating of entertainment programming and thought that Cuban television produced quality shows across genres.[59] Nonetheless, regardless of the critics' differing views of "high-culture" and "low-culture" programming, they all agreed that government control of radio and television content was detrimental to Cuba's democracy.

When the Ministry of Communication began to attack the CRE's judgment of television morality, and when a legislator proposed drafting a law to institutionalize an office to review scripts (the Comisión Revisora de los Programas Novelizados Radiales y Televisados), television critics, advertisers, and media owners underscored the dangers of censorship. For instance, the *Bohemia* critic, who in several of his columns had previously denounced the

CRE's Eurocentric views of culture, promoted the organization's work in an attempt to dissuade the government's intrusion into television.[60] Conversely, Emma Pérez, who had described CMQ-TV's programs as "grotesque" and who had also accused the Mestre brothers of having a monopoly, strongly campaigned against a new law.[61] "We have already seen what has happened with entertainment and amusements when these have been controlled by totalitarian regimes (Nazism and communism)," Pérez wrote in one of her *Bohemia* features.[62] Whereas Pérez did not describe Batista as a dictator, she hinted at the possibility of an authoritarian path.

Television owners and advertisers followed a similar rhetoric, categorizing government intervention as a threat to democracy. In addition, they emphasized the work that the CRE conducted in dealing with morality on television, thus suggesting that government involvement with the medium was unnecessary. In one of the speeches in honor of the Day of Advertising, a publicist observed, "It is important to mention that in this moment when demagoguery is damaging freedom of expression in advertisement, we have always maintained a moral tone thanks to the close vigilance of the Commission of Advertisement Ethics and the Commission of Radio Ethics."[63] Also, using another approach, advertisers and media owners reproduced the U.S. Cold War rhetoric regarding capitalistic democracy. "As an institution, advertisement plays a pivotal role in countries that maintain their economies and politics as a way to achieve freedom," an advertising executive declared in a speech.[64] In a period when the front pages of Cuban newspapers were covering the U.S. fight against "the reds" and when the Cuban government joined the "anti-red" campaign by creating a state office to monitor communist infiltration, consumption—as an integral component of capitalism—was seen as a staple of a healthy democratic state.[65] And advertisement, as Cuban publicists noted, was a key ingredient for inciting consumerism and thus promoting democracy. By censoring television and thus, indirectly, the sponsors that conceptualized the shows, the government would create hurdles in the chain of promotion, consumption, and democracy.

The most politically daring commentaries, however, came from Nuñez Rodríguez, who dissected the political motivations behind the government's interest in entertainment programming.[66] The following two examples demonstrate how the *Carteles* critic employed his television criticism to expose the government's undemocratic practices and the inefficiencies of the state. In an April 1955 column, Nuñez Rodríguez accused the government of utilizing entertainment programming as a political maneuver to avoid public confrontation regarding Cuba's problems. Furthermore, he suggested that the debate about immorality on television was intended to silence public political dialogue:

> What really has been happening is that there was a time, during the first years of the de facto regime, when Cubans were obliged to keep their opinions about political problems quiet. Even though the government said the right to criticize was safeguarded, this criticism was subject to a series of previous conditions. It was possible to speak, but one had to speak softly. So speaking against radio and television began to "look good." . . . That was when the public began to believe that radio and television were the main source of the moral crisis.[67]

With this column, the *Carteles* critic brought to light the ideological machinery that formed the spectacles of decency. In other words, the emphasis on decency was a way to obscure any class, racial, and gendered elements that might question the broadcasting of Cuban modernity, a modernity that, culturally speaking, was associated with European norms of bourgeois conduct. But, in particular moments during the Batista regime, the spectacles of decency (as with the other spectacles) also operated as a disguise to conceal the flaws of Cuba's democracy. Nuñez Rodríguez's words disclosed the political project behind the spectacles. Three months after publishing the aforementioned commentary, the *Carteles* critic discussed how the opening of an office to monitor scripts would be a misuse of funds during a moment of economic crisis: "At a time when the Republic is hurting from massive firings, when public employees are feeling a drastic reduction in their salaries, when telegraph operators, for example, are fighting hard not to have their longevity pay lowered, the creation of a new expensive and ineffectual agency would overwhelm the budget with unnecessary expenditures."[68] In this case, Nuñez Rodríguez's column foregrounded the uncertainty some sectors of the population felt about Cuba's economic stability and growth.[69]

The fact that the *Carteles* critic was able to openly criticize Batista's government was a product of the political moment. In 1955, as Marifeli Pérez-Stable writes, the likelihood of reestablishing Cuba's democracy was high. The temporary reinstatement of the 1940 constitution, the amnesty of political prisoners (including Fidel Castro), and the acceptance of political exiles into the country showed what appeared to be a transformation in the Batista government's tactics.[70] Whereas the political opposition questioned the elections of 1954 in which Batista, as the sole candidate, was named president of the Republic, the momentary reestablishment of the constitution "opened up the possibility of dialogue" across different political sectors.[71] Hence, the temporal space for public debate allowed the *Carteles* critic to intersect his political views with his television criticism. And it was also via the restoration of the constitution that, as Nuñez Rodríguez wrote in one of his columns, the proposed commission to regulate entertainment content was deemed unconstitutional: "The Reviewing Commission for Radio and Television Serialized Programs does violate Article 33 of the Constitution because it refers to the free expression of ideas in the form of radio and TV novels [radio and television soaps]. Unless Senator Illas believes that novels, be they emitted on radio, on television, or as books, do not express ideas."[72] Anchored in Cuba's modernity and a supposed path toward a democratic present and future, the plans to legally intervene in television did not materialize in 1955.[73]

But the absence of a legal office to scrutinize scripts did not preclude the Ministry of Communication from supervising entertainment shows. Even though the CRE highlighted its strong hand in fighting indecency on television, and even as critics forcefully advocated for the state not to intervene in entertainment programming, they were unsuccessful in stopping the government's close surveillance of the medium.[74] By the summer of 1955, the Ministry of Communication was in full force, assessing morality on entertainment shows.[75] Three main areas dominated its battle against indecency and immorality on television: racialized dance performances, child actors, and men in drag. While this echoed some of the CRE's morality rules, as seen in the ministry's focus on female dancers' movements, clothing, and Afro-Cuban rhythms,[76] for the most part, the government office set morality standards that the CRE then appropriated.

The minister of communication's interest in Afro-Cuban music and dance was associated with some of the performances that were broadcast on variety shows. Although in 1954 the CRE banned the "transmissions of programs that stimulate beliefs against civilization" and "choreographed dances associated with cults or religious beliefs," some Afro-Cuban religiously derived dances still made it onto television.[77] For example, in one of his reviews of programming during 1955, Alberto Giró chastised television producers for allowing children to perform music associated with Afro-Cuban religious practices: "The Commission on Radio and Television Ethics, which has achieved so many successes in its brilliant work of refining the radio and TV programs, . . . would do well to pay a little attention to the need in this environment to watch over children's programs, thus protecting the moral health of children. . . . In some children's programs we have seen beautiful children dancing to African rhythms and even singing a lyric that not even adults who are familiar with barbaric sects can understand."[78]

Besides openly expressing his racist attitudes, Giró's words underline the complexities of censoring television. The live broadcast technology made it difficult to effectively control content. Hence, to help with the eradication of racial, religious, and sexual indecencies, the Ministry of Communication joined forces with the CRE. The two organizations worked together to suppress televised signs linked to the nation's mulataje and noncontained blackness. In the words of the *Bohemia* critic: "It was not only the [dancers'] garments that worried those who were severely judging our television. Dance also suffered the effects of the regulations. . . . Our dances—rumbas, conga, mambo, chachachá—that made the interpreters move according to those rhythms would be also affected. Those rhythms that, because of their exotic amalgamation of the tropics and their African influence, have been a success across different latitudes would have, it seems, to be adulterated in their place of origin."[79]

It should be clear that black singers and musicians continued to participate in variety and musical shows. The problem was not the presence of black bodies on television; it was the types of performances enacted on television. Anything that digressed from European languages, religious traditions, and bourgeois norms of sexual conduct provoked racial and sexual anxieties and, as a result, could not be aired.

The fixation of the Ministry of Communication and the CRE on elements associated with Afro-Cuban vernacular cultures occurred in a moment when black communities and religious traditions were at the center of intellectual dialogues. In 1954, Cuban intellectual Lydia Cabrera published her seminal work, *El monte*, a book that documents Afro-Cuban religious traditions. A meticulously researched anthropological work, *El monte* made a mark by uncovering religious practices and ceremonies from Santería and other African-based religions.[80] This exposure of rituals most likely influenced choreographers, who, responding to the intellectual dialogues of the time, exalted Afro-Cuban folklore in televised dance performances. Furthermore, throughout the 1950s, the renowned Casino Tropicana choreographer "Rodney" (Rodrigo Neyra) had been including Afro-Cuban cultural elements in his cabaret shows.[81] High-profile cultural attention like this probably influenced the citation of Afro-Cuban religious references on television. Of course, not all Cubans appreciated this aspect of the island's society and culture. The debate over the morality and value of Afro-Cuban culture, then, demonstrates the dichotomies between the intellectual and artistic spheres and the economic elite, even though, in most cases, Cuban intellectuals came from those same elite groups (as Cabrera did). Still, given that television was seen as an important site to display Cuba's European/cultural modernity, not even the folklore exalted by upper-class intellectuals could be screened.

The topic of Afro-Cuban folklore and racialized sexuality trickled down to other areas beyond mamboletas and musicians: as the *Diario de la Marina* critic noted, "we have seen beautiful children dancing to African rhythms."[82] Children, based on this quote, were not merely watching immoral content on television; those working in the industry were confronting immorality on a daily basis. Thus, to protect their well-being, the Ministry of Communication banned child actors from working in the industry. This new rule surprised television owners, critics, and audience members. Even the most conservative of the television reviewers, Alberto Giró, expressed his dissatisfaction with the measure, indicating that it was "excessively drastic and unfair."[83] Others, including an audience member, worried about the financial stability of child actors, some of whom used their salaries to help sustain their families.[84] Although the CRE publicly explained that child actors did not participate in shows that contained adult content, the organization was unsuccessful in its attempts to stop the ban. After 1955, the youngest actors on Cuban television were fourteen years old.

The third area of censorship—men in drag—was more controversial than the exclusion of children. Here the debates not only related to the elimination of characters that the audience loved, or the CRE's possible favoring of a particular network; the act of cross-dressing introduced a new topic into the discussions about morality on television: sexual orientation.[85] By screening men in drag, censors argued, television promoted homosexuality. This connection between men in drag and homosexuality could be seen as a product of Latin America's *machista* culture, which, as literary scholar Ben Sifuentes-

Jáuregui writes, permeates ideologies of gender, sexuality, and sex. In this regard, masculinity is hegemonically heterosexual, invariably situating any gender transgressions as signs of sexual aberrations. "Sexual difference and perversions—whether transvestism, prostitution, male homosexuality and lesbianism, even womanhood—are readily projected upon the transvestite's body."[86] Thus, following Sifuentes-Jáuregui's argument, cross-dressing performers destabilized hegemonic notions of femininity, masculinity, and appropriate sexual conduct, positioning men in drag as symbols of homosexual behavior.

The merging of men in drag and homosexual desire was based on two main issues: the characters' inability to convey a real representation of women, and the messages that these imperfect representations might convey about sexual desire. Faulty gender performances were first enacted by Pirula, a character who made occasional appearances on a variety show. Performed by a man with a mustache, Pirula was frequently seen flirting with the show's master of ceremonies. In this particular case, the censors focused on how the imperfect performance of gender and femininity (i.e., a woman with a mustache supposedly cannot be a woman) created a space for homosexual desire.[87] Drag, as Katrin Sieg notes, "maximizes the demand on the spectatorial faculty of suspending disbelief if it is to be viewed as a plausible representation of reality."[88] Pirula's inadequate femininity exposed the performance act, opening the possibility for audiences to read sexual desire between two men. A similar logic was used for the other women characters performed by men (Mamacusa and Prematura). These characters did not have facial hair, meaning that, according to standards of femininity, they could "pass" as women. Nonetheless, the public was aware that men were behind the characterizations. Even though one television critic insisted that these characters were read as women ("Mamacusa is not a man, she is a tragic old spinster"), and another critic indicated that television was not to blame for sexual aberrations ("It is unfair to blame radio and television for the problem regarding sexual deviance. . . . One cannot accuse radio [and television] of being a vehicle that transmits or promotes that scourge which has its deep roots in medicine and the penal law"), the Ministry of Communication prohibited men in drag on television.[89] This prohibition repositioned television as a heteronormal space void of performative gender transgressions. Together with the previous decrees, men and women on television would now continue to act within socially constructed parameters of femininity and masculinity, which encompassed clothing styles, manner-isms, and interactions with the opposite sex. Those who tried to cross the boundaries—men in drag, dancers wearing inappropriate/revealing cloth-ing, or singers performing songs with sexual innuendo—were banned or suspended from television.

Proper behavior, as discussed earlier, also involved religious traditions. Anything that departed from Catholic/Christian religious practices could not be depicted or addressed on television. Hence, Afro-Cuban religiously derived songs and dances needed to be eliminated not only because they deviated from Catholic/Christian doctrines but also because they were vi-sual and oral reminders of the non-European ethnic/racial elements that were part of Cuba's culture and society. Even though Santería, for example, formed part of the vernacular, and even as intellectuals were learning, dis-seminating, and celebrating Cuba's African influences, television could not endorse these aspects of the island's culture.

The state's enforcement of morality and decency also included parenting. By banning children from working on television, the Ministry of Commu-nication was not just preventing a child from being exposed to immoral content but also becoming a parental figure. With the help of the state, now parents could learn how to raise a modern Cuban child who would know how to behave according to gender parameters and how to discern which elements of Cuba's culture should make him or her proud to be Cuban.

Policing Decency on the Screens

In August 1956, the Cuban Legion of Decency published a bulletin address-ing the "immorality plagues" that had battered the city of Havana.[90] Fo-cusing on bordellos, *hospedajes* (lodgings where couples met for sex), and pornographic magazines, the Legion demanded that the government ag-gressively battle all activities that were damaging Cuba's "Christian morality and good customs," traits that were at "the core of all civilized societies."[91] Even as the legion's complaints came from a highly conservative Catholic doctrine, the criticism was not off the mark. In the 1950s, sex ruled Havana, offering local and foreign clients an array of "price ranges, comfort, and dis-cretion."[92] Bordellos and sex locales, together with gambling, helped shape the characterization of Havana as a place where illegality was welcomed. But the Legion of Decency's focus on Havana's sex industry was not its only concern at the time. Since 1955, the Legion had been strongly advocating that the Comisión Revisora de Películas (Movie Review Commission, a government-run office) take a closer look at Hollywood and European films screened in Cuba and their public display of immorality. In a CMQ-TV *Mesa redonda* broadcast, the Legion demanded that the government institute a new law to monitor films.[93]

The Legion of Decency's call for a stricter look at the exhibition of immoral content (i.e., sex) in films related to the type of monitoring that had characterized the Comisión Revisora de Películas during Batista's regime. Since its establishment in 1944, the primary objective of the commission had been to verify that movie content was appropriate for children under the age of twelve. However, in the post-1952 period, the commission's censorship centered, for the most part, on films that endorsed rebellion, insurrection, and communism.[94] As mentioned in chapter 2, a year after Batista's coup, all cinema newsreels had to be approved by the Comisión Revisora de Películas before being shown in movie theaters. This surveillance practice did not mean, however, that the commission was able to detect the political messages in all films or, more important, anticipate how film critics would write about the texts. For example, as Megan J. Feeney's research demonstrates, a film such as *Viva Zapata*, whose main topic was the Mexican Revolution, passed the censors. And in terms of film criticism, it was common for reviewers to interject their political views against Batista and to criticize U.S. hegemony in their opinionated pieces.[95] Thus, in some ways, film reviewers, similar to some television critics, utilized various media outlets as channels for expressing their political commentary. Nonetheless, in a period when television was scrutinized for its so-called indecent content, some television reviewers, in an attempt to divert censorship away from local productions, echoed the Legion of Decency's call regarding film, thus distancing themselves from the film reviewers' highly critical views of Batista's censorship.[96]

Noticing the imbalance between the ongoing monitoring of local production and the lack of attention to Hollywood films aired on television, several television reviewers and producers suggested that the minister of communication change direction and focus on movies. Additionally, on its editorial page, the *Diario de la Marina* called for a closer look at films in movie theaters as well as those broadcast on television.[97] The government listened, at least partly. The mayor of Havana closed theaters that showed pornographic movies, and the minister of communication announced that his office would create a commission to inspect radio and television, paying particular attention to the movies broadcast on television.[98] Even though the commission to inspect films was not instituted, the government showed great interest in controlling the screening of sex in the years to come.

Following the morality campaign initiated in the 1955–56 period, the Ministry of Communication continued to monitor signs of "immorality" throughout the end of Batista's regime. Television shows depicting people dancing to rock and roll, telenovelas that insinuated improper sexual relations, dancers showing too much skin, comedians who made jokes that could be decoded as sexual, and movies that offended "public morality" were among the programs and people that the Ministry of Communication suspended.[99] Thus, even though by the end of the decade U.S. magazines were describing Havana as a bordello and Cuban journalists pondered the U.S. Mafia's control of Havana's casino industry, television had to be a puritanical space.[100] The regulation of sex and immorality operated in different coordinates and realities on television versus in Cuban society. But, as Ann Laura Stoler reminds us, "Sexual asymmetries and visions convey what is 'really' going on elsewhere, at another political epicenter. They are tropes to depict other centers of power."[101] The surveillance of televised sex that heightened in the 1955–56 period went beyond regulations of the body and sexual desire. The government's stern control of television coincided with the solidification of the anti-Batista movement.

Student protests and labor strikes flourished in Havana, and, in Gladys Marel García-Pérez's words, "increased confrontations between the people's sectors and the government in 1955–56 established the basis for civil war in Cuba."[102] At the same time, as García-Pérez's research indicates, the government began to repress people who were (or seemed to be) involved in an insurrection. These tactics of surveillance also applied to newspapers and magazines. Although the news censorship established in 1956 was not as severe as that which took place a year later, editors and journalists voiced their discontent.[103] Progressively, freedom of expression dwindled, and the partial reestablishment of the constitution that took place in 1955 halted. The imminent presence of a revolutionary movement and the alleged threats of a communist uprising (both student protesters and Fidel Castro were labeled as communists in 1956) were enough for the government to eliminate constitutional rights.[104]

In the 1955–56 period (and beyond), spectacles of decency mostly functioned as government-guided rhetorical and political actions to validate the control of the state in a moment of crisis. Through the regulation of televised racial, gender, and sexual performances, the state could claim not only concern for the moral well-being of its citizens but also assert its goal to promote a European-influenced cultural modernity. In that way, the government's scrutiny of decency and the political crisis did not completely alter the narrativization of success that characterized the spectacle of progress. Whereas the Association of Cuban Advertisers did not conduct its May 1956 survey due to the tense political situation and the suspension of constitutional guarantees, television owners and reviewers continued to praise the developments of Cuban television as a sign of Cuban modernity.[105] In other words, even as the suspension of the survey revealed part of the artifice behind the spectacles of progress, owners and reviewers continued to assert Cuban television's success.

In 1956, CMQ-TV, Televisión Nacional, and Telemundo expanded their signals to the eastern parts of the island. Although audiences complained about bad reception or not having access to television (recall the disgruntled *pinareño*), owners and reviewers celebrated the fact that Cuba had three networks.[106] In terms of television sets, Cubans owned 200,000 in 1956, positioning the island as the sixth country in the world—and number one in Latin America—in terms of ownership.[107] Renowned performers like Liberace, Roland Gerbeau, and Libertad Lamarque participated in local programming, and while these appearances mainly took place during the ratings season, reviewers covered their participation as examples of the excellence of Cuban television.[108]

To be sure, the crisis that began in 1954 continued to affect the industry. Popular shows lost their sponsors, others were canceled, and many media professionals migrated to other parts of Latin America.[109] However, without losing perspective on the crisis, television reviewers began to cover the successes of Cuban artists, media professionals, and television products off the island as examples of Cuban television's progress. Thanks to the emergence of television in various places throughout the region, the lack of trained personnel in the countries that set up this complex system, and Cubans' vast experience in multiple aspects of television production, the impact of Cuban television was felt outside the island. Stories about Cuban technical staff helping develop television in other parts of Latin America, news about Latin American media entrepreneurs' admiration for Cuban television, the success of Cuban scripts in the region, and the investment of Cuban radio and television owners in various Latin American nation-states (specifically CMQ-TV's Goar Mestre) became part of the spectacles of progress.[110]

Nonetheless, one important aspect that began to change in the narratives that formed the spectacles of progress was the blind admiration for the United States. While Cuban cultural elements and people were key to reviewers' acceptance of programs that originated in the United States, open rejections of U.S. influences were sporadic and mostly came from television reviewers. This reception of Americanness began to change in 1956, and, interestingly, some of the questioning of U.S. influences came from audience members. This included incredulity regarding the fact that many Cuban programs were adaptations of U.S. shows, offense at learning that the upper classes preferred U.S. cigars to Cuban ones (which affected sponsorship), and distrust over claims about Cuban television's top position in the world when Hollywood movies began to dominate the schedule.[111] Similar to previous years, audience members' letters fragmented the discourse of progress that television owners and some reviewers embraced. The main difference between previous challenges and those initiated in 1956 was the audience's rejection of the United States' role in Cuban commercial television and the blind adoption of U.S. culture by certain sectors of the Cuban audience. These reactions can be seen as part of the changes taking place in Cuba's narrative of nationality. As Louis A. Pérez writes, "New narratives on nationality were taking form. The dominant cultural motif of the 1950s addressed matters of representation, a process that necessarily involved the affirmation of Cuban as distinct from and independent of things North American at a time of deepening economic dislocation and political crisis."[112] If the 1940s embodied both the promise of utopia and the threat of dystopia, by the late 1950s the utopian ideals of democracy and economic abundance that defined the 1940s had collapsed.

It is in this temporal moment that the spectacles of democracy excelled and that, concomitantly, a preamble to the spectacles of revolution appeared on the international scene. Thanks to a series of *New York Times* articles published in 1957 focusing on Fidel Castro, a May 19, 1957, CBS News Special Report covering Castro and his army in Cuba's Sierra Maestra, and Batista's legalization of media censorship in 1957, the spectacles of democracy moved to center stage. Even though these were already part of the national arena, the existence of an organized militant group and the Cuban citizens' engagement with the revolutionary movement revealed the cozenage of Bastista's government. At the same time, photographs and stories in the *New York Times* about Fidel Castro's activities in Sierra Maestra brought international attention to the political situation in Cuba. Staged for a foreign public, the U.S.-made preamble to the spectacles of revolution introduced new imagery of and narratives about Cuba, presenting some of the elements that would constitute the spectacles of revolution.

CHAPTER 4

Spectacles of Democracy and a Prelude
to the Spectacles of Revolution

Taking a general look at television programming and media business trends during 1957 and 1958, one could conclude that Cuban commercial television was business as usual. In fact, for some producers and television owners, the future looked quite bright. Indigenized U.S. shows such as *Queen for a Day* and *The $64,000 Question* (aired on Telemundo) and locally conceptualized versions of giveaway programs (e.g., *Pepe pregunta y paga*, on CMQ-TV) took over the Cuban television airwaves, challenging the dominance of musical and variety shows. While some critics debated the pros and cons of *Reina por un día* (Queen for a day), others indicated that Cuban television's new genre promoted healthy competition between Telemundo and CMQ-TV, the two most powerful networks at the time.[1]

Cuba's trailblazer status in Latin American television continued, and, consistent with the past, some technological advances were interconnected with U.S. economic and political interests in Cuba and the surrounding region. In 1957, the American Telephone and Telegraph Company (AT&T) established the "Over the Horizon" telephone service between the United States and Cuba.[2] In addition to increasing the number of potential simultaneous phone conversations between the two countries, the connection technology, referred to as "tropospheric scatter," introduced the possibility of direct television transmissions between the United States and Cuba. For example, in 1957 the baseball World Series was transmitted from the United States to Cuba using the new technology, and in 1958, to celebrate the inauguration of Televisión Habanera (channel 10, which had just become affiliated with the National Broadcasting Corporation), Havana's Cabaret Tropicana broadcast directly to 180 stations across the United States.[3]

The potential for transnational television initiated by "Over the Horizon" technology also opened up political possibilities for the region. According to the Pan American Union, Cuba was going to be the first "chain" in the creation of a television network that would link the United States and South America.[4] If radio, film, advertisements, and travel were used to create "hemispheric solidarity" as part of the Good Neighbor policy during the Cold War era, a transnational television network could help build a collective front against the threat of communism.[5] As a Florida senator remarked in 1958 while celebrating "Pan American Week," "The United States has yet to come up with a bold plan to make the hemisphere a real stronghold of the free world."[6] According to the Pan American Union's plans and the "utopian discourse of global television" that, as Michael Curtin explains, characterized government and corporate discussions about the medium, a transnational television network could help fortify U.S.–Latin American alliances against the Red Menace.[7]

The casino industry would also benefit from Cuba's television advancements. The Hotel Havana Riviera, inaugurated in December 1957 and funded mostly by U.S.-based Mafia boss Meyer Lansky, planned to install a closed-circuit television so guests could gamble from their rooms (guests would watch the casino tables on television sets in their rooms and place a bet via phone). As a journalist stated, "Cuba, the most advanced country in the area of television in all Latin America, was also going to be the first in the world to use the most modern and wonderful medium for gaming."[8] Whereas neither the Hotel Havana Riviera's nor the Pan American Union's plans materialized, other events maintained Cuba's standing as a television pioneer in the region. For instance, in 1958 Gaspar Pumarejo launched the first color-television station in Cuba and Latin America. Pumarejo's channel 12 joined Havana's two existing stations (channels 7 and 10), providing innovative news and human-interest stories to those who owned one of the approximately ten thousand color sets available on the island.[9]

Cuban television's presence across Latin America also expanded from 1957 to 1958, particularly through Goar Mestre's investments. As one of the two television owners who survived the 1954 crisis (the other being Amadeo Barletta), Mestre thought the region was full of business possibilities. Mestre's primary goal, as he expressed in 1954, was to create a "television network beginning with Mexico City and ending with the capital of Peru," and to this end, he began to invest in media projects in the region (e.g., in Puerto Rico and Colombia).[10] In addition, in 1958 he initiated the process to create Televisión Interamericana S.A. (TISA), a consortium with other Latin American television owners (particularly Mexican media mogul Emilio Azcárraga Vidaurreta) with the objective of exporting kinescopes and films across the region. Closely connected to Mestre's transnational business plan was the development of the dubbing industry in Cuba. Whereas Puerto Rico, Mexico, and Spain dominated the industry, Mestre began dubbing projects a year prior to the revolution with the goal of adding extra competition to the market by providing intermediary prices between those in Mexico and Puerto Rico.[11]

The need for dubbing hints at the proliferation of imported Hollywood films and television shows in Cuba and the progressive elimination of drama and comedy shows, a process that began during the 1954 crisis. While this trend benefited television owners financially, it drastically diminished job opportunities for actors, scriptwriters, directors, and musicians. Most of the programming on CMBF-Cadena Nacional S.A. network and Havana's channels 10 and 7 was imported from Hollywood, and although CMQ-TV kept producing fiction, the network negotiated new contracts that reduced the salaries of performers and writers.[12] Furthermore, even though local programs still dominated the ratings during 1957, by 1958 U.S. shows such as *Jungle Jim*, *Rin Tin Tin*, *Highway Patrol*, and *Lone Ranger* had moved to the top of the list, beating many local productions, including the now-legendary Cuban telenovela, *El derecho de nacer*.[13] With the importation of programming and its rating success, some television critics finally realized the relevance of legally establishing percentages for local talent, live shows, and recorded programs.[14] Changes in the Cuban television industry were a direct product of the Broadcasting Law of 1953 (see chapter 2).

The dominance of Hollywood programming did not change how television critics approached local productions. In other words, they did not soften their reviews in an attempt to boost the ratings of locally produced shows. It was quite the opposite. Some television reviewers blamed creative personnel for alienating the public and causing a "regression" from the initial "golden age" of Cuban television.[15] Others noted that local television's only chance for survival was to present new genres and artists in addition to legally reintegrating quotas for recorded programs.[16] Interestingly, for one critic, the only hope for the Cuban public (evidently limited to the middle and upper classes) was the potential for "pay television," where audiences could watch "excellent movies, news programming, or sports, without the annoyance of commercials."[17] This critic not only predicted the future of global television but also rejected the localism of other reviews. Other critics, similar to their predecessors, continued debating the existence of high-culture programming in Cuba and the diminishing of popular-culture genres.[18] In sum, the highly critical eye of the previous years persisted, even when local programming was vanishing.

Previous observations seem to indicate that, with the exception of the invasion of Hollywood films and shows, nothing was out of the ordinary during 1957 and 1958. Obviously, this was not the case. Fidel Castro's ship landing in Cuba in December 1956, Herbert L. Matthews's *New York Times* articles on Fidel Castro and the 26th of July Movement, and the violence that erupted across the island all impacted how the state reacted to the presence of an insurrection. Media censorship was legalized in 1957, affecting both news and entertainment programming. In just one year, the government enacted two decrees to solidify the state's control of radio, television, cinema newsreels, and newspapers and to modify the Broadcasting Law of 1953.[19] News stories covering political dissent and insurrection were rare (particularly after August 1957), and the incisive politically engaged commentaries of television critics such as Emma Pérez (*Gente de la Semana* and *Bohemia*) and Enrique Nuñez Rodríguez (*Carteles*) disappeared. For news programming, as Michael B. Salwen writes, "censorship became so severe after 1957 that the media could no longer even mention that their reports were censored."[20] In terms of entertainment programming, as I discuss in the following pages, morality and decency dominated the minister of communication's attention to television.

This chapter focuses on Cuban and U.S. television and media events that stressed the spectacles of democracy while, at the same time, revealing the emergence of the spectacles of revolution. I begin by analyzing some of the suspensions of news-related programming, the discourse of democracy that was part of the 1957 amendment to the Broadcasting Law of 1953, and the minister of communication's fixation with morality on television. According to the narrative that formed the spectacles of democracy, legalization of media censorship and the minister of communication's suspension of shows (for subversive and/or allegedly immoral content) were understood as necessary courses of action to combat the communist menace that was threatening the island. I then move to the United States and examine *Rebels of the Sierra Maestra: The Story of Cuba's Jungle Fighters*, a May 19, 1957, CBS documentary covering Castro and his army. While the documentary did not attract as much attention as Matthews's pieces in the *New York Times*, it nonetheless brought Fidel Castro and the revolutionary movement into the homes of many Americans. Sponsored by the Prudential Insurance Company, *Rebels of the Sierra Maestra* began selling the Cuban Revolution on television; it was a prelude of sorts for the spectacles of revolution. Even as this U.S.-made introduction would differ from the spectacles produced in Cuba, it nonetheless presented Fidel Castro, the principal protagonist, to the United States and the world. Equally important, the "made in the USA" preamble and, more specifically, *Rebels of the Sierra Maestra*, developed some of the visual and narrative cues that would form the spectacles of revolution.

Staging Democracy for a Local and Global Audience

On March 10, 1957, five years after Fulgencio Batista's coup d'état and approximately two months prior to the legalization of censorship, *Carteles* published an article titled "During the Censorship, Many Things Happened," recounting events that occurred during the previous months when the government closely monitored newspapers, radio, and television news.[21] In addition to including a summary of Matthews's *New York Times* articles and the picture of Castro published by the New York–based newspaper, the piece presented a monthly account of newsworthy events from January to March. From the censoring of U.S. and Cuban newspapers; to brutal deaths, bombs, incarcerations, and fires; to a government statement questioning whether Castro was alive, the story did not shy away from controversial topics. In effect, in a text box labeled "Without Censorship" the journalist declared, "Once again the Cuban press has suffered censorship. Censorship is a comfortable means usually used by governments when they find themselves incapable of confronting the reality of the facts."[22]

Carteles confirmed the events that some people had learned of via word of mouth and underground sources, and that U.S. newspapers had reported. With the temporary elimination of legal censorship in the final days of February, the truth came to the surface; for some, this might have been the last bit of evidence they needed to confirm that Fulgencio Batista was a dictator. At the same time, the temporary halting of legal censorship from March to July 1957 could be seen as one of the government's last attempts to convince Cuban citizens and the world that it was a democracy threatened by communist rebels. Thanks to censorship, incarceration, death, and fighting, the spectacles of democracy were in the limelight, attracting both local and global audiences.

Trying to persuade the United States and the global public that Cuba was a democracy was a difficult, if not impossible, task. Since his rise to power in 1952, news stories had been describing Batista as a dictator who was somewhat peaceful and efficient, but a dictator nonetheless. He was a friend of the United States who "kept down communism and nationalism at home and [had] been entirely loyal to the democratic world at the United Nations."[23] The events that began to take place in 1957, however, altered this representation. Matthews's articles from February 1957 not only contradicted Batista's claims that Fidel Castro had died after his ship landed on the island but also charted government corruption and the collective efforts of various sectors of the population (many from the middle and upper classes) to reestablish Cuba's democracy. Moreover, the articles denied any connections between communism and Castro's 26th of July Movement, the main explanation Batista used to justify media censorship and multiple assassinations.[24] After Matthews's pieces were published, other stories followed that described the battles taking place in Cuba and the repression of Batista's government.[25] The narrative that had sustained the spectacles of democracy and the new lines of defense that became part of that narrative (e.g., associating Castro with communism) were probably not enough to convince the U.S. audience of Batista's approach to governing, even though some might have had doubts about Castro's communist agenda.

On the island, journalists and media owners were not convinced by any of the minister of communication's excuses for censorship. After all, the policing of the media had been part of Batista's regime since 1952; as a result, journalists and media professionals had become accustomed to the government's array of pretexts. Thus, as soon as the first censorship decree was struck down, they voiced their dissatisfaction with the repressive tactics that were being used even during the months when censorship was not mandated. For instance, in April, Goar Mestre, in his capacity as president of the Federation of Cuba's Broadcasters, denounced the minister of communication's unexpected three-day suspension of Radio Progreso. One month later, Mestre, again representing the Federation of Cuba's Broadcasters, together with journalists, protested the government's closure of Radio Mambí and asked the minister of communication to emulate U.S. broadcasting laws, which protected freedom of expression. In June, in response to Vasconcelo's censoring of newsreels and news programming (all of which, as in 1953, needed to be approved by the Comisión Revisora de Películas), the Federation of Cuba's Broadcasters sent out a press release condemning the "unjust and arbitrary" actions.[26] Then, in July, to convey a clear message of disapproval for the two-week suspension of the television program *Ante la prensa*, Mestre produced a show called *El estudio vacio* (The empty studio), which, airing in the same time slot as *Ante la prensa*, depicted an empty studio and used a narration to tackle the importance of freedom of expression. According to one television critic, *El estudio vacio* was "one of the extraordinary programs" of that year.[27]

The minister of communication came up with a range of justifications for his censorship acts, all of which were supposedly meant to protect Cuba's democracy. For example, in reference to the closing of Radio Mambí, Vasconcelos explained that he wanted to minimize "distressful news" that, aside from exaggerating a series of events, was affecting Cuba's tourism industry. In the same piece, he responded to Mestre's call for the Cuban government to implement measures similar to the ones in the United States by indicating that "in North American democracy, like ours, all industries can use—and here they even abuse—radio and television frequencies."[28] Thus, closing Radio Mambí was not censorship per se but a response to manufactured news stories that were threatening Cuba's economy. Similarly, in reference to the partial suspension of one radio news show, Vasconcelos indirectly accused Mestre of fabricating stories for ratings and commercial profits.[29] Lies posing as news and subversive attitudes were also justifications for the suspension of *Ante la prensa*. Paraphrasing a telegraph from Vasconcelos, one newspaper reported, "The Minister of Communication regrets having to suspend [*Ante la prensa*] but he explains that it was the only alternative given the subversive attitude of two of the program's participants."[30] During that same period, Vasconcelos wrote a column to discuss a story published in a Mexican newspaper that had foregrounded Cuba's freedom of expression.[31] Neither the Mexican journalist nor Vasconcelos believed that suspending *Ante la prensa* was a violation of that freedom.

For Vasconcelos, all necessary measures had to be taken to safeguard what he described as Cuba's democracy. Consequently, the killing of one of the island's most important revolutionary figures (Frank País) by the police, and the workers' strike that followed in protest of the murder (one of the most significant events in the history of the Cuban Revolution) were enough for the minister of communication to suspend constitutional guarantees and reinstitute legal media censorship. From August 1957 to January 1958, censorship was mandated by law, and even though the government publicly reestablished constitutional guarantees and abolished censorship in early 1958, the state's silencing of the press/news programming from Cuba and abroad continued until the victory of the Cuban Revolution.[32]

The August decree was a carbon copy of the January 1957 decree. Both pieces of legislation cited national security as the primary reason for abolishing constitutional guarantees and for the inclusion of censors at all radio and television networks and stations. Together with the suspension of news shows that took place between March and July, the decrees brought to light the theatricality that formed the spectacles of democracy. In other words, if, as Ronald Inglehart and Christian Welzel write, "The institutional presence of civil liberties is a necessary element of liberal democracy . . . , for democracy is a constitutional phenomenon based on legal rights," then the aforementioned legislation eliminated the final scenes that sustained the spectacles of democracy.[33] By officially striking down civil liberties, the government's claims about Cuba's democracy collapsed. Still, other legal stipulations in the broadcasting arena presented a more complicated picture of the government's approach to censorship and the state's intent to maintain parts of the narrative that formed the spectacles of democracy.

Quickly after censorship was reinstated, Batista amended the Broadcasting Law of 1953. Creating legal mechanisms to avoid monopolies and expanding the percentage of educational and cultural programming, segments of the new broadcasting legislation repositioned Batista's government as one that not only expanded communication channels to allow multiple voices to exist but also was interested in the educational enrichment of its citizens and their moral well-being.[34] In terms of ownership, the amendment prohibited a person or a corporation from holding multiple stations that, because of their power and territorial reach, "could influence national broadcasting."[35] Although this change could be seen as a strategic move against Goar Mestre (the most powerful broadcasting owner at the time and a passionate critic of Batista's government), the legal stipulation opened up possibilities for the future diversification of stations, programming, and ideological positions. In terms of education, Article 12 changed the proportion of educational/

cultural programming from 2 percent (as established in the Broadcasting Law of 1953) to 5 percent and required all networks and stations to include these types of shows during hours when "an average-sized audience" tuned in.[36] Additionally, the regulation required networks and stations to provide free-of-charge broadcasting space for programs produced by the minister of education.

The objectives presented in the articles that addressed monopolies and educational/cultural programming resembled the tone of the 1930s and 1940s broadcasting regulations, in which the government envisioned radio as a channel for the cultural enrichment of the Cuban citizen. That said, contrary to previous legislation, the overbearing power of the state was also part of the amendment. For instance, one stipulation required broadcasters to provide a yearly list with the names of all media professionals working at their networks and stations, thus extending the policing of content to the policing of personnel. Another section of the amendment indicated that the minister of communication had the power to intervene at all broadcasting networks and stations, something that, technically, he had been doing for quite a while. Finally, a couple of articles limited the time during which news and editorials could be broadcast and prohibited negative discussions and accusations focused on people and/or institutions associated with the government.

The 1957 amendment exemplifies the duality that characterized Batista's approach to government in general and the broadcasting industry in particular. Some chapters and articles presented the government as in agreement with the practices of a democratic society, while others hinted at Cuba's repressive political environment. Nonetheless, one particular article (number 14) mixed morality with politics, accentuating the ways in which defining what was moral and immoral became part of Batista's circuitry of control. Concealed behind the call for civility, ethics, and nationalism, political censorship reached beyond news programming.

Article 14 begins by noting that Cuba's broadcasting should "respect the ethical principles that are the basis of our civilization, as well as the dignity of the individual, the family, society, and the values of [Cuban] nationality."[37] This interconnection of civilization, nationalism, and morality in broadcasting regulations was not new. As discussed in chapter 1, the decree of 1939 set the parameters for the cultural and moral norms that would define radio programming in Cuba while also highlighting Cuba's standing as a modern, culturally European nation. Furthermore, later legislation tackled issues of morality and programming. For example, the broadcasting laws of 1942 and 1953 included articles that prohibited the use of bad language and, in the case of the 1953 law, the inclusion of immoral images. Hence, the topic of moral content and the connection between civility, morality, and Cuban modernity had been ingrained in Cuba's broadcasting laws since the late 1930s. What was new about the 1957 amendment relates to the specific description of what was considered immoral and indecent. The legislation outlawed the following: "Obscene images, phrases with double entendre and obscene expressions . . . , dramatizations that promulgate evil desires, that praise delinquent conduct, or that despise the authority or the law; everything that tends to cause depression or upset people, for example, the justification of suicide, adultery, incest, cruelty, superstition; . . . the staging of bloody scenes and of arm[ed] robbery; and interviews of incarcerated people without previous permission of the authorities."[38] In addition to delineating immoral themes, Article 14 established that all movies broadcast on television had to be approved by the Comisión Revisora de Películas (Movie Review Commission). Prior to broadcasting, networks and stations were also required to include a warning indicating whether movies were appropriate for children. By supervising movies, the article addressed concerns that the Cuban Legion of Decency had expressed years earlier and responded to journalists and artists who claimed that the government had different standards of morality for local and imported movies and shows.

These stipulations produced two outcomes. First, they opened up the possibility that the Commission on Radio Ethics could be eliminated. Once the minister of communication was legally entitled to intervene in entertainment shows, the CRE became unnecessary. Second, they created venues for the removal of entertainment content that might present political positions that differed from the government's by labeling them as immoral. With topics such as "the praising of delinquent conduct" or "interviews with incarcerated people," the minister of communication had the power to deem almost any content indecent. The 1957 amendment legalized the minister of communication's interposition on entertainment programming, an area that broadcasters and advertisers had strategically reserved for the CRE.

As discussed in previous chapters, since the late 1940s the CRE had established standards for defining immorality in radio and television programming. Through press releases and industry codes, the CRE provided a detailed explanation of what the organization considered immoral, steadily strengthening its standards based on programs' and artists' alleged immoral conduct as well as the progressive intervention of the state. In the mid-1950s, however, the minister of communication became more involved in matters of entertainment programming, taking the lead in describing what he considered indecent and in suspending artists and programs. By 1956, the CRE was in the shadows of the minister of communication.

Vasconcelos's preoccupation with morality on television intensified at the beginning of 1957, and in some of his initial suspensions, politics was transposed with immorality. For example, in February, Vasconcelos suspended the afternoon movie broadcasts on Havana's channel 7 and, specifically, the Mexican movie *El rey del barrio* (The king of the barrio), starring Mexican celebrity and comedian Tin Tan.[39] On the surface, the suspension did not make much sense, since the 1949 movie is a comedy in which Tin Tan plays a Robin Hood–type character. However, as John Mraz observes, most, if not all, of Tin Tan's films "rendered a critique of the status quo. . . . . In film after film he ridicules the wealthy and those who govern."[40] Following this thematic trend, in *El rey del barrio* Tin Tan directly critiques the corruption in Mexico's government during the late 1940s. Thus, by censoring this film, Vasconcelos asserted *El rey del barrio*'s political subtext and its potential to be transposed to Cuba's revolutionary movement. Nevertheless, his justification for suspending the film was its "immoral content."[41] Political rebelliousness transmuted into indecent content, positioning any ideological contestation to the status quo as immoral.

Also classified as immoral were programs that could be read as mocking the government or government officials. For instance, in May, Vasconcelos suspended the show *Las cosas del senador* (The senator's affairs) because it "ridiculed the senatorial post by presenting the character of the senator as a grotesque and uncultured individual."[42] Locally inspired humor, somewhat similar to Tin Tan's socially engaged comedies, was seen as a threat. The Cuban *choteo*, which had contributed to the successful ratings of comedies and variety shows since the early 1950s thanks to its satiric take on Cuba's contemporaneity, had to be diluted.

Similar to previous years, music and dance were also targeted prior to the 1957 amendment, but one particular genre received the minister of communication's full attention: rock and roll. In early February, Vasconcelos sent a press release to newspapers and magazines indicating that rock and roll challenged the decency norms established by the Broadcasting Law of 1953. Described as a "choreographic deformation" that "causes morbid states of excitation," dancing to rock and roll was briefly banned from Cuban television.[43]

Vasconcelos's actions might not have been a surprise for people following the anti–rock and roll campaign that took place in the United States during the mid-1950s. As Matthew F. Delmont writes, fear of racial integration and miscegenation fueled the movement against rock and roll and the outlawing of the musical style in various parts of the United States.[44] In addition to the racialized associations, the genre was also linked with juvenile delinquency. According to Delmont, "A wide range of critics argued that mass media, especially comic books, Hollywood films, television crime shows, and rock and roll music, incited young people to violence and illegal behavior."[45] Considering the connection between rock and roll and youth rebellion, as well as the fact that young people mostly filled up the ranks of the revolutionary movement, Vasconcelos's censorship may have been responding to the subversiveness associated with the genre. Still, the racialization and sexualization of rock and roll might have also influenced its prohibition on television, given the minister of communication's preoccupation with race and bourgeois norms of conduct since the mid-1950s.

To be sure, rock and roll dances did not disappear from Cuba's public sphere. In fact, the dances were again allowed on television as long as the young people performing them modified what some officials considered a series of sexually suggestive steps that threatened "public morals."[46] Furthermore, the same month in which Vasconcelos banned such dancing, rock and roll–themed films such as *Juventud desenfrenada* (Mexico, 1956) and Elvis Presley's *Love Me Tender* (United States, 1956) were screened in Havana movie theaters and advertised in newspapers. Also, U.S. films such as *Rebel without a Cause* and *Blackboard Jungle* were screened in Havana's cine clubs, introducing the "bad boy" of the Cold War era to Cuban audiences.[47] As literary scholar Leerom Medovoi argues, the bad boy image that populated U.S. Hollywood films symbolized the suburban youth who refused to be domesticated and "thereby ensur[ed] the continuity of American freedom in an age of three worlds."[48] At a time when the Soviet Union and the United States were fighting an ideological war for geopolitical control, the United States needed to maintain its representation as a progressive, revolutionary, free nation in contrast to the Soviet Union's politically restrictive and regulatory way of life.[49] The bad boy image, then, preserved some elements of the Cold War containment (in terms of class, race, and notions of masculinity) while concomitantly capturing the notion of freedom ingrained in the United States' Cold War ideological propaganda. As such, the bad boy symbolized "dissent, defiance, or even insurrection mounted against a social order of conformity."[50] Hence, even as the minister of communication paid close attention to rock and roll dances, the rebelliousness of the music and the nonconformity associated with the commodified yet politically charged U.S. movie culture were part of the Cuban popular-culture imaginary. More important, Cubans already had their own "bad boy." Even as some people thought Fidel Castro was dead, others, in various places across Cuba, were defying the government. Similar to previous years, Vasconcelos's focus on rock and roll repositioned television beyond Cuba's social and political realities in an attempt to police the broadcasting of Cuban modernity.

The ban on rock and roll was the first in a series of consecutive suspensions before the 1957 amendment went into effect. Models who made immoral gestures while advertising products; female dancers who moved their bodies indecently; telenovelas that promoted sexual relations before marriage and whose characters spoke about immoral topics; and the hiring of a girl (who in reality was seventeen years old) to act in a television drama were all cited by the minister of communication as indecent actions that required suspension.[51] A seemingly overreaching indecency menace took over Cuban television, forcing the state to intervene. What the amendment did, then, was legalize the minister of communication's intrusion into entertainment programming on TV, a process that began in 1955 and intensified over the years.

Some commentators verbalized their dissatisfaction with the minister of communication's actions, indirectly hinting at the lack of freedom that defined Cuban society and the government's conservative trend. In reference to the outlawing of rock and roll on television, one journalist wrote, "We are opposed to any imposition that limits any individual right such as making music and dancing," while another indicated that the banning of "North American rhythms" was an example of the "parochialism" that had invaded Cuban society.[52] In some ways, similar to discussions that had taken place in Cuba's public sphere about suspending news shows and stations, debating the exclusion of the musical genre helped question the government's claims of democracy and modernity. Another reviewer, in reference to multiple suspensions during the first months of 1957, described the events as a once-in-a-lifetime moment in the history of Cuban television. This critic also explained how the suspensions affected the industry financially.[53] Other reviewers noticed the silence of the CRE and commented on the fact that the minister of communication was directing all of the suspensions and defining morality. These reviewers wanted the CRE to take the lead in monitoring indecency, highlighting the fact that not every journalist or television reviewer opposed the policing of morality.[54] But what they all seemed to agree on was the notion that the CRE was supposed to be in charge of supervising, not the minister of communication.

Vasconcelos's emphasis on morality in broadcasting crystallized how Batista's government was attempting to control all types of programming as his political regime began to crumble. It not only targeted the topics of sex, religion, and crime in entertainment programming but also content that questioned the political order. This thematic focus further distanced what was being broadcast on Cuban television from what was happening in Cuban society, where, for example, bodies covered in blood appeared on the streets, bombs exploded in the early morning hours, and prostitutes performed sex acts at Havana's Shanghai Theater.

Furthermore, concurrent with the minister of communication's enactment of two censorship decrees and the close monitoring of news and entertainment programming during the months when censorship was legally lifted, the publication of the 1957 amendment articulates the contradictions of Batista's government. On the one hand, he legitimately enforced his power by legalizing censorship. On the other hand, he crafted new regulations that envisioned diversified programming content and ownership. And, in between these legal enactments, there were months when some public expressions of dissent were possible. The broadcasters' complaints against the suspensions of news programming and a show entirely devoted to the importance of freedom of expression (CMQ-TV's *El estudio vacio*) attest to Batista's erratic government. This trend of imposing and lifting censorship, as Jorge I. Domínguez writes, reveals that "Batista was an inefficient dictator. His press censorship and his constitutional manipulation were distinctly inconsistent."[55] The pressure to maintain good standing with the United States and, closely interconnected, the need to promote Cuba's modernity most likely played a role in Batista's contradictory handling of broadcasting.[56] The 1957 amendment should be interpreted as one of the final scenarios in the spectacles of democracy.[57]

This scenario, nonetheless, was not sufficient to keep U.S. audiences convinced by and fully involved with the spectacles of democracy. While the minister of communication was imposing and lifting media censorship, another representation of Cuba began to evolve in the U.S. media. Herbert L. Matthews's *New York Times* articles and the May 1957 CBS News Special Report *Rebels of the Sierra Maestra* introduced a heroic figure into the Cuban narrative and provided a U.S.-made preface to the spectacles of revolution to come. These U.S.-made introductions presented another understanding of Cuba and provided a glimpse of how Cuban modernity would be broadcast in the early years of the Cuban Revolution.

A Rebel with a Cause: Fidel Castro and U.S. Youth in *Rebels of the Sierra Maestra*

Taking him, as one would at first, by physique and personality, this was quite a man—a powerful six-footer, olive-skinned, full-faced, with a straggly beard.

The personality of the man is overpowering. It was easy to see that his men adored him and also to see why he has caught the imagination of the youth of Cuba all over the island. Here was an educated, dedicated fanatic, a man of ideals of courage and of remarkable qualities of leadership.—Herbert L. Matthews, "Cuban Rebel Is Visited in Hideout," *New York Times*, February 24, 1957

Herbert L. Matthews's *New York Times* articles on Fidel Castro and the 26th of July Movement marked, according to Anthony DePalma, a new period in the history of the Cuban Revolution.[58] With these pieces people in the United States and around the world not only learned that a thirty-year-old man named Fidel Castro was fighting in the mountains of Sierra Maestra to overthrow Fulgencio Batista but also became familiar with a young leader who was capable of mobilizing the masses. First taken by Castro's physical appearance and then by his personality (as the preceding quotes demonstrate), in his first interview Matthews introduced some of the elements that would become part of the spectacles of revolution. As discussed in the next chapter, the images of the Cuban Revolution—a bearded Fidel Castro wearing combat fatigues, smoking a cigar, and carrying a rifle next to his *barbudo* rebels, also wearing fatigues and holding rifles—presented in Matthews's February articles and, two months later, in the documentary *Rebels of the Sierra Maestra* became key components of the revolutionary iconography.[59] Even though both media artifacts were developed with a U.S. audience in mind and were constructed by journalists' perceptions of Castro (and in the case of Robert Taber's CBS television program, by commercial imperatives), parts of these U.S.-framed pictures traveled in time and geographic space and were cemented in the spectacles of revolution.

Matthews's interview was the first media artifact to present Castro's personality and political objectives to a local and global audience. Described as an eloquent, magnetic, highly intelligent and educated man, Castro was depicted as a mixture of El Zorro and Robin Hood (in terms of fighting for the poor) but with very specific political goals for his country. As Matthews writes, "He has strong ideas of liberty, democracy, social justice, the need to restore the Constitution, to hold elections. . . . The 26th of July Movement talks of nationalism, anti-colonialism, anti-imperialism."[60] Whereas the truthfulness of Castro's intentions and words, together with Matthews's political views and objective approach to the subject, have been questioned over the years, the most intriguing part of Matthews's description—particularly in the context of the Cold War—relates to the terms he used to describe the revolutionary movement. Even though Matthews made it clear that Castro and the 26th of July Movement did not embrace communism, ideologically loaded terms such as "anticolonialism" and "anti-imperialism" highlighted the Popular Front and its political movement, characterized by "a social democratic electoral politics; a politics of anti-fascist and anti-imperialist solidarity; and a civil liberties campaign against lynching and labor repression."[61] Although in 1957 it was too soon to predict the success of the revolutionary movement and thus its political impact in the geopolitical sphere, Castro's leadership and his ideals for social justice were appealing enough to attract young American fans, as *Rebels of the Sierra Maestra* demonstrates.

Included as part of the highly prestigious CBS Reports series, *Rebels of the Sierra Maestra: The Story of Cuba's Jungle Fighters* aired on the CBS network on Sunday, May 19, 1957, at 6:30 PM. The main objective of the documentary, which came from a tradition of journalism in the United States that embraced professionalism and objectivity but that, at the same time, was engaged with and commented on social problems affecting different parts of the world, was to introduce U.S. viewers to Fidel Castro and his revolutionary movement.[62] Following an "expository mode" of documentary narrative to convey distance and objectivity, the twenty-six-minute documentary positions journalist Robert Taber and his cameraman, Wendell Hoffman, as the principal storytellers of the "jungle fighters'" chronicle.[63] Through voice-overs, shots, and interviews, a nameless master narrator, together with Taber and Hoffman, guides viewers into the mountains of Sierra Maestra to find "rebel leader Fidel Castro" and learn about the motivations behind the revolution.

Sonically, the documentary begins with unidentified parts of the 26th of July Movement hymn visually accompanied by a drawing of a barefoot campesino (farmworker) wearing a sombrero and carrying a rifle and a string of bullets across his chest. The campesino image is a visual citation of the *bandido* characters that had populated U.S. films since the silent era; however, this Cuban figure was more sympathetic than the bloodthirsty, rugged, and tough bandido villain. Even as his clothing and bare feet conveyed primitivism and backwardness, the right hand placed on his chest and the seriousness of his look depicted a dignified, honorable man (see fig. 4.1).

The linguistically and culturally distant music and illustration are followed by a shot of the Sierra Maestra. A flamenco guitar substitutes for the 26th of July Movement hymn, presenting culturally appealing and somewhat familiar music that, once again, transports the audience to previous representations of Latin America in Hollywood films. This time, though, the audience is not going to watch beautiful señoritas dancing flamenco (the other type of image that, in addition to the bandido and the Latin lover, had been used to depict the region since the silent era); instead, as the next shot illustrates, they are going to learn about a group of jungle fighters. Even though the shot presents a somewhat threatening image of a group of young men emerging from behind the foliage, all looking and pointing their rifles at an undefined target in the distance, the theatrically staged poses sonically framed with flamenco guitar reconstruct the image and story of the jungle fighters as an adventure tale similar to those presented by Hollywood (see fig. 4.2).

In an attempt to allure the audience, the beginning of *Rebels of the Sierra Maestra* borrows a series of sonic, visual, and narrative cues from Hollywood, reaffirming both the constructedness of the documentary and the commercial imperatives that define U.S. television. To borrow film scholar

FIGURE 4.1. Opening, CBS documentary *Rebels of the Sierra Maestra*, May 19, 1957.

FIGURE 4.2. Jungle fighter, CBS documentary *Rebels of the Sierra Maestra*, May 19, 1957.

Bill Nichols's words regarding the fictionalization of reality in the documentary genre, the U.S. audience would get a "reference to a 'reality,' that is a construct, the product of signifying systems."[64] Mediated by Robert Taber and Wendell Hoffman's perspectives as well as by previous representations of Latin America in Hollywood films, *Rebels of the Sierra Maestra*'s purpose was to educate and entertain the public. As Michael Curtin explains, television documentaries in the late 1950s and early 1960s sought to cultivate an understanding of U.S. and worldwide social problems. *Rebels of the Sierra Maestra* took up that educational mission and framed it using Hollywood's cinematic conventions. As a commercial product, *Rebels of the Sierra Maestra* had to attract the audience; thus, besides reframing the jungle fighters' tale as a Hollywood-style adventure story, the narrator quickly establishes why Americans should pay attention to these unknown rebels.

The island's geographic closeness to the United States ("approximately one hour from Miami") and the existence of the "strategic U.S. naval base, at Guantanamo Bay" are the first pieces of information the film presents to highlight the importance of Cuba for a U.S. audience. After the Cuba-U.S. connection is established, the viewer learns basic information about the island's political situation: Fulgencio Batista's route to power, the U.S. recognition of his government, and some Cuban citizens' support for "a government by a strong man." The narrator also notes that, according to Batista, those fighting against his government have communist affiliations. The film neither supports nor denies this piece of information, though no one from Batista's cabinet is included to provide the government perspective. It is clear which side the documentary is going to represent and support; the focus is on the revolutionary cause. Nonetheless, it is not until Taber and Hoffman arrive at the 26th of July Movement's camp (after a long and difficult journey, as the audience learns via narration and shots) that the documentary's primary political objective stands out.

At the camp, all the revolutionary soldiers pose once again for Hoffman's camera, although this time the young men are not preparing to fire at an invisible target. Instead, they are assembled as a group, almost immobile, posing for a photograph. Fidel Castro is then introduced via a close-up and a brief description by Taber that emphasizes his educational accomplishments ("This is Dr. Fidel Castro, thirty-one, holder of four university degrees"). Up to this point on Taber and Hoffman's journey, the audience has had the chance to see key figures of the Cuban Revolution. Leaders such as Haydeé

Santamaria, Celia Sánchez, Camilo Cienfuegos, and Raúl Castro are among the jungle fighters who guide the journalist and his cameraman through Sierra Maestra's rough terrain. Yet these leaders (mostly referred to by their first names) are silent, as are all of the other Cuban revolutionaries. The only rebels, besides Fidel Castro, who speak in *Rebels of the Sierra Maestra* are U.S.-born Michael Garvey, Chuck Ryan, and Victor Buelhman—fifteen, twenty, and seventeen years old, respectively—who left their families at the Guantanamo Bay Naval Base to fight for Cuba's freedom. "We came to do our part for the freedom of the world, mostly," Chuck Ryan, explains. "We just heard so much about how Batista was so cruel and how he had a dictatorship, . . . how the people were fighting for freedom, we felt moved to do our part. So here we are."[65] Influenced by their Cuban friends' stories about the political situation, the three young adults left the base to become revolutionaries.

Somewhat similar to the 1940s, when Cuban radio signals interfered with the base's radio station, the legal-territorial division between Cuba and the U.S. Guantanamo Bay Naval Base is breached in this scenario. If during World War II, Cuban radio signals crossed the imaginary line that affected transmissions when national security was at risk, in the late 1950s ideological messages of revolution, anticolonialism, and anti-imperialism carried over by people were penetrating the minds of some U.S. youth. And, contrary to the more manageable radio signals, no modern technological apparatus could control the appeal that the Cuban Revolution had for some U.S. adolescents. Through personal interactions (as in the case of the three young men) and U.S. newspaper stories, Fidel Castro and his cause began to impact various sectors of the U.S. population, opening a space for a new type of political affiliation. As historian Van Gosse argues, before the triumph of the Cuban Revolution, Castro and his cause attracted middle-class adolescents who were distanced from the political discourse of the Popular Front but mesmerized by the idealism and nonconformity that the revolution symbolized.[66] Castro was a foreign rebel with a very appealing cause who was turning young Americans into real bad boys.

Nonetheless, for one of the three young men, Fidel Castro and the revolutionary movement were not the only reasons for joining the rebels. For Ryan, the spokesman of the group and the oldest of the three U.S. jungle fighters, the main inspiration to become a revolutionary came from a book he had read some years before. In response to Taber's question regarding his main encouragement for joining Castro, Ryan explains, "Yes it was a book put out by *Reader's Digest, Reading for Americans*. It has many stories about American men, other short stories about the world in general, freedom fighters, different jobs that people could get, things on education, just general American readings." According to Ryan, the message of freedom that was part of the *Reading for Americans* stories echoed the accounts of his Cuban friends. In the eyes of this young man, Cubans were fighting for the same principles Americans had fought for over the years: freedom and democracy. Indeed, the short pieces in *Reading for Americans* highlight U.S. democracy against other "tyrannies." As noted in one of the essays, "Today, various tyrannies are challenging liberty, each in its own way. How can Americans protect ourselves? . . . Your fathers, mothers and distant ancestors believed in the reality of duty. Upon that, they built the world."[67] The six-part compendium emphasizes the United States' route to freedom and the value of democracy, resonating with the ideological doctrine of the period.[68] In many ways, Ryan and his friends follow the teachings of *Reading for Americans* even as the people behind *Reader's Digest* most likely did not intend to promote this type of citizen engagement.

Taber asks Ryan to send a message to the worried parents of Michael Garvey and Victor Buehlman at the Guantanamo Bay Naval Base (the State Department was also trying to bring the young men back to the United States). "They should be proud of their sons. I hope they realize that their boys are fighting for an idea. This is for world peace," Ryan responds. Then, Fidel Castro, who for the first time is given a chance to speak, agrees with Ryan. "I am very happy and grateful to them. They have learned very much here. They are brave. They will be good soldiers." Through Taber's narration the audience learns that the two underage teenagers were "honorably discharged" and returned to the United States. The oldest stayed with the 26th of July Movement soldiers.

The rest of *Rebels of the Sierra Maestra* focuses on the soldiers' daily life in the mountains. Through Taber's voice-over narration and Hoffman's shots, the audience discovers how the rebels got their rifles and general supplies and learns about their day-to-day chores. In the last part of the documentary, Taber, Hoffman, and all the soldiers hike to Pico Turquino, the highest mountain in Cuba. At the top of the mountain they test their weapons and pray in front of a bust of José Martí. It is in this last part of *Rebels of the Sierra Maestra* that Castro becomes the main speaker in the documentary. In his dialogue with Taber and the U.S. audience (via the camera), Castro stresses two main themes. The first is the importance of reporters (implicitly from the United States) in divulging information Batista has censored: "We will always get someone who will let people know what is going on, because there will always be a reporter, like you, who is willing to risk [his life], for seeking the truth." The second is the inability of Batista's government to stop the revolution: "We have demonstrated that the tyranny is incapable of defeating the fight for liberty. . . . This is only the beginning. The last battle will be fought in the capital. You can be sure about that." The documentary ends with all the men, including Taber, posing for the camera. The rebels lift their rifles and then wave the Cuban flag. The hymn of the 26th of July Movement is played again, accompanied by the drawing of the campesino and the presentation of the credits.

Bill Nichols reminds us that documentaries are "fictions with plots, characters, situations, and events like any other. They offer introductory lacks, challenges, or dilemmas; they build heightened tensions and dramatically rising conflicts, and they terminate with resolution and closure."[69] In *Rebels of the Sierra Maestra*, the plot is the Cuban Revolution. Nevertheless, even though at the beginning of the narrative Taber explains that his journey is "to find a rebel leader named Fidel Castro," the audience soon discovers that the main heroes of the story are the three young American men who joined the revolution. In the words of Van Gosse, "The significance of Taber's film, hard on the heels of Matthews' discovery, is that North Americans who had been shown only rebels minus causes, as a pose or a form of social 'delinquency,' now had a full-fledged rebellion playing itself out in their living-rooms, at the center of which were their own teenage compatriots."[70] Through the media, the jungle fighters become a modified version of the Hollywood bad boy. They are rebelling not against the confines of suburbia per se but against social injustice and political oppression. *Rebels of the Sierra Maestra* pluralizes the image of the "bad boy" while concomitantly, as Gosse argues, fostering the gestation of the New Left.

An exchange of bad boys took place between Cuba and the United States during 1957–58, and the imagery, narrative, and ideological aspects that were part of this transaction were transferred through and structured by the media. In other words, the cultural industries—particularly film and television—were the channels and, in some ways, the creators. On the one hand, the bad boy who came to Cuba from Hollywood went from being a young rebel in U.S. suburbia to becoming—at least in the eyes of Cuban censors—a threat to the norms of social and sexual conduct. Even though the Hollywood bad boy imagery and narrative is a fictionalized compendium of a U.S. Cold War ideological formation of freedom and democracy, part of the symbolism associated with the image represented a threat. In the political and social context of Cuba in the period 1957–58, the influence of the bad boy image (in terms of nonconformity and sexuality) was a menace to the Cuban state. On the other hand, the bad boy who came to the United States from Cuba (first via Matthews's *New York Times* stories and Taber's *Rebels of the Sierra Maestra* and later by way of newspapers, newscasts, and magazine stories) became the epitome of freedom for many youths and activists. With Fidel Castro and the revolutionaries of the 26th of July Movement, the core ideas of freedom and defiance that were part of the U.S. Cold War rhetoric merged with the call for social justice and activism on a global scale that was part of the U.S. Left during the 1930s and 1940s. Whereas Castro and his soldiers were real-life rebels, their representation in the media was framed by a series of codes associated with both heroic and fictionalized figures that were popularized by Hollywood and its previous representations of Latin America. The mediated figure of Fidel Castro blurred reality and fiction; past and present; and U.S., Cuban, and international social and political struggles.

U.S. commercial culture's creation of the Cuban bad boy "with a good cause" image (as Gosse describes it) had a long-lasting influence on the visual construction of the revolution. Pictures of Fidel Castro and the rugged combatants dominated the visual-photographic narrations of Cuba in the United States and around the world from 1957 to 1958, and with the triumph of the Cuban Revolution, these images continue to be used as representations of the new Cuban nation. Fidel Castro and his army became "celebrities," adding what literary scholar José Quiroga refers to as "revolutionary glamour," a glamour that was then appropriated by the state.[71]

Changing the Backdrop for New Spectacles

On January 19, 1958, NBC broadcast *The Steve Allen Show* from the Havana Riviera Hotel in Cuba, taking advantage of the "Over the Horizon" technology launched less than a year earlier on the island.[72] The luxury of the hotel and the sophistication of its guests framed this enclosed depiction of

FIGURE 4.3. *The Steve Allen Show,* NBC, January 19, 1958.

Cuba, presenting a drastic departure from the images of *Rebels of the Sierra Maestra*. The only similarity between the two television artifacts was their emphasis on the geographic closeness between Cuba and the United States. While in *Rebels of the Sierra Maestra*, the voice-over narrator mentions that Havana is "approximately one hour from Miami" and then proceeds to reference the Guantanamo Bay Naval Base and a summary of Batista's route to power, in *The Steve Allen Show*, the host, with the help of three attractive Cuban women holding large cue cards with information, notes the short territorial distance between the two countries and the size of the island and its population, before quickly commenting on its economy. Whereas the purpose of *Rebels of the Sierra Maestra* was to introduce the revolutionary struggle and some young Americans' engagement with the movement, *The Steve Allen Show* was designed to encourage tourism, particularly for the Havana Riviera, which had been christened a month earlier (see fig. 4.3). As the *New York Times* television reviewer wrote, "The gambling industry in Cuba and a new Havana Hotel were the chief beneficiaries of last night's visit to the island by Steve Allen and his company."[73]

With the exception of the hotel workers and some musicians (a couple of drummers and the Quinteto de Facundo Rivero, as the last performers on the show), most of the artists and people seen on the program were tourists who, like Allen, came to Havana to enjoy the weather, the lavish hotel, and the casinos. The only signs of "Cubanness" offered by the program are a rustic wagon pulled by a burro (which is shown as Allen's mode of transportation to the Havana Riviera Hotel), campesino hats and attire worn by some of the show's comedians, and the Spanish language used to introduce the show's guests and sponsor, Johnson's Wax. *The Steve Allen Show* functioned in many ways like a television sequel to some of the Good Neighbor policy–inspired films in which Cuba and its citizens were used as props and scenery for the American protagonists and stories.[74] To be sure, *The Steve Allen Show*'s portrayal of Cuba was uncommon in the U.S. media scene during 1957 and 1958, when national and local newspapers and newscasts covered the Batista government's censorship, the revolutionary battles, the abuses of power (including footage of Batista's police beating protesters), and most of all the figure of Fidel Castro.[75] Casinos, luxury hotels, and their shows did not seem to be the main interests of U.S. newsrooms and networks.

The NBC variety show's politically aloof and culturally insensitive depiction of Cuba clearly made an impact on the Cuban reviewers who protested the show. "We need to regulate the transmissions offered from Cuba," an offended reviewer wrote. "We need to protect our prestige and demand that we get the respect we deserve. We cannot continue being a village for Jewish and North American people."[76] Although framed by an anti-Semitic tone that not only rendered Cuban Jews nonexistent but also created a bifurcated identity for Jewish people in the United States, the strong nationalistic sentiment that pervaded Cuban culture and society in the last part of the decade was clearly manifested in the reviewer's words. *The Steve Allen Show*'s portrayal of *Cubanness* was decoded as an insult to Cuba and its people.

But programs like *The Steve Allen Show* were not the only products of U.S. culture and influence that Cubans resented. Toward the end of 1958, many newspaper and magazine columns commented on the dominance of Hollywood imports and the failure of the government and the CRE to monitor the Hollywood films that aired on Cuban television. Reviewers and unionized performers demanded regulation, particularly given that the Ministry of Communication (under the leadership of Alberto García Valdes, beginning in mid-1958) and the CRE (following the government's lead) kept suspending local programs, dancers, singers, and comedians for being "immoral."[77] The minister of communication provided a partial solution to the problem in late 1958, when he announced that the CRE would be in charge of regulating movies broadcast on television. The CRE's new task provided some hope for reviewers and performers who believed regulating imported shows would ease the focus on local artists and programs.[78] Still, Hollywood's imports on Cuban television continued to be an important topic of discussion during the early months of 1959.

The government attempted to accommodate some of the media professionals' requests in other areas as well. In a last attempt to convince Cubans and the world of his commitment to democracy and freedom of expression, Batista released another broadcasting decree in June 1958.[79] While on paper the decree reduced the state's power to censor, it did not alter the government's intrusion in programming. In fact, one month before releasing the decree, Batista declared another forty-five-day "state of national emergency."[80] Batista's erratic form of governing continued throughout his last months in power.

It is important to note that despite the state's monitoring of programming, media creators did manage to introduce political messages into entertainment shows. For example, a *radionovela* from 1957, *El dictador de Valle Azul* (The dictator of the Blue Valley), told the story of a terrible dictator and the birth of an insurrection led by a man named Taguary.[81] In addition, Delia Fiallo, one of the most important radionovela and telenovela writers in Cuba and Latin America, indicated in a 2013 interview that she had always tried to incorporate subversive messages into her scripts. When asked about Batista's dictatorship and the artists' involvement in politics in 1950s Cuba, she acknowledged her participation in this type of hidden politics. "I did it. For example, *Cuando se quiere a un enemigo*'s [When one Loves the Enemy] action took place in France, when Maquis were fighting against the German occupation. There was also *Soraya*, which took place in India. . . . in these *novelas* I reflected an oppressed people's anxious desire for freedom. I mirrored this by using strong phrases."[82] During an era when word of mouth and transmissions from the 26th of July Movement's Radio Rebelde (broadcasting from the Sierra Maestra since February 1958) were the main sources of information regarding the state of the Cuban Revolution, writers and media professionals also involved themselves in the revolutionary fight through their creative work, though their participation did not have the same impact as that of those fighting in the Sierra Maestra. To paraphrase one of the sentences from the documentary *Hasta el último aliento* (1995), television and radio were "palpitat[ing] together with the Cuban people" and the revolutionary movement.[83] This "palpitation" continued with the victory of the Cuban Revolution. Nonetheless, as the revolution was radicalized, some media professionals began to distance themselves from politics. What it meant to be Cuban and modern changed, and with this alteration the broadcasting of modernity and its spectacles was detached from previous conceptualizations of progress, decency, and democracy. The revolution became the main source for what it meant to be modern.

CHAPTER 5

Spectacles of Revolution
A Rebirth of Cubanness

Casino de la alegría could finally present a program with authentic Cuban roots, without censorship, without authoritarian regulations. And the same for all of national television and radio. Because, once again, we have a free and sovereign Republic, and that is the only way that art can be expressed in its full truth.—Alberto Giró, "Patriótico programa ofreció el 'Casino De La Alegría,'" *Diario de la Marina*, January 10, 1959

Minister of Communications Dr. Enrique Oltuski, in one of the most interesting personal revelations of the new regime, in a recent televised interview strongly disapproved of our radio and TV for abstaining from explaining the doctrine of the revolution to the people.—"Ondas, doctrina, y cultura," *Carteles*, April 19, 1959

Everyone knows about the large number of revolutionaries who appeared after January first. How could it have happened that even the characters on a radio soap opera became revolutionaries upon moving to television after that date!—Mariana Romeu Calderón, Holguín, Oriente, "Nos dicen," *Bohemia*, September 27, 1959

The three preceding quotes illustrate the ways in which a reviewer, a state representative, and an audience member conceptualized the changes taking place on Cuban television during 1959. The first quote reflects the euphoria of the moment, when citizens' massive support for the Cuban Revolution began to influence television's singular focus on revolutionary themes and Cuban culture. The second quote hints at a change in the trajectory of the Cuban Revolution, when the new government began to envision the medium as a tool for political indoctrination. The third quote demonstrates that even though the government was unsatisfied with commercial television's engagement with the "doctrine of the revolution," television was immersed in the historical moment. In effect, the problem was not commercial television's detachment from the revolution but, rather, Fidel Castro's ongoing articulation of new political, social, and cultural discourses.

Within approximately three years, the revolution moved ideologically from democracy to Marxist-Leninism, drastically changing the future of the nation. Yet, even though Castro did not acknowledge his position as a Marxist until 1961, events such as the nationalization of locally owned and foreign property, the silencing of criticism against the revolution, business arrangements with the Soviet Union, and the government's endorsement of Cuba's communist party (which moved from a peripheral position to a central place in the state) hinted at both the revolution's political course and the messianic stature of its leader, Fidel Castro. A revolutionary movement that was originally formed to reinstate Cuba's constitutional democracy changed its course and adopted a socialist doctrine between 1959 and 1960, only to be redefined again in 1961 when Castro declared himself a Marxist-Leninist. Supported by many Cuban citizens who, after years of government corruption, U.S. economic and cultural dominance, and drastic class discrepancies, saw the radicalization of the revolution "as a militant struggle for collective redemption," the revolutionary government—that is, Fidel Castro—became the sole voice of and for the Cuban nation.[1]

In the year and a half during which television was privately owned following the triumph of the Cuban Revolution, the government went through three ideological shifts: democracy, *humanism* (a term coined by Castro, as explained later), and nationalism/socialism. Even though the political transformations taking place between 1959 and 1960 should be viewed as shifting tides of ideas and actions rather than drastic ruptures, scholars have identified specific stages marked by events in the history of the revolutionary regime.

The first stage, democracy, was the force behind the revolutionary movement throughout the 1950s, including the first year of the revolution. Many leaders of the 26th of July Movement and Cuban citizens wanted to reinstate Cuba's constitutional democracy and hold elections. During 1959, Fidel Castro and his leaders invited important figures from all the major political parties to participate in the new government. In addition to this initial pluralization of voices, Castro and his allies enacted a series of legal and governmental changes that benefited Cuba's disenfranchised citizens. These early transformations included increasing wages, stabilizing rent based on income, ending racial discrimination in private business, and discussing the distribution of farmland, which in May 1959 became the Law of Agrarian Reform. As Louis A. Pérez observes, "The reform measures were dramatic and historic, and all provided immediate relief to those sectors of Cuban society that demanded relief immediately."[2] Marginal sectors of Cuban society and most members of the middle and upper classes welcomed these renovations.

In terms of media, two policy changes during the early months of 1959 influenced broadcasting and film: the establishment of the Ministerio de Recuperación de Bienes Malversados (Ministry for the Recovery of Ill-Gotten Goods) and the launching of the Instituto Cubano del Arte y la Industria Cinematográficos (ICAIC; Cuban Institute of Cinematographic Art and Industry). The Ministry for the Recovery of Ill-Gotten Goods began to operate in January with the initial objective of confiscating property and businesses owned by people affiliated with Fulgencio Batista. By way of the ministry's appropriation of businesses, land, and funds, the government developed a range of projects to support the country's poor. With the radicalization of the revolution in 1960, the Ministry for the Recovery of Ill-Gotten Goods nationalized all private property, making the government the sole force behind economic development, services, cultural enrichment, education, and other aspects of Cuban society. During this process of nationalization, Gaspar Pumarejo's channel 12 became the first state-managed television station (in April 1959), and Goar Mestre's CMQ-TV network became the last television industry to be nationalized in September 1960. Due to political unrest, Mestre left the island in March 1960, followed by his brothers soon after.[3] The ICAIC was established in March 1959 and represented the first effort of the Castro-led government to advance cultural productions that would combine ideological, aesthetic, and pedagogical functions. Initially producing newsreels and, to a lesser extent, documentaries for local and global audiences, in its first period (1959–60) the ICAIC celebrated the triumph of the revolution while also screening the corruption of Fulgencio Batista's regime.[4]

A speech that Fidel Castro gave in the United States in April 1959 marks the beginning of the second stage: humanism. Through a series of interviews and speeches, Castro described the revolution as a call for social justice and equality for all Cubans, stressing that the meaning of democratic humanism "was neither capitalist nor communist but sought to find its own way."[5] Castro's conceptualization of democracy in the second stage echoed the views he expressed to Herbert L. Matthews in a *New York Times* interview in 1957. As Matthews wrote, "He has strong ideas of liberty, democracy, social justice, the need to restore the Constitution, to hold elections. . . . The 26th of July Movement talks of nationalism, anti-colonialism, anti-imperialism."[6] The main difference between Castro's 1957 political goals (per Matthews) and his conceptualization of democratic humanism in 1959 was his lack of interest in holding elections. Castro's government did not demonstrate any urgency in restoring the electoral process during the first year of the Cuban Revolution, causing distress among some 26th of July leaders and Cuban citizens. However, the majority of Cubans—many from the working class—were not concerned with the lack of elections and embraced the multiple policy changes taking place at the national level.[7]

The nationalism/socialism phase began when a revolutionary leader (Huber Matos) denounced Fidel Castro's involvement with the communist party, leading to Matos's subsequent trial and incarceration in December 1959. This stage marked an important shift in the history of the Cuban Revolution. The characterization of the United States as an imperialistic force, the nationalization of all private properties, the beginning of diplomatic relations with the Soviet Union, and the end of diplomatic relations with the United States (between December 1960 and early 1961) dramatically distinguish this phase from the previous two periods. Cuba's civil society was banished while, concomitantly, the government appealed to Cuban citizens to devote themselves to the revolutionary cause and, more important, to Fidel Castro. In the words of Lillian Guerra, "Replacing all discussions of humanism were messianic calls to abandon traditional values associated with political liberalism in favor of an all-encompassing revolutionary morality based on personal courage, selflessness, and unwavering faith."[8] *Fidelismo*, that is, the view of Fidel Castro as a Christlike figure in charge of the moral guidance of the Cuban nation, was solidified during the nationalism/socialism stage.

During these three phases, the government began to develop new ideas about progress, democracy, and morality, situating the Cuban nation in a liminal stage wherein, while not totally abandoning previous conceptualizations of modernity, it began to parallel the modernization ethos of communist regimes.[9] Traces of another style of modernity were foreshadowed by an initial redistribution of wealth that was later reformulated as a class-based battle against economically solvent people; the redefinition of democracy by situating a singular figure (and later a central-party state) to oversee every aspect of Cuban society; the control of the press; and the use of different platforms (such as education, mass rallies, and the media) to communicate the "doctrine of the revolution." In the liminal stage, Cuban modernity encompassed dominant, residual, and emergent notions of what it meant to be modern.[10]

This chapter centers on the first year of the Cuban Revolution and explores how the government's understanding of Cubanness and modernity began to alter the uses and function of television in Cuban society. I begin by analyzing the effects of the revolution on television, focusing on how various genres addressed the political changes taking place at the national level. Fidel Castro himself also used the medium to address those issues, and reviewers reacted. I closely examine his participation on television, paying particular attention to the ways in which reviewers read his ongoing on-air appearances and how his reliance on the panel-show genre influenced his televised political persona. I also analyze Castro's appearances on U.S. panel shows to demonstrate how language, politics, and control of production influenced his televised performances.

My goal in the following pages is to demonstrate how the spectacles of revolution served a dual role. First, they began to accommodate notions of progress, morality, and democracy emanating from ideologies and discourses rooted in Cuba's long fight for independence.[11] Combining speeches that quickly turned into government policy changes, Castro and his revolutionary leaders began looking inward instead of outward, gradually dismissing the United States and Europe as inconsequential points of comparison.

Hence, rather than forcing a drastic rupture, the broadcasting of modernity during the first year of the Cuban Revolution placed alternative views of Cuban modernity at the center of programming themes and discussions about the medium. In other words, commercial television incorporated conceptualizations of modernity that were already part of Cuba's culture but that occupied a marginal position in the national imaginary. Second, as a result of this look inward in terms of Cuba's present and past, the spectacles of progress, the spectacles of decency, and the spectacles of democracy were swiftly subsumed, leaving the spectacles of revolution as the only force behind the broadcasting of modernity. The spectacles of revolution then, operated as a transformative phase, offering a visual and narrative glance at some of the new types of representations that would define Cuba's televised culture in the early 1960s.

The Revolution's Seduction of Commercial Television

The Cuban Revolution dominated the television schedule after January 1, 1959. From the coverage of Fidel Castro's speeches, rallies, and celebrations of important dates in Cuban history and the revolution, to the afternoon court trials of people associated with Fulgencio Batista, to variety shows and dramas, to the production of *telenovelas*, nearly everything was about Fidel Castro, the 26th of July Movement, and the exaltation of Cuban culture.[12] And the novelty was not just that throughout 1959, commercial networks, stations, and advertisers—mostly on their own initiative—began to produce current affairs programs and entertainment shows that focused on the revolution. Also unique in these television offerings was that the topic of the revolution made an appearance in a range of genres, providing multiple revolutionary experiences for the audience.

On prime-time news, journalistic programs, and panel shows, the anchormen, hosts, and guests covered events and policies, providing so-called objective accounts of the revolution and happenings in the country. In January, the new minister of communication (Enrique Oltuski) opened the doors to journalists to demonstrate the revolutionary leaders' "respect for the freedom of expression" (an opinion echoed by Fidel Castro during a trip to the United States in April 1959). This gesture most likely influenced the public's understanding of Cuban news and news-oriented shows as depictions of facts and reality.[13] Even though, as journalism scholar Michael

Schudson reminds us, a news story is not "reality itself" but "a transcription" that is influenced by the historical moment, Cuban news and news-oriented programs were constructed as representations of the "real."[14] In a similar way, the panel show—Castro's preferred television genre for communicating with the Cuban public—was associated with promoting meaningful interrogation and debate regardless of the possible consequences. The seeming transparency of these news efforts contrasted with the censorship that panel shows were subjected to during the Batista years.

On entertainment programs such as dramas and variety shows, the revolution reached audiences through textual, visual, and aural cues, creating another revolutionary experience. In dramas such as the adaptation of Ernest Hemingway's *For Whom the Bell Tolls* and the telenovelas *Tu vida y la mía* (Your life and mine) and *La rebelión de la juventud* (The rebellion of the youth), the texts reenacted stories and battles of Fidel Castro and the 26th of July Movement rebels in the Sierra Maestra, in addition to including some of Castro's speeches.[15] By depicting the revolution's history in the making—and thus constructing some moments as historic—dramatic programs immersed the audience in revolutionary battles and clandestine associations. Although audience members might not have actually witnessed these moments, because of their temporal, national, and sentimental proximity, they most likely also became part of their own revolution. In other words, through dramas, the revolution's not-so-distant past merged with the audience's revolutionary present.[16] Each drama or telenovela episode provided new information about the revolution, a series of fictionalized facts that would constitute the history of the new Cuban nation in the years to come. Hence, as Guerra argues, while certain public spaces and events provided Cuban citizens "with a superhuman awareness of their own individual importance as actors" during the revolution, television dramas served as pedagogical tools that, by recounting the revolutionary past, helped enhance the audience's participation in the revolutionary present.[17]

Dramas and telenovelas that addressed the revolution and programs that, for the most part, centered on Fidel Castro also became part of the iconization of the leader and the ritualization of watching him on television. Whereas photography and the ICAIC's documentaries and newsreels (beginning in 1960) presented Castro in "moments of scripted intimacy," television dramas offered audiences corporeal-performative citations of Castro's gestures, voice, intonations, and words.[18] As one reviewer observed regarding an actor's depiction of Castro, "We have seen many wonderful imitations performed by Tito Hernández, our great actor, but the one presented this past Saturday . . . which revived the moment when Doctor Fidel Castro Ruz took the podium at Camp Columbia, obtained such a fidelity that many people believed they were actually seeing the maximum leader of the Cuban revolution."[19] By representing heroic moments of the not-so-distant past, portrayals of the character Fidel Castro provided audiences with renewed cathartic experiences and began engraving words and gestures from his political persona into their memories. Through dramas and telenovelas, the character Fidel and the "real" Fidel merged—highlighting his stellar role in the spectacles of revolution.

Variety shows became the primary genre for exalting Cuban musical culture. While a few international figures appeared on variety shows such as *Casino de la alegría* and *Jueves de Partagás* (although to a much lesser extent than in the prerevolutionary years), after the triumph of the revolution, musical genres and performers that underscored Cuba's traditions dominated the genre.[20] It was on variety shows that many of the popular-culture songs dedicated to the Cuban Revolution (such as "Como lo soñó Martí," "Canción de libertad," "Sueño de un guajirito," and the Puerto Rican Daniel Santos's song "Sierra Maestra") were performed.[21] In addition, with the state's and citizens' impetus for the Agrarian Reform, Cuban folkloric themes addressing the countryside became highly popular during 1959. As a reviewer noted, "In terms of music and variety shows, we have observed a sudden peak of peasant folkloric themes, always nicely modulated with patriotic and revolutionary improvisations."[22] Poetry readings that exalted the nation, the revolution, and Castro also became part of variety shows.[23] The genre offered audiences an aural, musical, and lyrical experience of the Cuban Revolution.

The comedy genre also incorporated the topic of the revolution, although, based on several reviews, comedians and scriptwriters had to be cautious about the target of the joke. In fact, when discussing the influence of the revolutionary moment on television, a reviewer observed that comedy "is radio and television's Cinderella."[24] Any comedian or variety show's host who made (or allegedly made) fun of, for example, Fidel Castro or the soldiers' appearance, was seen to be insulting the revolution. Writing for *Cinema*, a reviewer declared, "We disapprove of some imitations of Fidel Castro. . . . In this moment of happiness, the *choteo* is not pertinent. Ridiculing is a very dangerous weapon."[25] While two of the most popular songs of 1959 ("Ensalada rebelde" and "Carta a Fidel") were performed by comedians (the comedic duo of Pototo and Filomeno), the lyrics praised the revolution and its leaders, transferring the brunt of the joke to one of the characters who, in his usual demeanor, mispronounced words or used them out of context. Furthermore, the songs ended on a highly patriotic note, thus eliminating any possible connotation of disrespect.

The thematic focus on the Cuban Revolution that dominated all television genres also permeated the ways in which critics discussed the medium. With article titles like "Patriotic Program," "Cuban and Emotional," "A Tribute to Our Art," "Radio and Television in the Revolutionary Movement," and "Show Business and the Revolution," reviewers extolled the efforts made by all commercial networks to keep the audience informed.[26] In addition, reviewers praised the artists and writers who conceptualized fictional programs and variety shows that managed to capture the nationalistic sentiment inspired by the revolutionary victory. Revolutionary Cuba became the epicenter of all discussions about the medium, transforming what was produced, said, and envisioned for television. Unavoidably, engagement with the revolutionary moment and the government's political actions affected what was conceived as television progress, morality on television, and the purposes of television in the new Cuban nation.

Having the most advanced television system in the region, establishing new businesses in Latin America, or implementing U.S. technological innovations ceased to be the main indicators of the medium's progress. The victory of the Cuban Revolution became the principal evidence of Cuba's capacity to excel; thus the search for symbols of television's progress revolved around the revolution. The combined efforts of the networks and media professionals to transmit, for example, the trials of ex-Batista officers; a network's broadcast of a marathon to raise money for the Agrarian Reform and the country's peasants; and the production of shows focusing on Cuban culture became examples of Cuban television advancement. Throughout 1959, Cuban television's progress was measured not by technological superiority in comparison to the outside world but by how well the technology and technological skills could be put to work in the service of the revolutionary cause. The new parameters for progress emerged from within the nation.

The revolution also influenced what was perceived as television morality. To be sure, the topic of sexuality (mostly associated with women's attire and programs that addressed themes such as infidelity and incest) and acts that transgressed dominant norms of masculinity and femininity continued to be seen as immoral after the establishment of the new regime. In fact, a few years after the rebels' victory, gender and sexuality norms were strengthened, combining the control of the body and mind with the moral duty to serve the revolution. However, with Fidel Castro's goal of fighting racial discrimination—a key mandate of the young revolutionary government in 1959—the narration of blackness as a symbol of the primitive and uncivilized did change. With the revolution, Afro-Cubanness suddenly had a place on the television screen.

During a March 1959 speech, Fidel Castro condemned antiblack racism in Cuba, calling on all citizens to fight discrimination. This, according to Alejandro de la Fuente, became "a central principle of the revolution's program" and "created unprecedented opportunities to challenge traditional patterns of race relations in Cuba."[27] Even as, with the establishment of a communist state, the government named racial discrimination a class-based malaise prevalent only in capitalist societies (and thus nonexistent in Cuba), Castro's antidiscrimination speech projected the subject of racism into Cuba's public sphere.[28]

The government's call to end racism influenced television in three ways. First, it allowed for the introduction of programs that focused on Afro-Cuban religious traditions, musical styles, and dances that were previously banned by the Commission on Radio Ethics (CRE) and Batista's minister of communication (Ramón Vasconcelos). For example, a few weeks after Castro delivered the speech targeting discrimination, Telemundo began to air *Carnaval en Cuba libre*, a program under the guidance of a renowned musicologist (Odilio Urfé) who used the space to talk about Afro-Cuban cultural traditions. In addition, variety shows began to incorporate Afro-Cuban folklore, including songs and dances in honor of Santería, a topic that had been forbidden by the CRE and the previous government.[29]

Second, the state's fight against racial discrimination modified the ways in which reviewers discussed race and Afro-Cuban performances. For example, contrary to his chastising of musical styles associated with Cuba's black populations and his advocacy for the CRE's and Vasconcelos's censoring of Afro-Cuban folklore, the *Diario de la Marina* critic Alberto Giró celebrated Castro's mandate. In several of his reviews of *El alma no tiene color* (The soul is colorless), a popular Cuban telenovela set in the U.S. South that addressed racism, Giró highlighted the importance of the telenovela topic and how it could be applied to Cuba. Following a similar trend, in a review of a variety show that included Afro-Cuban folklore, Giró described the Santería-inspired performance as a representation of "good taste."[30] Although some of his descriptions regarding black performers and Afro-Cuban musical styles were still problematic (e.g., in his reviews of popular singer Celia Cruz, he recurrently described her as one of the best "Afro," instead of "Cuban," singers), the racist commentary present in many of his pre-1959 reviews disappeared. Throughout 1959, each of Giró's columns showed massive support and enthusiasm for the Cuban Revolution, Fidel Castro, and television's involvement with the revolutionary cause.

Third, the revolution's commitment to ending racism also eradicated the CRE's campaign against Afro-Cuban culture. Even though the CRE did not announce any formal change to its ruling, Castro's words and broad discussions about the subject seemed to be enough to silence the organization. The CRE was not very active during 1959, only suspending a few female performers for wearing "provocative clothing."[31] The theme that dominated the schedule was the Cuban Revolution and its leaders; thus, heroism and nationalism substituted for topics that could be seen as crossing the line in terms of gender and sexuality. And, given that Afro-Cubanness was seen as integral to the new Cuban nation, the CRE, similar to television reviewers and media professionals, accepted the call for racial equality and the fight against racial discrimination.

This certainly did not mean that all commercial television projects specifically targeting the issue of racism were well received. For example, following the success of CMQ-TV's *El alma no tiene color*, an independent production company (Promotora Panamericana) began to broadcast *Una voz en la calle* (A voice on the street), the first telenovela featuring black actors in principal roles. Despite its innovative casting selection and theme, the "integrationist" *telenovela* broadcast on Telemundo was not able to acquire a sponsor, forcing it off the air two months after its first broadcast (November 1959–January 1960). According to the telenovela's producer, problems finding a sponsor and some people's characterization of the program as "racist" (because of its casting of black actors) attested to a persistent racial problem on the island.[32] The case of *Una voz en la calle*, similar to other areas in Cuban society where the government saw some resistance to change (private clubs, schools, and organizations), showed the difficulties of abolishing an ideology that was ingrained in Cuba's culture. Still, the fight to end discrimination, along with the government's efforts to help Cuba's poor, brought marginal sectors of Cuban society to the center of policy debates, the nation, and television.

The government's impetus for helping Cuba's poor also renewed discussions about the possibility of it sponsoring educational programs. Television critics, returning to a topic that had been important to them for approximately ten years, explained how the technology of television could help further the revolution's goal of revamping Cuba's education system. "With a medium as extraordinary and powerful as television, [the government] could teach thousands of Cubans, especially in the rural areas," a critic wrote, connecting television to discussions about the Agrarian Reform.[33] Similarly, in an "open letter" to CMQ-TV's Goar Mestre, an audience member asked the media mogul to follow the revolutionary moment and its leader, Fidel Castro (who, according to the audience member, was always talking about "schools, schools, and schools"), and reinstitute a Saturday show dedicated to the adaptation of literature and theater classics.[34]

This time, the government and media owners listened. Besides creating a commission to explore the development of educational programs on television, the minister of communication (Enrique Oltuski) announced his plans to launch a network for the country's peasants. Oltuski also stated that the new broadcasting law (a law that began to be discussed in the early days of the revolution but did not materialize until 1962) would require a minimum of 10 percent of educational programming on commercial television. Furthermore, following a similar path, the Ministry of Education produced a culturally oriented program on CMQ-TV, while television networks, influenced by the collective enthusiasm for the revolution, expanded their adaptations of literary classics in addition to producing shows that centered on aspects of Cuban folklore and cultural traditions.[35] Nonetheless, the leading transformation regarding television and education came with changes to channel 12, the first station nationalized by the government.

Channel 12 was a Havana-based television station dedicated to news programming. When the channel began operations in 1958, it received a lot of attention from television reviewers for being the first color-television station in Cuba. None of the stories covering its inauguration, however, provided a list of investors; they listed only Gaspar Pumarejo as the proprietor.

Yet, within weeks of the revolutionary government's establishment, rumors began to spread that Pumarejo had received financial backing from people associated with Fulgencio Batista, and as a result, the station was confiscated. With a new name decreed by Fidel Castro, Tele-Rebelde/channel 12 became the first government-run station.[36]

The station's new name underscored its programming connection to the revolutionary state, which began using government-produced public affairs shows to explain its actions to segments of the Cuban public. For example, *El Ministerio de Recuperación informa* (The Ministry for the Recovery of Ill-Gotten Goods Informs) provided information about government-confiscated businesses and properties, their owners, and how these individuals and industries were connected to Batista's regime, while *El fórum nacional de la Reforma Agraria* (The National Forum for Agrarian Reform) addressed various aspects associated with the Agrarian Reform. A different strategy was used in *El pueblo pregunta* (The people ask), a panel show in which Cuban citizens had a chance to ask questions of government officials. Although none of the program reviews explain how the citizens and questions were selected, the description of the show emphasized an open dialogue between government officials and Cuban citizens.[37]

Tele-Rebelde/channel 12 also presented educational and entertainment shows, expanding the topic of the revolution and Cubanness to other genres. For instance, shows such as *La universidad popular, Teatro del sábado*, and *¿Qué sabe usted de Cuba?* (The popular university, Saturday theater, and What do you know about Cuba?) tackled various aspects of Cuba's culture and history. Of these three, *Teatro del sábado* offered something new in Cuban television's history by providing a space for Cuban playwrights to present their work. The history of the Cuban Revolution was covered in *Así se escribió la historia* (This is how history was written) and *Anécdotas de la revolución* (Anecdotes of the Revolution). An innovative aspect of *Así se escribió la historia* was the incorporation of real revolutionaries (mostly as narrators) into the dramatic reenactments. This inclusion of "real" people added veracity to the stories being re-created by mixing documentary genre cues with drama. Furthermore, by including the voices of different *revolucionarios* and by narrating stories beyond emblematic moments, these programs pluralized the history of the Cuban Revolution. In other words, while commercial television dramas tended to reference principal actors and accounts, Tele-Rebelde programs integrated many men and women who were part of the 26th of July Movement, highlighting the collective effort to liberate Cuba.[38]

Although most of Tele-Rebelde's programming had political and educational content, a few shows were disconnected from the revolution and the historical moment. This was the case with the program *Grandes comedias* (Great comedies), where viewers had the opportunity to watch adapted theater pieces. Also, the telenovela *Amor y orgullo* (Love and pride) was described by one reviewer as presenting "romance and intrigue," with no reference to politics.[39] Even though in the early years of communism on the island the telenovela was viewed as a symbol of U.S. imperialism, in 1959 the genre was still a suitable form of entertainment for Tele-Rebelde.[40]

Tele-Rebelde's programming combined various genres, most of which foregrounded the importance of education for the new Cuban government. In addition, the channel's programming illustrates the significance of Cuban culture and history for the revolutionary state and its efforts to highlight the multiple social actors who were part of the revolution. Cuban citizens interested in learning more about particular policies, and writers looking for opportunities to present their work also had a space on Tele-Rebelde. The station allowed for a more participatory approach to production in addition to placing the nation and its people at the center of its programming. Inadvertently, Tele-Rebelde followed some of the public-station guidelines of the 1934 radio law, legislation that had been enacted during a moment of revolutionary transformation. Whereas none of the stories covering Tele-Rebelde/channel 12 mentioned the earlier broadcasting law, and even though, during 1959, Tele-Rebelde mostly functioned without a clear objective, the improvised programming schedule combined education, information, and entertainment, modeling the guidelines for a public station according to the 1934 law.

Still, Tele-Rebelde's programming also introduced a key aspect of the government's future uses of television: political indoctrination. Based on the description of shows such as *El fórum nacional de la Reforma Agraria* and *Así se escribió la historia*, the government employed television to explain and sell the Cuban Revolution to sectors of the Cuban public. And, contrary to commercial networks, which also promoted the Cuban Revolution through dramas, variety shows, and public affairs programming, at Tele-Rebelde there was no mediation; the government was in total control of the message. With Tele-Rebelde, the government built the foundation for the new uses and functions of television in Cuban society. We could see the station as the main stage upon which the state rehearsed the televised culture of communist Cuba.

Nevertheless, one of the main problems with Tele-Rebelde was its limited reach. As a local Havana-based station originally intended for color-television broadcasting, the channel did not attract a big sector of the Cuban audience. According to the two surveys conducted in 1959, CMQ-TV programs obtained the highest ratings, including the network's news, a novelty in terms of top-rated shows.[41] Based on the numbers, no one seemed to be watching Tele-Rebelde. This lack of popularity most likely influenced Fidel Castro's preference for communicating with the Cuban public via commercial television networks. Sometimes invited to be a guest on panel shows and at other times simply showing up at a television studio unannounced, Castro was all over television, practically on a weekly basis. It was no coincidence, then, that there was no artistic revelation in 1959, as one reviewer observed. Fidel Castro was the star of the revolution and of television.

Fidel Castro: The Protagonist of the Spectacles of Revolution

In the past year no figure reached the category of artistic revelation. Maybe this was a result of the triumph of the revolution. A nation that produces a Fidel has satisfactorily contributed to its advancement.—"El año de 1959, en radio y televisión," *Carteles*, December 20, 1959

In all of the "end of the year" 1959 television summaries, Prime Minister Fidel Castro was named the most important television personality. As a man who ended a seven-year dictatorship with the creation of a grassroots movement, who promised to restore Cuba's constitutional democracy, and who, as soon as he took power, worked to help the marginal sectors of Cuban society, Fidel Castro became an instant national hero. Yet, being considered a hero and a man of the people does not necessarily translate into being named the television figure of the year. In Castro's case, nonetheless, the correlation with television emerged through his recurrent on-camera appearances. Prime Minister Castro informed and guided the nation through television; thus, the citizens who owned (or had family or friends who owned) one of the approximately 365,000 sets available in

Cuba in 1959 had the opportunity to watch the *comandante* almost on a weekly basis.[42]

Combining television programs and televised speeches, Castro's participation during a single year ranged from one to eight television appearances per month, with interviews lasting from thirty minutes to six hours. In some cases, program hosts were responsible for extending the television interviews. As one television critic observed, "It is logical and up to a certain extent understandable, the fixation on retaining Fidel Castro Ruz for the maximum time possible in front of the cameras. But, when the really important themes have been exhausted and when the Premier begins to show signs of tiredness, one should not insist on retaining him."[43] As a highly popular figure, television owners provided Castro with an open platform; hence, while Castro employed the medium for political purposes, some program hosts, television owners, and sponsors promoted his on-screen appearances both for ratings and to demonstrate their political support for him. Even a critic like Alberto Giró, who refrained from commenting on political leaders, promoted Castro's appearance on television, suggesting how beneficial it would be for the Cuban people to see Castro on television each week.[44] That also seems to be precisely what Fidel Castro believed, given that the revolutionary leader used television as his main outlet for communicating with the Cuban people. Thus, while media professionals advocated for his extended appearances on television, in most instances, Castro requested unlimited on-air time to discuss particular political issues.

For example, during his February 19, 1959, appearance on CMQ-TV's *Ante la prensa*, Castro used the live broadcast to talk about Agrarian Reform, unemployment, political asylum, Latin American dictators, Cuba's relations with other countries, his attitudes toward the United States, education, tourism, and Cuba's future elections. "[Fidel Castro] appears literally capable of talking forever, on any subject under the sun. He is a dynamic, forceful speaker, with that rare quality of fixing and swaying his audience regardless of the contents of his words."[45] That is the way a U.S. Foreign Broadcast Information Service journalist explained Fidel Castro's performance style and, more important, the fascination of the *Ante la prensa* studio audience with the comandante. Castro's television charisma even mesmerized conservatives who had questioned his political agenda early on: "This young man disconcerts me. . . . He looks so sincere, so fervent, totally immersed in his cause, so passionate about his hope for justice, equality, and the well-being for all people. . . . Yes, he is a Cuban miracle."[46] This was how a man described as politically conservative evaluated one of Castro's television appearances.

The television ratings reflected the audience's enthusiasm for Fidel Castro. For instance, after his trip to the United States and various parts of Latin America, Castro showed up unannounced at Telemundo's *Telemundo pregunta*. When the May 10, 1959, program began at 8:00 PM, the show had a rating of 12 points. By 9:00 PM, the ratings were at 36.82 points, and by 10:00 PM, they had soared to 50 points, equivalent to half a million viewers watching the show.[47] There are no data on the remaining four-hour broadcast of *Telemundo pregunta* that night (Castro remained on the air for a total of six hours); nonetheless, the ratings survey provided interesting demographic information about who tuned in to watch Fidel Castro. In terms of class, the majority of viewers were part of what advertisers designated as Class D and Class E, the most modest and poorest sectors of Cuban society, respectively. According to the survey, Class A and Class B, which constituted the upper-class and upper-middle-class sectors of the population, respectively, represented only 8 percent of the viewers. In contrast, Class C, Cuba's middle class, constituted 38 percent of the audience. In terms of gender, more than 50 percent of the viewers were women. The remainder of the audience was divided between men (39 percent) and children (9 percent).

The survey, similar to most conducted by the Asociación de Anunciantes de Cuba (Association of Cuba's Advertisers), exclusively covered La Gran Habana, that is, the City of Havana and the municipalities of Marianao, Regla, and Guanabacoa. Consequently, no information was gathered about other Cuban provinces. That said, while one cannot make a direct correlation between viewership and revolutionary support, the data regarding the class spectrum of the *Telemundo pregunta* audience coincide with scholars' arguments that the working class (or *las clases populares*) was the force behind the revolutionary movement and that, at least during the early stages of the Cuban Revolution, the middle class also backed Castro.[48] Additionally, the gender composition of the audience signals women's general endorsement of the revolution, which, as several scholars have documented, was tied to the pro-woman measures the newly instituted government enacted.[49] Thus, broadly speaking, the social and gender composition of the *Telemundo pregunta* audience could be read as a sign of certain sectors of Cuban society's growing endorsement of the revolution, and as a reflection of Castro's popularity. Equally important and interrelated, Castro's impromptu appearance on Telemundo signals his reliance on television to talk to the people.

More than radio or film, television emerged as the medium of the Cuban Revolution in 1959. Beginning with the transmission of Fidel Castro and the *barbudos'* (bearded ones) caravan from Santiago de Cuba to their triumphant entrance into Havana, and continuing with Castro's program appearances and televised speeches, television merged revolutionary imagery and political performance. Live television represented an ideal media outlet for Castro's intelligence, wit, improvisational skills, energy, and political persona. As a critic observed in August 1959, "In Cuba, the television receptor has obtained an importance never imagined before. The peculiar style of Fidel Castro, . . . has made the television screen the center of the citizens' attention. . . . Fidel Castro has found an adequate and immediate medium to create an open-door government. And that medium is television."[50] Exclusively targeting the national public, the televised Fidel Castro complemented the photographic and filmic imagery of the Cuban Revolution.

After 1959, as literary scholar José Quiroga writes, Cuban photographers began to treat Fidel Castro and his army as "celebrities," creating a "revolutionary glamour" that the state then appropriated. However, photography, according to Quiroga, was not simply art or reportage; the medium "had a duty to perform: it was a document and, as such, it contained a certain kind of *knowledge* that would be used to produce more *knowledge* in turn."[51] Whereas the level of political indoctrination intensified with the adoption of Marxism, photography's iconization of Castro and its focus on masses of people attending political rallies were part of the revolution's propaganda imagery from the early days. Similarly, the ICAIC's documentaries also became integral to the state's ideological propaganda by presenting Fidel Castro in "scripted moments of intimacy," as mentioned previously, as well as showing multitudes of people at rallies and government events. Under total control of the state and following a "hypodermic needle" type of communication strategy, wherein messages contained in media artifacts would be injected into the people's minds, the ICAIC's early documentaries highlighted the collectivity of the revolution.[52]

In concert with the work of photography and film, commercial television produced a multiplicity of images about Fidel Castro and the revolution. On television, however, the oral, kinetic, and "unpredictable" elements associated with broadcasting live, the physical copresence of Fidel Castro and the studio audience, and the temporal simultaneity of transmission and reception made the audience feel like it was watching the real Castro.[53] Although these representations operated through Castro's constructed political persona (from his style of dress, to the smoking of cigars, to conversation themes) and were mediated by television's technology (cameras and microphones), the broadcasts of the revolutionary leader functioned through the code of "liveness" that characterized 1950s television. In other words, because of the live broadcast, the in-house studio audience (in the case of panel shows) and the television audience watched a real and thus spontaneous Fidel Castro. Not only did these live performances of spontaneity make it possible for the revolutionary leader to perform various roles (the altruistic leader, the educator, the common man, the maximum leader, etc.), but many of these depictions were then subsequently captured in photographs and published in newspapers and magazines. As Lillian Guerra observes, with the triumph of the revolution and with Castro's popularity, "illiterate and semi-illiterate people who might not formerly have picked up a newspaper started doing so."[54] Hence, in an attempt to expand Castro's reach to those who did not have access to a television set and/or were illiterate, Castro's television images reappeared as continuous frames in newspapers, usually one day after his appearance on television.

With each televised transmission, audiences witnessed spontaneous aspects of the leader, and they could also read and see sequences of Castro's verbal and bodily spontaneity in newspapers and magazines. Through photographs and captions (as well as performances of Castro's character in commercial television dramas), fragments of Castro's "repertoire"—namely, his live televised gestures and verbal performances—began to be incorporated into the revolutionary "archive."[55] Sometimes representing the prime minister in dramatic moments and at other times simply reproducing an image of him sitting in front of the microphone, the photographs and captions of Castro's live broadcasts together with the broadcasts themselves documented the leader's performances as major attractions in the spectacles of revolution.

For example, on July 17, 1959, after the government-affiliated newspaper *Revolución* announced Castro's resignation as prime minister, the comandante participated in a combined four-hour TV and radio hookup to explain the motivations behind his decision. On camera, Castro accused his appointed Cuban president (Manuel Urrutia Lleo) of betrayal, made it clear that he (Castro) "[would] never abandon the revolution" and ended by declaring: "I do not wish to be dramatic, but the hour of decision has arrived and there is no alternative but for me to resign."[56] As Cuban newspapers and magazines reproduced the images and phrases of this televised moment, they not only deferred to television's authority to report the news but also to its power to become the news. "Television," as one Cuban journalist noted, "made history." Reconstructed and narrated as a melodramatic saga, the journalist wrote, "The hours of anguish that the Cuban people lived—from the moment in which the resignation of Doctor Fidel Castro was announced until his appearance on television—are part of the most emotional pages of our convoluted process as a republic."[57] The drama and spectacle of Castro's appearance were not just a result of his message; they also were a product of his delivery on television, where Castro's live voice, gestures, and presence strengthened the relevance of his political intentions and views. After watching the broadcast, Urrutia Lleo resigned as president, and a new president, Osvaldo Dorticos Torrado, was selected the next day. Castro remained in his position as prime minister (he announced that he would continue as prime minister in a July 26, 1959, speech). In this particular instance, television played a central role in the *making* of a historical event, rather than simply in the narrating of a historical event (see figs. 5.1 and 5.2).

Not all televised performances of spontaneity were as theatrical as Castro's resignation. In other instances, segments of Castro's broadcast that depicted simple and unexpected sides of the leader were reproduced in newspapers and magazines. For instance, in one of his *Ante la prensa* appearances, Castro joked about the Dominican dictator, Rafael Trujillo. A few days later, the Cuban magazine *Carteles* reconstructed a sequence of images and quotes from the televised *Ante la prensa* describing the shots as Prime Minister Castro's "minute of humor" (see fig. 5.3).[58] Each of the three photographs published in *Carteles* included a caption citing the words Castro used during the broadcast. Most of Castro's television appearances, nonetheless, were devoted to explaining policies and government changes. Thus, the majority of Castro's time on television functioned as a place for him to represent himself as a leader-educator. From these policy-related appearances, newspapers and magazines usually reproduced one or two images with summaries of the most important points. Regardless of the topic, newspapers and magazines devoted significant attention to Castro's television appearances.

The perception of Fidel Castro's spontaneity and realness associated with live broadcasting was also influenced by the conventions and trajectory of the panel show as a television genre. As Jason Mittell writes regarding the meanings of genre, "In any given moment, a particular set of assumptions may emerge as the foremost incarnation of the genre in cultural circulation. While there will probably be contradictory texts and discontinuous discourses active in the generic cluster, a generic dominant functions as the primary connotative implication of generic terminology."[59] In Cuba, similar to its U.S. predecessor, panel shows such as *Ante la prensa* devoted their discussions to political, social, economic, and cultural issues confronting the nation. However, as mentioned previously, in Cuba, panel shows gained added stature under the Batista regime due to the hosts' interrogation of government policies regardless of possible censorship. This representation of panel shows as a television site for serious debate defined the genre. Thus, critics and audiences understood that journalistic integrity would inform the dialogues taking place on this type of programming. As a result, even though in 1959 some of the panel shows' participants and hosts, similar to most of the population, were mesmerized by Castro's leadership, and even as Castro took control of those televised spaces by talking for hours, the genre had the prestige of serious journalistic interrogation.[60]

Another aspect that influenced the perception of Castro's frankness and approachability was the simplicity of the panel shows' setting—participants sat behind a table, with signs indicating their name and position. The set created a level of intimacy between the host and the panelists. Hence, as a genre, Cuban panel shows were viewed as promoting one-on-one dialogue and debate in a close environment where panelist, the studio audience, and the general audience were all invited.

The industrial, political, and historically situated processes that defined the 1950s Cuban television panel show produced an aura of openness for Castro's televised political persona. Additionally, Castro's use of simple language to explain policies, economic processes, and international issues influenced the perception of accessibility attached to the revolutionary leader. Through his interactions with the show's host and panelists, as well as his speeches directed at the camera, Castro was perceived (according to some journalists and commentators) as communicating on a "one-on-one" basis. As a journalist observed in October 1959, "Once again, the maximum leader of our revolution presented himself in front of the people, via television,

"Hay principios fundamentales que debe tener el hombre público y un hombre revolucionario, de que el último interés es el interés propio; que antes del interés de uno debe estar el interés de los demás, debe estar el interés del pueblo".

"Renunciar a la lucha, jamás, porque por pruebas muy duras hemos sado y nadie nos vió nunca vacilar. Renunciar a un cargo que no es premio, que no es una prebenda, que no es sino un lugar de trabajo, lugar en donde se ha estado cumpliendo el deber".

"Las discrepancias son de tipo moral, de tipo cívico, de tipo revolucio-nario, —no de tipo ideológico—, porque en definitiva todos estamos en el deber de coincidir en el mismo camino que hemos coincidido hasta aquí. Son diferencias morales. Diferencias insolubles".

"Para ser Presidente de la República sólo se requieren honradez, la político, sólo se requiere un sentido claro de la vida; ciertos princi, morales inflexibles que hagan que un hombre jamás se vuelva contra país, que se vuelva contra los intereses del pueblo".

FIGURES 5.1 (*above*) and 5.2 (*right*). "En la Televisión se hizo historia," *Bohemia*, July 26, 1959. Courtesy of the Cuban Heritage Collection, University of Miami Libraries, Coral Gables, Florida.

to explain and orient us to the laws, plans, and changes that have been surrounding us in the last weeks."[61] By addressing the camera, the Castro monologue was rearticulated into a conversation between Castro and the Cuban people. Television, specifically panel shows, facilitated the perception of Castro's immediacy.

However, Fidel Castro's political persona changed when the leader appeared on U.S. panel shows. Issues of language, control of the communication process, empathy, and politics (particularly in terms of journalists' distrust of the leader's intentions regarding elections in Cuba and questions about his support of communism) influenced how Castro was able to present himself on these programs. For example, during the January 11, 1959, broadcast of *Face the Nation* recorded at CMQ-TV studios for the U.S. audience, Castro appeared somewhat uncomfortable, cutting off the panel-

todos estamos para defender esta revolución sea cual fuere el lugar que nos corresponde en esta lucha. Renunciar a un cargo no quiere renunciar a la revolución, al cumplimiento de un deber. Nosotros no tenemos otra razón en la vida que defender la revolución".

"Yo personalmente, no tengo ni me interesa tener nada. Sólo llevo conmigo el interés a toda prueba que me ha acompañado hasta hoy y al que no renunciaré. Hay cosas que están por encima de todo lo demás en el orden de los valores que al pueblo le interesa".

miras pedíamos a los obreros azucareros que fueran a trabajar renunciando a todas sus demandas, la Presidencia de la República está, (es devengando el mismo sueldo que el dictador, —que había sido exactamente aumentado en cien mil pesos. Eso no es moral".

"Este proceso revolucionario —que es fruto de sacrificios de la Nación Cubana— y en el cual la Nación tiene puesta toda la esperanza, es tan sólido que no podrá frustrarlo nada ni nadie. Tengo fe absoluta en la revolución. La revolución no corre ningún peligro".

que ser muy amargo ver cómo se fueron gestando las condiciones que desembocara en una crisis. ¡Qué no hubiéramos dado para evitar el problema, en el instante en que se está viendo crecer la obra de la revolución. Se ha estado al borde de la traición".

"Al combate corred bayameses que la patria os contempla orgullosos. No temáis una muerte gloriosa que morir por la Patria es vivir". En la voz del doctor Castro evocamos la mañana luminosa en que Carlos Manuel de Céspedes entonó nuestras inmortales estrofas.

FIGURE 5.3. "Minuto de humor," *Carteles*, July 12, 1959. Courtesy of the Cuban Heritage Collection, University of Miami Libraries, Coral Gables, Florida.

ists who were trying to ask questions.[62] Whereas in some instances Castro seemed to make fun of himself for his lack of familiarity with English words, in reality, he was out of his element, lacking control of his political persona. In reviews, Castro was described as answering questions with "obvious sincerity"; however, he failed to persuade journalists to accept his explanation of some of the Cuban government's actions (particularly the executions of Batista's men and the prospect of future elections).[63] The format of *Face the Nation* coincided with the Cuban panel-show genre, where journalists interviewed the guest. By incorporating new journalists/people speaking in an unfamiliar cultural, political, and linguistic tongue, the same set used for *Ante la prensa* became a type of judicial arena for Castro's politics. Empathy and revolutionary passion were also out of the equation, creating a different televisual result.

Four months after the *Face the Nation* interview, a more eloquent Castro appeared on *Meet the Press* (see fig. 5.4). The April 19, 1959, program was broadcast simultaneously in the United States and in Cuba, becoming an important event in the Caribbean nation. In most of the interview Castro acted calmly and was respectful of the journalists' questions. In fact, a couple of the panelists/journalists were the ones who seemed impatient, particularly when addressing Castro's position on communism and the Soviet Union. The only moment in which the revolutionary leader looked uncomfortable occurred early in the broadcast when the host, in his program introduction, asserted that (as if Castro were not sitting next to him) "Castro's problems both internally and externally have multiplied." Visibly aggravated, Castro quickly responded, "There are no problems in Cuba," and then briefly ex-

FIGURE 5.4. Fidel Castro as a guest on NBC's *Meet the Press*, April 19, 1959. On the left, Ned Brooks, moderator. Courtesy of the Cuban Heritage Collection, Cuban Photograph Collection, University of Miami Libraries, Coral Gables, Florida.

plained the island's political situation.[64] Except for this aside, he appeared relaxed, providing intelligent, sharp, and witty answers to the journalists' questions. Still, although Fidel Castro's performance on *Meet the Press* showed U.S. audiences the leader most Cubans adored, it did not produce the same results as panel shows in Cuba. For Castro, Cuban panel shows were a platform for political communication instead of sites of political interrogation. As CMQ-TV owner Goar Mestre observed in an interview with journalism scholar Michael B. Salwen, "When Castro came into Havana we simply turned the television over to him lock, stock and barrel. . . . He was the prime-time show."[65] It was difficult (if not impossible) for the U.S. audience to sense the revolutionary leader's magnetism through U.S. panel shows, where Castro lacked control of the production and representation.

If the Cuban panel shows presented Castro as an approachable leader dutifully helping the public understand the transformations his revolutionary government was enacting, the televised speeches portrayed him as a larger-than-life figure. Through shots of Castro and the thousands of people who attended the rallies, the power of the televised speeches resided in the

FIGURE 5.5. Fidel Castro's televised speech in favor of the executions of Fulgencio Batista's supporters, January 22, 1959. *American Experience*, Fidel Castro. PBS, January 31, 2005.

FIGURE 5.6. Crowds of people at Fidel Castro's televised speech in favor of the executions of Fulgencio Batista's supporters, January 22, 1959. *American Experience*, Fidel Castro. PBS, January 31, 2005.

pluralization of the Cuban Revolution and the representation of Castro as a maximum leader who could move the masses. In other words, even though Castro was the primary speaker and the center of attention at the televised rallies, the depiction of the various cabinet members alongside Castro at the podium and of the multitude of people in attendance visually represented the revolution as a unified movement guided by numerous leaders and supported by all Cuban citizens. Watched by local and, in many instances, foreign audiences (via foreign correspondents' newscasts and the ICAIC's newsreels), televised speeches formed part of the revolutionary imagery designed for local and global viewers (see figs. 5.5 and 5.6).

The combined transmission of panel shows and televised speeches together with the newspaper and magazine reproductions of Castro's televised appearances, positioned Fidel Castro as a ubiquitous leader, a man devoted to the revolution and to the Cuban people. As Marifeli Pérez-Stable writes, "Fidel Castro emerged as the bulwark of the revolution—the mediator between the people and the government."[66] Following Pérez-Stable's argument, I would add that in 1959 Castro's role as a mediator was created and magnified via television. Through his panel-show appearances, Fidel Castro explained the revolution to large segments of the Cuban people. In addition, television and live broadcasting catalyzed the reproduction of Castro's images and speeches across a range of media outlets. To use John Corner's theorization of the performance of political figures, the "intensity" of Castro's interaction with television and the theatricality of his political persona made him the center of the televised revolution and the protagonist of the spectacles of revolution.[67]

Fully aware of his own charismatic persona, Fidel Castro used television as his primary communication tool to sell the revolution to local segments of the Cuban public. At the same time, commercial television owners—in hindsight, unwittingly—used Castro and the revolution to promote their own interests. By providing a space for Castro's appearances on panel shows, by transmitting his speeches, by broadcasting dramas and telenovelas that reenacted what had been defined as emblematic moments of the Cuban Revolution, and by sponsoring variety and musical shows that integrated the latest songs about the revolution, commercial television, together with Fidel Castro, marketed the revolution. Through television, Castro and the revolution were commodified and sold—making politics and capitalistic imperatives important components of the spectacles of revolution. Yet, as television saturated the public with the topic of the revolution, a transformation was occurring within its structure. Television began to move from being a technology at the service of owners, advertisers, and transnational corporations to being a tool of the state.

The effects of transmitting Fidel Castro live both formed and transcended the realm of political performance. These broadcasts—specifically those that pushed the established schedule—disrupted the commercial television programming flow and foreshadowed the flow of the post-1960, state-run television system. Beginning with the January 1, 1959, news event when, during a course of three days, all networks and television stations documented Fulgencio Batista's escape from Havana and the triumph of the revolutionary army, and continuing with the temporally extended panel shows and televised speeches for which Fidel Castro controlled the length of his appearance, the televised Castro and the revolutionary news represented ongoing *disturbances* to commercial television's programming.[68] These disturbances operated as time-conflicting units that challenged the "intervals between programs" that, as Raymond Williams observes, shape commercial and public television programming flow.[69] In other words, if the "interruptions" between programs are set to mark the beginning and ending of a show and the overall experience of watching television, the disturbances created a continuous stream wherein one program or television event monopolized the schedule. These sporadic disturbances obstructed the sequence of programming and advertising, thus initiating the dismantling of Cuba's commercial television flow.[70]

The obstruction of programming/advertising fluidity was the first step in the gestation of a new television experience. The unlimited and temporally elongated transmissions of Fidel Castro, political events, and newscasts would define the first years of the newly established communist nation-state's television programming. If in the commercial era (as Horace Newcomb observes regarding U.S. television), narrative seriality was central to attracting audience-consumers, in the postrevolutionary era, the screening of Fidel Castro, the revolutionary government's plans, and the fight to maintain Cuba's sovereignty incentivized viewers/revolutionary citizens to stay tuned in.[71] What began as programming disturbances during the commercial era would become the norm in the state-controlled televised era. Screening Fidel Castro and discussing the revolution was the new television routine.

Spectacles of Revolution and the Gestation of a Revolutionary Modernity

Beginning in January 1959, commercial television was integrated into the Cuban Revolution and thus became an essential part of the revolutionary experience. Cuban television "became an authorized historian" (to borrow Daniel Dayan and Elihu Katz's conceptualization of the medium), narrating episodes of the revolution's present while fictionalizing the not-so-distant past that was forming the core of Cuba's new history.[72] Indeed, television became an archivist of the historical moment.

The initial association between commercial television and the government gave hope to some reviewers and citizens who, just months after the 26th of July Movement's victory, wished that the state would use television to educate Cuba's citizens. The Cuban Revolution was seen as a new beginning for the nation, and many reviewers and audiences visualized television as part of the national rebirth. And, for the first time since television's inception on the island, the government valued the medium's pedagogical potential. The main difference between some reviewers' utopian imagining of television and the government's use of it as a pedagogical tool was the merging of politics and education. Revolutionary television was about educating the people in matters of culture and history while also teaching them about the revolution's political thought. Although it would take a couple of years for the government to design the ideological foundation of the new television system, the initial building blocks were already in place.[73] In 1959, Fidel Castro was the main architect testing the possible uses of television in Cuba.

As soon as Castro took control of the nation, he utilized television as his principal tool for communication. Appearing on panel shows such as *Ante la prensa*, *Telemundo pregunta*, and *Mesa redonda* (Meet the press, Telemundo asks, and Roundtable), Castro discussed various economic and sociopolitical issues, such as the Agrarian Reform, the appropriation of businesses tied or allegedly tied to Fulgencio Batista, and the government's goal of maintaining the nation's sovereignty. In this regard, and unlike during Batista's regime, government intervention on television operated not only behind the camera (via the Ministry for the Recovery of Ill-Gotten Goods' appropriation of stations) but also in front of it, by way of Castro's presence on the screen. Still, Fidel Castro's ongoing televised appearances were not the only revolutionary elements on commercial television. Public affairs programs, dramas, and variety shows kept the focus on the Cuban Revolution throughout the television schedule. As Mariana Romeu Calderón, an audience member from the Oriente province observed in a letter to *Bohemia*, "How could it have happened that even the characters on a radio soap opera became revolutionaries upon moving to television after that date [1959]!"[74] The revolution was everywhere on television, moving through various genres, networks, and channels.

The frequent appearances of Fidel Castro on panel shows, the mass rallies and speeches, as well as the dramas and variety shows focusing on the revolution projected a new picture of the Cuban nation on television. While an aesthetic associated with a U.S. and European style of modernity was still part of the medium, military fatigues, long and untamed beards, and rugged-looking men became part of the television screen. Revolutionary leaders and soldiers, some of whom were depicted in the CBS documentary *Rebels of the Sierra Maestra*, moved from the mountains and the countryside to the cities and the capital. Even as dramas and telenovelas depicted a more stylish picture of the revolution, what had been deemed barbarous and uncivilized (in terms of middle-class norms of conduct and Eurocentric ideas about race) became part of Cuba's new television culture.[75]

New images of Cubanness on television produced two distinct articulations of modernity. First, they weaved working-class masculinity into the tapestry of televised Cubanness. Even as most of the leaders of the revolution were from the upper class, their corporeal representation (bearded, with long hair and a shabby look), together with military uniforms, repositioned upper-class rebels-leaders (such as Fidel Castro, Camilo Cienfuegos, and Che Guevara) as working-class men. By selecting a working-class male aesthetic to represent their bodies, leader and soldier were visually merged, and the previously "uncivilized" became part of the new Cuban modernity (see fig. 5.7). This reconstruction of the modern was part of a larger process of redefining what being civilized meant. As Louis A. Pérez observes, "The power of the revolution resided in its capacity to rearrange in usable forms the standards by which to measure civilization and in the process, summon a vision of an alternative moral order. The notion of patria, free and sovereign, was reinvented around instrumental functions in which an egalitarian project served as the necessary condition of civilization."[76] The working-class rebels, together with other class-based marginal sectors of Cuban society (such as the country's peasants), were presented as pivotal participants in Cuban progress and civilization.

FIGURE 5.7. Revolutionary leaders. From left to right, Camilo Cienfuegos, Fidel Castro, Derminio Escalona, and Huber Matos, January 8, 1959. Photographed by José Suárez. Courtesy of the Cuban Heritage Collection, Cuban Photograph Collection, University of Miami Libraries, Coral Gables, Florida.

Second, the racial composition of some of the rebels, together with their limited education, not only brought to the forefront the geographically fragmented process of social and economic modernization but also highlighted what Michael Hanchard refers to as "racial time," that is, "the inequalities of temporality that result from power relations between racially dominant and subordinate groups."[77] According to Hanchard, those who experience "racial time" have limited or delayed access to education, resources, and services. Hence, the depiction of illiterate black and mulatto soldiers brought the different temporalities of Cuban modernization based on region, class, and race to the television screen. In this regard, then, one could say that the broadcasting of a revolutionary modernity was not only about representing nationalism and new conceptions of Cubanness but also about introducing new temporalities. On the one hand, Fidel Castro's and the state's *disturbances* of the television schedule fragmented the modes of production that were typical of capitalist societies in which the control of time and efficiency are associated with productivity and profits. By disturbing the schedule, the state controlled television's time and flow. On the other hand, by putting the rebels on television and, symbolically, the temporality associated with "racial time," the medium began to project those citizens who were literally and symbolically left behind by the processes of socioeconomic modernization. Whereas in the liminal stage, television mainly depicted the effects of "racial time," with the state's appropriation of all stations and networks in 1960, one of the new objectives of the medium would be to help eradicate the temporal disjunctions of Cuba's capitalistic modernization. Television would help educate Cuban citizens regardless of place and race.[78]

It is important to mention that, with the adoption of communism, the militarization of working-class masculinity associated with the barbudos intensified other ideologies such as machismo and homophobia. For example, in the 1960s and 1970s, the manual labor attached to working-class masculinity was juxtaposed with the idea of bourgeois masculinity, a type of manhood linked to U.S. capitalism, futile intellectualism, weakness, and homosexuality. To eradicate homosexuality and convert homosexuals into the "new men" of the Cuban nation, the state sent many gay men (together with other men and women labeled "antirevolutionary") to perform "hard agricultural labor so that the redeeming qualities of the rural atmosphere could cure their ills."[79] With the "virilization" of Cuban culture and the polity, homosexuality was represented as a threat to the nation.[80] Hence, images of the rebels that pervaded the television screen and public culture in 1959 were a symbolic snapshot both of emergent ideas about class, race, and masculinity that would form the new Cuba and of the pathologization and marginalization of any type of gender and sexual performance that threatened the state's legally regulated heterosexual and hypermasculine norms. Sexual morality became one of the components of the revolutionary morality.[81] Nonetheless, during the liminal stage, changes to what was reconceptualized as immoral and moral (particularly in terms of race and class) opened up some space for previously banned cultural practices and people to appear on television.

New ideas about morality and immorality were also woven into the reworked notions of progress. As noted earlier, progress began to be distanced from an exclusive view of capitalist advancement for the economic elite and started to be associated with the distribution of resources across different sectors of the population. Socioeconomic modernization continued to be an important component of progress; however, its goal was to help the nation's disenfranchised. As Lillian Guerra observes, "Revolutionary distribution simply implied putting the basic comforts of capitalist prosperity within reach of Cuba's most impoverished minority."[82] Following a similar trend, the push for consumption that had been present in Cuban culture as a symbol of progress and class status—particularly of U.S. and European goods—was revised to stress how buying Cuban products would help the nation. Echoing other processes taking place in Cuba, the revolutionary government used various strategies to, in the words of Castro, "Cubanize Cuba."[83]

The rebirth of nationalism that swamped the island during the liminal stage was reflected in television's programming and ratings. The Cuban Revolution and themes associated with Cuban culture, history, and society became the topics of all television genres. This passion for the revolution also influenced rating numbers. While U.S. imports such as *Rin Tin Tin*, *Highway Patrol*, and *Lone Ranger* did make it into the top twenty-five highest-rated shows, they were at the bottom of the list, a drastic departure from their positions just one year earlier (see chapter 4). Locally produced programs moved to the top of the list, with musical shows and comedies occupying the highest spots. That said, the programs that beat all records were those that hosted Fidel Castro.[84] In this regard, even though panel shows were not considered the most popular programs on Cuban television, the appearance of the leader assured network and station owners of a reliable audience. Yet, despite the popularity of local programs (including panel shows featuring Castro), the importation of U.S. shows and movies continued throughout 1959, which was a major concern for actors and writers alike.[85] Only after the state's appropriation of all networks and stations in 1960, and the restructuring of programming in the following year (which favored high-culture shows such as theater productions and adaptations of literary classics), did locally produced shows dominate the television schedule.

As discussed throughout this chapter, the changes taking place at the national level had an immediate and forceful impact on television. Even though Cuban media owners had tried to maintain distance from the government since television was introduced on the island, the enthusiasm that the revolution produced facilitated a symbiotic relationship between commercial television and the state. With the spectacles of revolution, a revolutionary modernity began to take shape and, in the process, absorbed the spectacles of progress, the spectacles of decency, and the spectacles of democracy. Thus, in the final days of the commercial television system, the spectacles of revolution gobbled up the other spectacles and took over the broadcasting of modernity. The grandiosity that formed the spectacles of revolution mesmerized audiences, all of them enchanted with the charisma of its star, Fidel Castro.

This does not mean, however, that the ideologies that formed the previous spectacles totally disappeared. As Raymond Williams observed regarding culture, "Certain experiences, meanings, and values which cannot be expressed or substantially verified in terms of the dominant culture, are nevertheless lived and practiced on the basis of the residue—cultural as well as social—of the previous social and cultural institution or formation."[86] Residual traces of the spectacles remained, yet these were, for the most part, subsumed by new ideas of progress, decency, morality, and democracy. Detached from associations with U.S. capitalism and liberal ideals of democracy, Fidel Castro began to construct a new vision of modernity and Cubanness. In this process of redefinition, Cuban television, as the next chapter explains, was born again. The spectacles of revolution prepared the terrain for the new "architecture of power" (to paraphrase Jonathan Crary) that was forming in 1960 when Castro embraced socialism, and a new external force—the USSR—stepped onto Cuba's stage.

CHAPTER 6

From Broadcasting Modernity
to Constructing Modernity

In 1960, three articles published in *INRA* magazine, a publication affiliated with the Instituto Nacional de Reforma Agraria (National Institute for the Agrarian Reform), symbolically conveyed the new function of television in Cuban society and the role of those working in the medium. The first article, devoted to the Soviet Exhibition of Science, Technology, and Culture that visited Havana in February 1960, included television as one of the areas in which the USSR had made an important technological impact. The description accompanying a photo that shows the electrical components of a television set highlights how the Soviets had used the technology in the domestic sphere as well as in other areas like surgery and fishing.[1] Dissociated from any reference to entrepreneurship and entertainment, figuratively, the image and caption reintroduced television to Cuba, positioning it as an apparatus that—similar to its uses in the USSR—would be at the service of Cuban society and the revolution.

The second article, also part of the February 1960 issue of *INRA*, focused on the first fictional film produced by the Instituto Cubano del Arte y la Industria Cinematográficos (ICAIC), *Historias de la revolución* (Stories of the Revolution). Featuring a series of photographs and short commentaries by the movie's performers, the image-oriented piece emphasized the role of the actor in the new Cuban nation. "An actor is another worker in society. . . . The 'Cuban actor' will be born again with the Revolution, and he will not be forced to perform foreign forms and characters, but instead he will perform a Cuban, a neighbor, a person he sees on the street."[2] Eliminating any signs of glamour, sophistication, and star status, the revolutionary actor would be the common man and woman in Cuba. Analogous to other cultural creators, such as writers, dancers, and artists, the performer would use his or her talents to enrich the collective revolutionary project.

The third article appeared in August 1960 and centered on the voluntary work offered by 1,450 teachers in the Sierra Maestra. In addition to helping build homes and facilities for the peasants residing in the area, as well as teaching them basic writing and reading skills, the teachers received three months of military training. In one of the photos included in the piece, a young man and a woman appear to be performing in front of a cardboard television camera. Along with referencing the materials used to "build" the camera (cardboard and three stakes), the caption reads, "Cubans' cheerful spirit never disappears."[3] Whereas the photo was probably used to illustrate that those who volunteered also enjoyed some leisure time after long days of hard work, the image of nonactors performing on "television" in the remote location of the Sierra Maestra signaled how the medium would be used in Cuba in the near future. Television would be a media outlet for and about all Cubans, regardless of geography, and the new televised culture would center on educating the people about matters of culture and the revolution. As the broadcasting law of 1962 indicated, the task of radio and television in Cuba was "to inform the people, promote people's education, elevate the socialist consciousness, disseminate political and scientific knowledge, and expand the people's culture, recreation, and sports."[4] Through images and captions, the three INRA magazine pieces repurposed television's technology, the roles of its professionals, its culture, and its reach while foreshadowing its new functions in Cuban society.

This chapter outlines the last phase of Cuban commercial television and the restructuring of broadcasting that took place in the early 1960s. More than an account of when each station or network was nationalized, the discussion maps the uses and functions of television in the young socialist nation-state, paying particular attention to how the medium was used to construct a new style of modernity. With the incorporation of a new system of values, Fidel Castro and his ministers began the process of redefining what it meant to be modern and Cuban. Television played a vital role in this transformative stage of tearing down ideological beliefs and building a different foundation. While the medium continued to broadcast the advances of the born-again Cuban nation and the citizens' massive support for the revolution and its leader (representations formed through the spectacles of revolution), building a socialist consciousness became television's main function. It was through this process of eliminating the commercial system and creating a state-run one that the spectacles of revolution faded, opening space for different narratives and representations. From a new administration to creative personnel to pedagogical and propaganda-oriented programming fare, helping to *construct* modernity became Cuban television's principal use and function. In the early 1960s, the broadcasting of socialist modernity scaffolded the construction of socialist modernity.

The Death and Rebirth of Television in Cuba

On May 8, 1960, the Cuban revolutionary government issued a press release announcing that Prime Minister Fidel Castro would host a weekly television show. Although the press release indicated that the first program would begin the following Friday, it provided no information regarding the time of day the show would air. In an attempt to explain the absence of a time slot to U.S. readers, a *New York Times* reporter wrote, "Dr. Castro is famous for irregular hours and as the duration of his speeches is unpredictable, no effort was made to announce the exact schedule."[5] With that simple explanation, the *New York Times* journalist partially captured the initial restructuring of Cuban television, a process that at the time entailed a programming flow based on Castro's and the revolutionary government's needs, the appropriation of a television station and network, and the production of educational programming. By May 1960, the revolutionary state had confiscated Telemundo, the second most powerful network in Cuba, and had banned foreign-made advertising. This was the first step in the total elimination of commercial sponsorship, completed in 1961.[6]

To be sure, in the early months of 1960, the government did not seem to have a clear plan for dismantling the commercial system. Unionized actors were still discussing a new advertising law to improve performers' salaries in March 1960, and *Bohemia* published a piece aimed at convincing the revolutionary government that advertising was financially important to the nation's economic growth (and offered benefits as a channel of communication between the state and the people). Both of these situations indicate that, despite envisioning television's use for education and politics, the revolutionary government did not initially conceive of an exclusively state-run system.[7] Furthermore, whereas in one 1990s interview, CMQ-TV owner Goar Mestre expressed that he and his brothers knew "it was just a matter of time" before the state confiscated the network, other interviews conducted in the 1990s with some of the revolutionaries behind the nationalization of media properties demonstrated that not even government officials were aware that the changes were going to develop "in a vertiginous and traumatic way."[8] Consequently, even as Telemundo (renamed Televisión Revolución) was already going through an internal transformation, the commercial system was still in place in May 1960.

For the most part, the state's intervention in matters regarding networks and stations came with some type of rationalization.[9] Initially motivated by suspicions of financial investments by people associated with Fulgencio Batista's regime, and later propelled by labor disputes between television owners and unionized media workers, the government usually explained why it confiscated media properties. Yet, despite changing from privately run to government-run stations and networks, the government-designed programming did not undergo drastic ideological transformations. In fact, similar to revisions at Tele Rebelde/channel 12 one year earlier, the programming that the government produced resembled the televised culture many reviewers had envisioned for Cuba before television's incorporation on the island.

For example, on Televisión Revolución, the Ministry of Education designed an instructive program dedicated to teaching school subjects, *Aprendiendo en televisión* (Learning on television), and produced culturally oriented shows such as *Enciclopedia cultural* (Cultural encyclopedia) and *Pueblo y cultura* (People and culture). Furthermore, the revolutionary government announced its plans to install television sets in all schools and provide them for the poor in both rural and urban areas. Also, as part of an effort to eradicate illiteracy, the government created a massive campaign titled "Enciendele tu televisor al alumno humilde" (Turn on your television for a humble student) to encourage financially solvent citizens to allow poorer people to watch educational programming in their homes.[10] Following Fidel Castro's directive to eradicate illiteracy, and most likely influenced by reviewers' and intellectuals' long-established views of the medium, the revolutionaries designing the programming focused on television's educational functions.

Throughout most of 1960, Cuban audiences received a hybrid programming fare of educational shows produced by the government and broadcast on Televisión Revolución (which became the main state-run network that year) and entertainment programming sponsored by advertisers and aired on CMQ-TV and CMBF-Cadena Nacional (partially owned by Mestre and, after nationalization, fused with Televisión Revolución). Nonetheless, by late 1960, it was evident that the television system that had thrived in Cuban society since 1950 could not continue in the new Cuba.[11] At a time when civil society ceased to exist, television had to undergo a metamorphosis as well. The new political stage of the Cuban Revolution—socialism—determined the government's appropriation of the last privately owned networks and reconfigured the system.

After the nationalization of CMBF and CMQ, larger discussions about programming took center stage in the already confiscated magazine, *Bohemia*.[12] Excited about the multiple possibilities of producing new programs and, to a certain extent, reproducing what a *New York Times* reporter categorized as "a solid monotone of praise for the regime and the revolution," a mixture of new and already established television reviewers discussed the medium's rebirth.[13] As the *Bohemia* piece titled "¡Ahora o nunca!" (Now or never!) indicated, "Now radio and television have a brilliant opportunity [to] eliminate their ancestral vices."[14] In this story, as well as in other articles published during the last months of 1960, writers commented on the possible elimination of genres such as *telenovelas* (which some claimed fomented sentimentalism) and the need to go beyond simple title changes of variety shows and tackle the "pretentiousness" that, according to one reviewer, characterized this type of programming. The reflections on revolutionary television also articulated a desire to utilize surveys to monitor the success of educational shows and to develop programs that would include theater, ballet, poetry, and literature.[15] The state's top-down reconstruction of the medium was designed to engage the audience in creating a new society. Yet, even though the imagined public was composed of people who, as Lillian Guerra writes regarding the majority of Cubans, "willingly and even joyfully, . . . surrendered their rights, including the rights to public protest, an autonomous press, and free assembly," the revolutionary audience seemed to be somewhat resistant to the changes taking place on television.[16]

In his short piece, "Más entretenimiento, más alegría" (More entertainment, more happiness), a *Bohemia* television reviewer revealed that he had received many letters from viewers complaining that "there is nothing to watch on television."[17] While the reviewer made it clear that he disagreed with this assessment, since he had seen media workers' "extraordinary effort[s] to offer new programs," he thought it was important to share some of the viewers' criticisms. Nonetheless, rather than including quotes from audience members' letters, the reviewer used the column to express what seemed to be his own take on the new television programming. "Maybe it is a problem of programming time slots . . . which gives a sense of emptiness. Also, there is too much repetition in the doctrinal programs. And, what is worse, the message is obvious, direct, and for that reason ineffective."[18] Then the reviewer offered a solution: combine genres and provide viewers with "more entertainment, more happiness." For this television critic (and the alleged letter writers), revolutionary programming was tedious.

Several factors most likely contributed to the reviewer's perception of the new television schedule. One of the characteristics of Cuban commercial television was its focus on entertainment. Cuban media professionals were highly regarded in Latin America not only for their knowledge of the technical and business aspects of television but also for their ability to adapt U.S. entertainment genres (such as variety shows, situation comedies, and game shows) to fit the Cuban and, to a certain extent, Latin American cultural landscape. Closely following U.S. production and programming innovations, Cubans mastered show business and the spectacles that formed it (these, as discussed in earlier chapters, were constituents of the spectacles of progress). It was precisely these connections between U.S. and Cuban television that positioned certain genres and genre elements as examples of Cuba's neocolonial formation and the modernity it represented. Thus, when a reviewer remarked that variety shows needed to go beyond title changes to eliminate their "pretentiousness" and "big spectacles," he was referring to aesthetic elements (such as sets and costumes) that symbolized the excesses of the commercial era, when Cuba embraced a U.S.-influenced concept of modernity. Any element that reminded viewers of that reality—a worldview that had been part of Cuba just one year earlier—had to be extracted. Genres needed to be purified to play a role on revolutionary television.

The purification that took place during the rebirth of Cuban television also included the elimination of U.S. shows, a highly popular programming component during the commercial era. Locally produced programs such as *Sombras del pasado* (Shadows of the past), which tackled Cuba's "ancestral blemish," and *Ventana al mundo* (Window to the world), a news-oriented program, replaced "filmed programs such as 'Bat Masterson,' and 'Mackenzie's Raiders' (authorized by the President of the United States to violate the Mexican frontier every time they pleased)."[19] Also missing from the schedule were the parade of international figures from Hollywood, Europe, and Latin America—entertainers who had previously performed at cabarets in Cuba's luxury hotels and on radio and television.[20]

The topic of international artists indirectly brings to light the massive exodus of Cuban television professionals across the region. In all probability, this migration contributed to the viewers' disenchantment with revolutionary programming. While most likely not fully aware of their relocation (government-run media outlets noted the departure of big names such as Gaspar Pumarejo and Goar Mestre, but not the exodus of lesser-known media workers or famous performers), audiences suffered the consequences of losing people with extensive experience in television production. As the revolution was redefined as socialist, the Cuban population became "completely polarized—between those who were in favor [of] and those who were against the revolution, who were called *contra-revolucionarios* (counterrevolutionaries) and *gusanos* (worms)."[21] This tense political situation initiated an extensive migration, first from the upper and upper-middle classes—including media owners, television professionals, and performers—and later, between 1961 and 1962, from middle-class individuals. Media professionals who left Cuba relocated to Buenos Aires, Caracas, Miami, New York City, Rio de Janeiro, and San Juan, becoming major figures in the development of commercial broadcasting and advertising corporations in Latin America and in the U.S. Spanish-language media scene.[22] For their part, the television and advertising professionals who stayed on the island not only had to step up and take the lead in managing and producing television but also had to retrain themselves to develop genres in which they had no previous experience. As a result, the media professionals' exodus, combined with the educational, propaganda-oriented programs favored by state operatives, led to a dearth in television production, management, and artistic creativity.[23]

Cuban television's rebirth—a process that began in late 1960 and continued throughout 1961—entailed a revision of production practices, a retraining of media workers, and a reassessment of taste. As an article published in *Bohemia* in 1961 states: "The habit, the mental attitude, of a pretty large number of people is well known. They traditionally have summarized their desires in these words: 'I don't go to the cinema or watch television to suffer, but to be entertained.' We have begun to fight against this habit and we must continue to oppose it intelligently because those of us working on contemporary television are interested, fundamentally, in what the public thinks."[24]

Relying on a series of binaries, revolutionary television was represented as the antidote to eliminating years of "frivolous entertainment."[25] Contrary to commercial television, an "evil instrument" that was "used to collectively stultify the people," revolutionary television had a "social meaning."[26] The renovated television system was used to fight illiteracy and develop the minds of revolutionary citizens. Through programs that showcased, for example, Cuban and world theater classics (with plays such as *Electra Garrigó*, *Oedipus Rex*, and *The Traveler without Luggage*) and a close examination of "the hidden structure of films made in capitalistic countries," television was repositioned as an apparatus that would help reshape the Cuban people's worldview.[27]

Revolutionary television was about demolishing all the spectacles that formed the previous era in order to use the medium to help rebuild Cuba. This was guided by a new, revolutionary way of thinking, a political language that, beginning in 1961, started to combine "ideologemes such as *people, homeland, nation, independence*, and *social justice*" with the Marxist-Leninism doctrine.[28] The end of diplomatic relations with the United States; the failed, U.S.-orchestrated Bay of Pigs invasion; Fidel Castro's public embracing of socialism; and his famous speech "Words to the Intellectuals," where his statement "within the Revolution, everything; against the Revolution, nothing" set the tone for the revolution's cultural policy, crystallized the path the revolution would take in the years to come. With a system of ideas centering on collective efforts to defend the revolution from internal traitors and from the United States, and a mandate to eliminate the ideological vestiges of U.S. imperialism, Cuba's fragmented process of modernization, as Cuban literary critic Rafael Rojas observes, reinforced the revolution's call for sovereignty, social justice, and the decolonization of the national imaginary.[29]

In this new architecture of power, television became a channel-instrument that would transmit revolutionary ideals and "penetrate" the minds of Cuban citizens. Following the Soviet model wherein radio and television were conceptualized as tools for "revolutionary transformation," Cuban television would "saturate" the public with the revolutionary message.[30] As César Escalante, one of the most important ideologues behind the propaganda campaigns of the early 1960s, stated, the media "are at the service of the Revolution," and as such, "we should all make our best and most sophisticated effort . . . so that they transform into the most effective media for achieving their important revolutionary, social, political and cultural function."[31] While in his speeches Escalante distinguished between advertising ("used to influence an individual" and "sell products") and propaganda (used to "promote revolutionary ideals"), the same techniques were employed to spread revolutionary ideology across all aspects of Cuban society. In the words of Escalante, "The revolutionary thought penetrates everything, it penetrates the pores of our body, the revolutionary thought penetrates production, penetrates defense, penetrates cultural labor; the revolutionary thought penetrates the information in the newspaper, it penetrates the newspaper's editorial content; the revolutionary thought penetrates the soap opera that is on the radio, the revolutionary thought penetrates the newscast, the information in all radio, television, or newspaper activity."[32] Crucial to this aggressive "penetration" was the centralization of radio and television, another influence of the Soviet model of broadcasting.[33]

The process of organizing and bureaucratically establishing a direct connection between the government and television began in 1961 with the transfer of media-confiscated properties to the Ministry of Communication. An important aspect of this new arrangement was the creation of the Office of Orientation and Coordination of Radiobroadcasting and the Office of Publication, agencies that, under the guidance of revolutionaries (some with extensive experience in advertising), developed propaganda campaigns and designed programming.[34] The last stage of this restructuring occurred in 1962 with the crafting of a broadcasting law that established the Instituto Cubano de Radiodifusión (ICR; Cuban Institute of Radio Broadcasting). This legislation was designed to create a bureau whose main purpose was to manage the administrative, technical, and programming aspects of radio and television. Describing both media outlets as the "broadest and most effective" channels to promote the socialist consciousness, the legislation officially positioned radio and television under Cuba's Council of Ministers, thus making broadcasting an arm of the government.[35]

According to Mirta Muñiz, one of the principal figures of Cuban television's rebirth, this centralization helped in the spread of Cuba's revolutionary consciousness across the population, in the "denunciation of imperialist aggressions," and in the reach of Cuba's literacy programs.[36] The renewed medium was dominated by Fidel Castro's "long and frequent" interventions on television, by the broadcasting of rallies and ceremonies, and by programs that promoted "the understanding and unity of the revolutionary force."[37] Serials with a revolutionary message, the adaptation of literary and theater classics (e.g., *The Diary of Anne Frank* and Bertolt Brecht's *Mother Courage*), and news-oriented programs occupied the television schedule.[38] Thus, some of the elements that were part of the spectacles of revolution (such as Castro's participation on television and the broadcasting of rallies) were set in the born-again television system. At the same time, new cultural and linguistic performances also began to appear on revolutionary television, introducing a new group of international friends and allies to the Cuban people.

Cultural acts and visitors from countries in the communist bloc began to appear in Havana's venues, and many were featured on Cuban television.[39] These visits, together with the political and economic affiliations between Cuba and the USSR, initiated new types of associations (physical, social, economic, and imaginary) that transcended language and culture and were formed through a common worldview of citizenry under socialism. In the early 1960s, the first building blocks were established for Cubans to begin "dreaming in Russian," situating the USSR and other bloc countries as idealized places where they could study, work, and even travel.[40] The communist bloc began to be constructed as a location and an inspiration for socialist modernity.

In the first few years of the 1960s, the vision of progress that began to be linked to socialist countries came via cultural acts; visits from "technicians, businessmen, and advisers"; stories published in INRA magazine; and science and technology exhibitions.[41] It was at those exhibitions that television was highlighted as a testament to socialist advancement. For instance, the caption to a photo included in an INRA article covering an exhibition from East Germany visiting Havana in December 1961 read, "Television sets with modern design and manufacture are a real draw in the exposition. Both radios and TV sets represent a powerful development in electronics within the RDA [East Germany], which is constantly advancing scientifically."[42] Having first been reintroduced as a technology used for practical purposes (via the Soviet Exhibition of Science, Technology, and Culture in February 1960), television was now being *re*-presented as an emblem of socialist progress. Television—the apparatus and, indirectly, the minds and hands behind its electronic and aesthetic design—became a symbol of socialist modernity.[43]

Unquestionably, these new ideas about socialist modernity that began to infiltrate Cuba's national imaginary were out of tune with U.S. television.

From the Nixon-Kennedy televised debates of October 1960 in which Cuba was described as "lost" and Fidel Castro was characterized as a "dictator," to documentary-style programs such as *Bell & Howell Close-UP!* and CBS *Reports* that tackled the repressive tactics being used in Cuba, according to U.S. television programs, there was nothing modern about the changes occurring on the island.[44] The brave, highly educated, and inspiring leader who appeared in CBS's *Rebels of the Sierra Maestra: The Story of Cuba's Jungle Fighters* (1957) turned into an aggressive individual who stole U.S. properties and profits, threatened to spread communism across the region, and later, in 1962, almost caused the extinction of the U.S. (and Cuban) population with the Cuban missile crisis. Fidel Castro went from being a rebel with a good cause to being an enemy of the state and a destabilizing force in the geopolitical order.

Certainly, not all U.S. citizens saw Castro as the dangerous dictator that U.S. television and media promoted. For those behind the gestation of the New Left and for many African American militants, the revolutionary leader was a victorious rebel who had defeated U.S. imperialism. Of these groups aligned with the Left, the Black Panthers established a special connection with Fidel Castro and the Cuban Revolution. As Van Gosse observes, "That a new African-American militance would translate so readily into solidarity with Castro should hardly be surprising.... [T]he undeniable fact that Cuba abolished its own Jim Crow practices with no 'deliberation' and a maximum of 'speed,'" in addition to Castro's multiple gestures of solidarity toward African Americans, generated sympathy and admiration.[45] Civil rights activist and militant Robert F. Williams moved to Cuba in the early 1960s, and African American leaders such as Stokely Carmichael and Angela Davis visited the island and expressed support for the revolution. These signs of camaraderie would strengthen the "Afro-Cuban-American" cultural and political connections for years to come.[46]

Dissenting political views regarding the Cuban Revolution, together with the visual and aural narrative structure of some U.S. television programming that focused on the Cold War, opened up the meaning of these television texts. As Michael Curtin demonstrates in his analysis of television documentaries of the early 1960s, in some cases, "the journalistic and narrative conventions" of presenting different sides of a particular issue provided audiences with opportunities to perform alternative readings.[47] This was the case for the April 18, 1961, episode, titled "Ninety Miles to Communism," of the ABC program *Bell & Howell Close-UP!*[48] Although the program's main objective was to denounce Castro's dictatorial government and the lack of freedom in communist regimes, probably in an attempt to justify the Bay of Pigs invasion that was taking place at the time of the broadcast, it did include black Cuban peasants discussing how the revolution had benefited their lives. This provided space for alternative readings by African Americans and those favoring desegregation and equality in the United States. What Curtin categorizes as an "excess of meanings," together with the audience's positionality, allowed for oppositional readings of such Cold War–inspired programs.

Of course, if available, the most divergent readings most likely would have come from Cuba, as demonstrated in a two-page *INRA* magazine article discussing the Nixon-Kennedy televised debates.[49] Reproducing an image of Nixon and Kennedy on television as well as two photographs of African American protesters, the piece, titled "Yankees' Elections: A Spectacle in Decadence," used the debates to criticize U.S. capitalism, racial segregation, and U.S. policy toward Cuba. Describing U.S. leaders as compliant with monopolistic interests, the medium and the messages were reinscribed as spectacles of a political system that sustained racial and class inequalities. Cuba, in contrast, had freed itself from the main forces that created those spectacles: U.S. representative "democracy" (included in the article in quotes to emphasize the ironic tone) and the corporations that controlled the political system. In Cuba, the revolution took the spotlight off the spectacles.

By 1962, when the ICR was legally established, the spectacles of television's commercial era were a thing of the past. As a *Bohemia* writer observed: "Stripped of its former commercial logic by the revolution, completely eradicating the vices of centralism, vulgarity, and programs devoid of an artistic sense and an orienting message, television today advances along new paths in our country and quickly moves forward toward important work in collective education, so that such an important vehicle completely fulfills its true social functions. . . . Television and radio are also actively working to construct our new socialist society."[50] Combined with propaganda spots incorporated throughout the programming schedule, revolutionary television was used to reeducate the people about matters of culture, history, socialism, and the benefits of the revolution.[51]

Television became an instrument for the edification of Cuba's socialist modernity, a modernity that entailed the reinterpretation of the nation's history, heroes, and national holidays.[52] It was in this process of reconstruction that items, practices, and cultural artifacts traditionally associated with the Cuban elite—from sophisticated clothing and hairstyles (as Lillian Guerra astutely analyzes) to the opera, ballet, and theater broadcasts on television— were redefined, reframed, and reintroduced as within reach for all Cubans.[53] In characterizing Cuba's capitalistic era as promoting "underdevelopment," the revolution was bringing "modernity and progress" to all by "implement[ing] equalitarianism and a collective orientation."[54] The revolution was represented as providing basic needs such as education and housing to Cuban citizens, as well as offering cultural productions that, under capitalism, had been accessible only to a few. Thanks to socialism, the television audience, composed of "laborers, peasants, workers, [and] all the people," would enjoy high culture, education, progress, and modernity.[55]

In early socialist Cuba, television was represented as a technology to help build the revolutionary consciousness, as a channel to culturally and politically form (and reform) the Cuban citizen, and as a place open to all Cubans. Through its revolutionary and high-culture content designed to benefit all citizens, television was broadcasting a new conception of modernity and, in the process, constructing a socialist modernity. Working as an ideological loop, the broadcasting and constructing of modernity would define Cuban television in the years to come.

EPILOGUE

When I traveled to Havana to conduct the research for this book, I had a very specific television routine. In the evenings I began with the one-and-a-half-hour program *Mesa redonda*, a politically dogmatic panel show that, in addition to addressing national and regional issues, devoted significant attention to *los imperialistas Yankees* (Yankee imperialists). I then watched locally produced shows, including the evening news, a *telenovela*, and culture-oriented programming. On some weeknights when I was able to stay awake until midnight or so (the "so" here is in reference to Cuban television's sometimes unpredictable programming schedule), I enjoyed subtitled episodes of *Grey's Anatomy*, *The Sopranos*, or whatever Hollywood series was being broadcast. Occasionally, during the afternoons when my allergies forced me to take a break from old documents, I joined my *compañeras/os* (comrades) at the Centro de Investigaciones del Instituto Cubano de Radio y Televisión and watched whatever Brazilian telenovela was on. This television viewing experience was complemented with occasional chats about television with other researchers at the Centro. It was during one of these conversations that I confessed to them my latest guilty pleasure, *24*.

To my surprise, many people at the Centro also liked *24*, and given that I had missed several episodes while being in Cuba, one of Centro's researchers was kind enough to bring me a DVD with the latest episodes. I still have no clue how this compañera had access to episodes that had aired in the United States for the first time only a couple of weeks earlier. Still, one thing was evident—like myself, my Cuban companions highly enjoyed U.S. television. It did not matter that U.S. shows were broadcast late at night, many Cubans patiently waited to watch them. As a Cuban friend once told me, "I wonder what Gillian Anderson [costar of *The X-Files*] would say if she knew that *la Scully* had a devoted fan-club in Cuba." In fact, a researcher affiliated with the Centro disclosed to me that, based on a nationwide survey conducted between 2006 and 2007, the most popular show in the Cuban provinces was *Friends*. Even though it is not clear precisely when or why the Instituto Cubano de Radio y Televisión (ICRT; Cuban Institute of Radio and Television, the state organism that controls radio and television) decided to broadcast Hollywood television shows, recent research indicates that U.S. television began to reappear on the state-controlled medium sometime after the 1990s.[1] The availability of new technologies and the apparent "payback pleasure" (as someone described it to me) of airing U.S. programs without paying copyright fees have apparently led to the scheduling of many Hollywood television programs on Cuban television.

Neither the popularity of U.S. programming nor the resources used to obtain Hollywood products are discussed on local media outlets. Nor is the fact that, since the early to mid-2000s, people with illegal cable hookups have been disappearing inside their homes to watch shows broadcast on the U.S. Spanish-language network Telemundo. Also not disclosed is the fact that many Cubans stay up-to-date with the latest Hollywood blockbusters and TV shows by obtaining these products at underground video rentals operating across the island. References to these practices, however, appear indirectly within the national news in reports of sporadic police raids to close down illegal video-DVD rentals and to dismantle clandestine cable hookups.[2] Thus, while during the late 1950s (when Hollywood began to dominate the Cuban prime-time schedule), journalists raised concerns over the effect of television and movie imports on the local industry, the contemporary state-run media structure has preferred to ignore the ideological contradictions of criticizing U.S. imperialism while concomitantly broadcasting Hollywood products.

Global media flows that have characterized other parts of the world for decades have become part of contemporary Cuba, a nation-state that until the early 1990s was a closed society politically and economically connected to the countries of the socialist bloc. The consumption of local, pro-socialist television shows such as *Mesa redonda* and of foreign TV programs such as *24* present Cubans with a plurality of political, cultural, and economic worldviews. New or, more accurately, historically reconstituted regional and global formations inform today's post-Soviet Cuban material and popular-culture conditions. Anthropologist Anna Cristina Pertierra observes as much, noting, "As Cubans lost the socialist connections that had previously informed many of their opportunities for travel, their television and musical choices, and the material culture of their homes, new global configurations have become important, linking Cuban residents to tourists and emigrants living in the United States, Canada and Western Europe."[3] The dismantling of the Soviet Union and the beginning and development of what is generally referred to as the Special Period are the direct and indirect forces behind these local and global intersections and the reconceptualization of media flows. As scholars have documented, the collapse of the Soviet Union after 1991 radically destabilized Cuba's economy and the lives of Cuban citizens.[4] While in one way or another postrevolutionary Cuba had always suffered from a shortage of material goods, by the 1980s the nation's citizens were able to meet their basic needs, and there was a general expectation of a soon-to-be "comfortable standard of living."[5] Thus, the 1990s crisis represented an unexpected turn.

To improve the economic situation produced by the elimination of trade exchanges with former socialist countries, the Cuban state initiated a series of measures that challenged the principles of the revolution as a capitalistic-free, egalitarian society. Legalization of the dollar and of self-employment in certain professional areas, together with the opening of Cuba's economy to foreign investors, began to create class divisions based on access to dollars (or foreign currency) via family in the United States and tourist-related ventures. Legalized businesses such as *paladares* (semiprivate restaurants) and *casas particulares* (semiprivate homes where foreigners rent rooms), together with illegal underground jobs such as prostitution and the selling of Cuban goods on the streets, represent some of the tactics Cubans have utilized for economic survival. It is within the realm of an illegal/underground economy that the video-DVD rental businesses and the cable hookups began to operate in Cuba.[6]

The interplay between local and global programming in contemporary Cuban television tells a story. This story goes beyond the telenovelas' diegesis or *Mesa redonda*'s attacks on the United States. Cuban television is a palimpsest, a technological-cultural artifact that circuitously interconnects Cuba's political, economic, and cultural past and present. "The palimpsest," as José Quiroga writes, "does not reproduce the original, but it dismantles it, writes on top of it, allows it to be seen."[7] As a palimpsest, Cuban television and its programming disclose the multiple connections that have defined this Caribbean island and its media systems. Shaping the foundation of the television/palimpsest is Cuba, a nation-state that during the twentieth century and through drastic political and socioeconomic transformations, has been linked to the West/First World and the East/Second World while remaining in the Third World periphery.

Considering Cuba's unique political history in the region and recent revolutions occurring in Latin America (for example, in Venezuela), a historical look at Cuban television serves as a starting point for future analysis of how, even in closed societies, television has always functioned as a space that is simultaneously local and global even though, at first glance, it appears to be exclusively local. Locality, as Arjun Appadurai reminds us, is "relational and contextual."[8] Cuba's television, genres, and programs operate in relation to the nation's present, but they also bring with them discourses associated with the nation's and television's local and global past.

Since the arrival of television in Cuba in 1950, the medium has been a chronicler of the nation-state's political, economic, social, and cultural circumstances. Cuban television's past and present challenge us to devise new ways to analyze the importance of the medium in transitional societies. Equally important, the Cuban case illustrates the ways in which television is a participant and sometimes also a creator of a nation's history.

NOTES

INTRODUCTION. Broadcasting Modernity, Spectacles, and Television

1 See Rodríguez, *The Havana Guide*; Hyde, *Constitutional Modernism*.

2 According to Kenneth Burke, people select specific ways to describe themselves and their surroundings, and their language selection (what he calls "terministic screens") unavoidably filters other ways of conceptualizing reality. As he writes, "Even if any given terminology is a reflection of reality, by its very nature as a terminology it must be a selection of reality; and to this extent it must function also as a deflection of reality." Burke, *Language as Symbolic Action*, 45.

3 For an extensive historical analysis of U.S.–Cuba relations before 1959, see Pérez, *On Becoming Cuban*.

4 *On Becoming Cuban*, 7.

5 *On Becoming Cuban*, 351.

6 Trouillot, "The Otherwise Modern," 224.

7 Kutzinski, *Sugar's Secrets*. For an analysis of race and the incorporation of black cultural elements as part of the Cuban nation, see de la Fuente, *A Nation for All*.

8 de la Fuente, *A Nation for All*, 12.

9 Kutzinski, *Sugar's Secrets*, 7; Arroyo, *Travestismos culturales*.

10 Arroyo, *Travestismos culturales*, 7.

11 Hanchard, "Black Cinderella?" See also Wade, *Music, Race, and Nation*, 3–7.

12 Moraña, Dussel, and Jáuregui, "Colonialism and Its Replicants," 2. See also Quijano, "Coloniality of Power, Eurocentrism, and Social Classification"; Mignolo, "The Geopolitics of Knowledge and the Colonial Difference"; and Quijano, "The Colonial Nature of Power and Latin America's Cultural Experience."

13 Gaonkar, "On Alternative Modernities"; Taylor, "Two Theories of Modernity"; Trouillot, "The Otherwise Modern." See also Eisenstadt, "Multiple Modernities."

14 Pérez, *On Becoming Cuban*, 459.

15 Sturken and Thomas, "Introduction," 1.

16 Domínguez, "The Batista Regime in Cuba," 126.

17 Debord, *Society of the Spectacle*, secs. 4 and 5.

18 Crary, *Suspensions of Perception*, 75.

19 Pertierra and Turner, *Locating Television*, 123.

20 For an analysis of the Cuban economy during the 1950s, see Farber, *The Origins of the Cuban Revolution Reconsidered*; Pérez, *Cuba*; and Mesa-Lago, *Market, Socialist and Mixed Economies*.

21 Pérez, *On Becoming Cuban*, 348.

22 López, "'A Train of Shadows,'" 149.

23 López, "'A Train of Shadows,'" 154.

24 As Jesús Martín Barbero observes, the historical circumstances that shaped Latin American nation-states and their political development (long periods under colonial rule, economic dependency, neocolonialism, and struggles to incorporate the popular classes into the political project) influenced their path toward modernization. Martín Barbero, *Communication, Culture and Hegemony*, 150–51.

25 Pérez, *Cuba*; and Arnavat, "The Cuban Constitution and the Future Democratic Transition."

26 In the words of Domínguez, "Batista believed that his tolerance of some opposition would gain him support, above all in the U.S. government. For this reason he authorized various 'dialogues' with civic groups to find a solution to the problem of political legitimacy, whose only plausible outcome was his own resignation." Domínguez, "The Batista Regime in Cuba," 126.

27 Guerra, *Visions of Power in Cuba*, 74, 76.

28 As Rafael Rojas explains, one of the first goals of the revolutionary leaders was to "destroy the experience" of the Cuban nation throughout the first part of the twentieth century. Rojas, *La máquina del olvido*, 72.

29 Debord, *Society of the Spectacle*, sec. 192.

30 Nye, "Technological Prediction," 171.

31 Jenkins, *Re-thinking History*, 11.

32 López, "Greater Cuba," 40.

33 As expected, this left-wing/right-wing dichotomy has had the effect of stifling the discussion of other areas beyond cinema and television. In reference to the limited research on the Visual Arts section of the Pan American Union (PAU) and on its influential leader José Gómez Sicre, Claire F. Fox remarks, "But the main reason, I believe, for the critical avoidance of the PAU arts programs is ideological, a legacy of the Cuban Revolution's polarizing impact on American intellectual sectors." Thanks to Fox's meticulous research, the complexities of this Cuban man and his contribution to the internationalization of Latin American art are appreciated beyond a simple characterization such as an agent of U.S. empire. Fox, *Making Art Panamerican*, 14.

34 For a recent analysis of the academic left's refusal to criticize the revolution, see Duanel Díaz Infante, "Revolución cubana, crítica latinoamericana, y academia

norteamericana," *Diario de Cuba*, April 28, 2013, accessed April 29, 2013, http://www.diariodecuba.com/de-leer/1367137602_2990.html.

35 Guerra, *Visions of Power in Cuba*, 2.

36 For information on newspapers in Cuba prior to the Cuban Revolution, see Salwen, "The Dark Side of Cuban Journalism."

37 Nichols, *Representing Reality*, 107.

38 González-Castro, *Hasta el último aliento*.

39 Zelizer, *Remembering to Forget*, 3.

40 For an excellent analysis of Cuban exile and Cuban American cultures, see Pérez Firmat, *Life on the Hyphen*.

CHAPTER ONE. Prelude to the Spectacles

1 Classen, *Watching Jim Crow*, 16.

2 Nye, *America as Second Creation*, 16; see also 1–42.

3 Here, I am referring to elements of U.S. modernity that emphasize technological and economic progress, not the particularities of American culture that foment individualism and secularism.

4 Similar legal practices took place in other colonized territories. See, for example, Larkin, *Signal and Noise*; and Mrázek, *Engineers of Happy Land*.

5 Both Oscar Luis López and Michael Salwen characterize Cuban broadcasting laws as copycat versions of U.S. laws. As López writes, "The government limited itself to adopt[ing] simple regulatory measures copying some dispositions that were prevalent in the United States of North America. . . . Everything was left to the private sector with the recommendation of 'respecting morality and good customs' although none of the legal codes defined what was moral and what the good customs were." See López, *La radio en Cuba*, 63–64; and Salwen, *Radio and Television in Cuba*.

6 Alfredo Zayas, President, "Secretaria de Gobernación," *Gaceta Oficial de la República de Cuba*, 1923, 3233–36.

7 See Slotten, *Radio and Television Regulation*; and Streeter, *Selling the Air*.

8 While advertisements were prohibited by law, some stations began to air ads in 1926, mostly from small local corporations. Additionally, the 1923 legislation did not include any explanation regarding membership and general duties of the Department of Communication. It was not until the 1934 Radio Law that the specific duties of this office were outlined. The Department of Communication would be in charge of regulating Cuban broadcasting for the next thirty-nine years. For information on Cuban radio, see López, *La radio en Cuba*.

9 Streeter, *Selling the Air*, 87.

10 López, *La radio en Cuba*. See also Salwen, *Radio and Television in Cuba*, 7.

11　"Hoover Forced to Limit Number of Broadcasters," *New York Times*, November 15, 1925, XX17.

12　For information about the first two periods of Cuban radio, see López, *La radio en Cuba*, 1–155.

13　Alberto Giró, "La Ley de Radio," *Diario de la Marina*, April 8, 1934, 7.

14　Carlos Mendieta y Montefur, Presidente Provisional de la República de Cuba, "Decreto-Ley Radio," *Gaceta Oficial de la República de Cuba*, 1934, 1–16.

15　Salwen, *Radio and Television in Cuba*, 8.

16　Streeter, *Selling the Air*, 97.

17　See McChesney, *Telecommunications, Mass Media, and Democracy*, 188–225; Hilmes, *Only Connect*.

18　Goodman, *Radio's Civic Ambition*.

19　López, *La radio en Cuba*, 83–84.

20　Pérez, *Cuba*, 268.

21　See de la Fuente, *A Nation for All*, 175–209; and Alexander, *A History of Organized Labor in Cuba*, 36–69.

22　de la Fuente, *A Nation for All*, 176.

23　In the 1940s the rumba performed in the upper-class casino cabaret shows went through various transformations to restructure traditional, noncommercial rumba's sexual musical and dance expressions. Moore, *Nationalizing Blackness*, 169, 185, 187.

24　These protectionist stipulations were present in the broadcasting laws of other Latin American countries. For instance, throughout the 1930s in Argentina, many citizens were in favor of adopting the British broadcasting model even as the industry was already defined as commercial. This view of broadcasting, together with U.S. influence in other Latin American countries, contributed to Argentina's legal requirements for radio owners to be citizens. See Agusti and Mastrini, "Radio, economía y política entre 1920 y 1945"; and Fox, "Media Policies in Latin America."

25　Mendieta y Montefur, "Decreto-Ley Radio" (1934), 1–2.

26　Mendieta y Montefur, "Decreto-Ley Radio" (1934), 2–3.

27　Mañach, "Introducción al curso," cited in Birkenmaier, *Alejo Carpentier*, 212.

28　Mañach, "Introducción al curso," 17.

29　López, *La radio en Cuba*, 90–91.

30　Federico Laredo, President, "Comunicaciones," *Gaceta Oficial de la República de Cuba* (1939), 5160–62. That same year, the Office of Communication released a short decree targeting channels and frequencies. See Laredo, "Comunicaciones" (1939), 5874–75.

31　Laredo, President, "Comunicaciones" (1939), 5160.

32　Laredo, President, "Comunicaciones" (1939), 5160.

33　Giddens, *The Consequences of Modernity*, 18.

34 See Hansen, "The Mass Production of the Senses"; Martín Barbero, *Communication, Culture and Hegemony*.

35 Cruz, "Patterns of Middle Class Conduct in Nineteenth-Century Spain and Latin America."

36 Stoler, *Carnal Knowledge and Imperial Power*, 45.

37 Federico Laredo, President, "Comunicaciones," *Gaceta Oficial de la República de Cuba* (1938), 2414–15. In 1941, the United States coordinated another conference to address the technical aspects of radio and the problem of interference. As a result of this conference, the government of Cuba reorganized its radio frequencies and reassigned channels to Cuban stations based on licenses and geographic location. See Fulgencio Batista, President, "Comunicaciones," *Gaceta Oficial de la República de Cuba* (1941), 2288–92.

38 Batista, "Comunicaciones" (1941), 2288–92.

39 Alberto Giró, "Dictó Comunicaciones dos importantes resoluciones sobre la radiodifusion," *Diario de la Marina*, March 29, 1942, 14.

40 The institutional dimension of modernity is divided into four areas: industrialism, capitalism, surveillance, and military power. Giddens, *The Consequences of Modernity*, 57–78.

41 For instance, the informative programs (news) were required to be produced by accredited journalistic organizations, while the variety shows could combine professional and aficionado performers.

42 Article 7 of the decree required radio owners to have professional artists in their programs, "at least fifteen percent of the programming" needed to be written by Cuban authors, and "at least twenty percent of the mechanical music" had to be Cuban. Additionally, radio owners needed to mention the names and artists of recorded songs played on the radio. Whereas the combined percentages required by the state for live or recorded programming featuring Cubans or foreigners residing in Cuba did not account for 50 percent of the programming, this provision establishes the state investment in endorsing Cuban culture and people. Federico Laredo, President, "Communicaciones," *Gaceta Oficial de la República de Cuba* (1939), 5161.

43 In his recent work, Michael Curtin attempts to expand the analysis of global media exchanges and the centrality of particular cities in the production and exportation of film and television products. Arguing that most interpretations of global media flows center on the relationship between film and broadcasting industries and the nation-state, Curtin proposes a new analytical framework in which scholars would consider "the web of relations that exist at the local, regional, and global levels, as well as the national level." By examining what he categorizes as media capitals, cities that have become important sites of media production, researchers could pay attention to "the spatial logics of capital, creativity, culture, and polity" without favoring any of these factors. Curtin,

"Media Capital," 204; and Curtin, *Playing to the World's Biggest Audience*, 23, 10–22.

44 Pérez, *Cuba*, 281.

45 Farber, *The Origins of the Cuban Revolution Reconsidered*; Pérez, *Cuba*, 283–88.

46 Birkenmaier, *Alejo Carpentier*; Díaz Ayala, *Música Cubana*; Lemogodeuc, "Orígenes, Ciclón, Lunes"; Moore, *Music and Revolution*.

47 Pérez, *Cuba*, 284.

48 Scarpaci, Segre, and Coyula, *Havana*.

49 Pérez, *On Becoming Cuban*, 132.

50 López, *La radio en Cuba*, 255; see also Dávila, *Latinos, Inc.*, 24–32.

51 Díaz Ayala, *Música Cubana*, 201.

52 López, *La radio en Cuba*, 205.

53 López, *La radio en Cuba*, 92.

54 Fulgencio Batista, President, Carlos Saladrigas, Prime Minister, and Marino López Blanco, Minister of Communication, "Reglamento general de radiodifusiones comerciales," *Gaceta Oficial de la República de Cuba* (1942), 1355–61. Two addenda to the January 1942 law were included in *Gaceta Oficial de la República de Cuba* in the months of March and July.

55 Batista, Saladrigas, and López Blanco, "Reglamento general de radiodifusiones comerciales" (1942), 1355.

56 Batista, Saladrigas, and Blanco, "Reglamento general de radiodifusiones comerciales" (1942), 1355.

57 López, *La radio en Cuba*, 245–46.

58 López, *La radio en Cuba*, 92.

59 Rivero, "Havana as a 1940s-1950s Latin American Media Capital." See also López, *La radio en Cuba*.

60 Manuel Fernández Paradela, "La Comisión de Etica Radial," *Carteles*, April 8, 1947, 58–59; Garcés, *Los dueños del aire*, 87, 124.

61 It is important to mention that some individual stations had regulatory parameters prior to the establishment of La Comisión de Etica Radial. According to Cuban television critic Mayra Cue Sierra, the radio stations O'Shea and CMQ Radio had their own regulations regarding morality and journalistic practices beginning in 1935 and 1942, respectively. Additionally, in 1943 the Cuban Advertisers Association published a list of regulations delimiting morality on radio. Nonetheless, La Comisión de Etica Radial's combined membership of advertisers, media owners, and the state gave weight to the organization and the power to regulate "morality" on the airwaves. For general information on individual stations' regulatory practices, see Cue Sierra, "El periplo de la ética en la radiodifusión cubana."

62 Fernández Paradela, "La Comisión de Etica Radial," 58.

63 See Alberto Giró, "Acuerdos adoptados por la Comisión de Etica Radial,"

Diario de la Marina, July 27, 1947, 37; Alberto Giró, "Suspenden el programa 'Cocktail Musical,'" *Diario de la Marina*; Alberto Giró, "Acuerdos adoptados por la Comisión de Etica Radial," *Diario de la Marina*, June 8, 1947, 37; Alberto Giró, "Noticias de la Dirección de Radio," *Diario de la Marina*, July 20, 1947, 37; Alberto Giró, "Tarajano no ha renunciado," *Diario de la Marina*, November 27, 1949, 18; and Alberto Giró, "Sanciones," *Diario de la Marina*, November 27, 1949, 18.

64 "Un aficionado abre el camino de la televisión en Suramerica," *Diario de la Marina*, August 6, 1944, 21; "Entregados los aparatos de televisión ocupados por la Dirección de Radio," *Diario de la Marina*, January 19, 1947, 14; Alberto Giró, "Cómo se realiza una transmisión de televisión," *Diario de la Marina*, May 4, 1947, 37; Alberto Giró, "Televisión en cantinas," *Diario de la Marina*, August 10, 1947, 37; Alberto Giró, "La música necesaria para la televisión," *Diario de la Marina*, September 28, 1947, 37; Alberto Giró, "Misterios de la televisión," *Diario de la Marina*, September 21, 1947, 37.

65 Alberto Giró, "Toscanini inicia una nueva era en la televisión," *Diario de la Marina*, November 13, 1949; Alberto Giró, "El éxito de los programas," *Diario de la Marina*, November 20, 1949; Alberto Giró, "La opera del 'Metropolitan,'" *Diario de la Marina*, November 27, 1949; Alberto Giró, "La televisión y los niños," *Diario de la Marina*, January 15, 1950; Alberto Giró, "Importancia vital de la televisión," *Diario de la Marina*, September 3, 1950; Alberto Giró, "Educación audiovisual," *Diario de la Marina*, September 29, 1950; H. Espinet Borges, "Pantalla televisora de aquí y de allá," *Carteles*, November 5, 1950; and "La NBC ofrecerá la primera ópera por televisión el domingo día 17," *Diario de la Marina*, December 12, 1950.

66 Giró, "Educación audiovisual"; Espinet Borges, "Pantalla televisora de aquí y de allá."

67 Pérez, *On Becoming Cuban*, 450.

68 Carlos Prío Socarrás, President, Manuel A. de Varona, Prime Minister, and Arturo Illas, Minister of Communication, "Reglamento para el servicio de Radio-Televisión," *Gaceta Oficial de la República de Cuba* (1950), 1587–99.

69 Socarrás, de Varona, and Illas, "Reglamento para el servicio de Radio-Televisión" (1950), 1593–94.

70 For example, in terms of jobs and expertise/knowledge, all the announcers and masters of ceremonies needed to be licensed, and only accredited doctors could address the topic of medicine.

71 de la Fuente, *A Nation for All*, 211–12.

72 According to de la Fuente, Afro-Cuban organizations and Communist leaders wanted clauses in the law that dealt directly with discrimination and the possible consequences of discriminatory actions. de la Fuente, *A Nation for All*, 214.

73 As Tasha Oren explains, the dialogues about Israeli television in the pretele-

vision era disclosed broader struggles regarding national and transnational politics, the definition of nationhood and people, and cultural-religious hierarchies. Oren, *Demon in the Box*, 3.

CHAPTER TWO. Spectacles of Progress

1 For a list of authorized television stations in Cuba in 1952, see Salwen, *Radio and Television in Cuba*, 50.

2 Walter Ames, "Snader Announces Switch to Color Production; Cuban TV Company Formed by Founce," *New York Times*, April 23, 1951, 26.

3 Unofficially, there were apparently many more, thanks to smugglers. H. Espinet Borges, "Pantalla Televisora," *Carteles*, December 24, 1950; and Alfred R. Zipser Jr., "TV-Set Smuggling Outlawed in Cuba," *New York Times*, May 29, 1953.

4 Pérez, *On Becoming Cuban*, 348.

5 See López, *La radio en Cuba*; Rivero, *Tuning Out Blackness*; Rodríguez and Tellez, *La telenovela en Colombia*; and Varela, *La televisión criolla*. For an elaborated discussion of these flows and interactions, see Rivero, "Havana as a 1940s–1950s Latin American Media Capital."

6 González-Castro, *Hasta el último aliento*.

7 Farber, *The Origins of the Cuban Revolution Reconsidered*, 7–8. See also Pérez, *Cuba*, 283–88.

8 Pérez, *On Becoming Cuban*, 450.

9 Farber, *The Origins of the Cuban Revolution Reconsidered*, 7.

10 Pérez, *Cuba*, 13. See also Farber, *The Origins of the Cuban Revolution Reconsidered*.

11 "To Regulate Broadcasting," *New York Times*, October 5, 1951, 23. See also "International Air Waves," *New York Times*, September 27, 1951, 20.

12 For information on the interconnection of U.S. and Cuban corporations, see de la Uz, *Los monopolios extranjeros en Cuba 1898–1958*.

13 Schwock, *Global TV*.

14 Cohen, *A Consumers' Republic*, 127.

15 See, for example, Coontz, *The Way We Never Were*; Spigel, *Make Room for TV*.

16 In the words of Anna McCarthy, "Television's structural separation from the federal government, coupled with its diverse modes of address, made the medium seem like an ideal tool for nondirective persuasion." Via the leadership of industry officials and philanthropists, television would guide the U.S. citizens to an understanding of contemporary social, political, and economic issues while keeping a distance from the state. McCarthy, *The Citizen Machine*, 24.

17 Cohen, *A Consumers' Republic*, 127.

18 For an extensive historical analysis of U.S.-Cuba relations before 1959, see Pérez, *On Becoming Cuban*.

19 Pérez-Stable, "Reflections on Political Possibilities."

20 Some of the new sections included "Tele-Radiolandia" (*Bohemia*); "Pantalla Tele-visora" (*Carteles*); "Radio y Televisión" (*Diario de la Marina*); and "Radio-TV" (*Gente de la Semana*).

21 Alberto Giró, "Primer programa 'TV,'" *Diario de la Marina*, October 19, 1950, 15.

22 Alberto Giró, "Micro-Onda," *Diario de la Marina*, October 25, 1950, 15.

23 Alberto Giró, "El éxito de los programas," *Diario de la Marina*, November 20, 1949.

24 Alberto Giró, "Como se realiza una transmisión de televisión," *Diario de la Marina*, May 4, 1947, 37; Herbert Asbury, "Televisión por teléfono," *Bohemia*, August 3, 1947, 10–11, 83.

25 Some journalists saw the baseball broadcast as the main cause for the rapid sale of television sets in Cuba. According to a journalist, after the end of the baseball series, television owners needed to pay attention to their shows and create "interesting programs" to stimulate the acquisition of more sets. See Alberto Giró, "Pelota por televisión," *Diario de la Marina*, November 1, 1950, 15; Carlos Guzmán, "Un golpe para la TV," *Gente de la Semana*, February 25, 1951, 40.

26 H. Espinet Borges, "Oyendo Radio," *Carteles*, September 24, 1950.

27 Alberto Giró, "No hay derecho," *Diario de la Marina*, March 21, 1951.

28 H. Espinet Borges, "Oyendo Radio," *Carteles*, December 3, 1950; and Alberto Giró, "Estudio 15," *Diario de la Marina*, September 7, 1951.

29 Alberto Giró, "El teatro del lunes," *Diario de la Marina*, August 1, 1951, 2.

30 The first telenovela was broadcast on the program *La novela en TV*, a short-lived show that was canceled in 1953. Plans to move the genre to prime time began in 1954 when Televisión Nacional discussed its objective to produce thirty-minute-long telenovelas, broadcast Monday through Friday, one month per telenovela. By 1956, telenovelas were one of the most popular genres on Cuban television. Emma Pérez, "Televerdades," *Gente de la Semana*, January 10, 1953; "Una dura prueba," *Bohemia*, September 26, 1954, 48; "Survey de TV," *Bohemia*, September 16, 1956, 40.

31 Alberto Giró, "'La novela en televisión' inaugurada ayer por CMQ-TV," *Diario de la Marina*, October 3, 1952, 12.

32 Alberto Giró, "La novela por video será programa básico," *Diario de la Marina*, November 23, 1952, 38.

33 Another example of this was the successful radio drama *La familia Pilón*, which, according to one critic, in its radio version discussed heated contemporary topics and on television turned out to be a "boring and moralizing sketch." M. Rodríguez Alemán, "Una catilinaria sobre el hogar," *Gente de la Semana*, June 24, 1951, 38. See also M. Rodríguez Alemán, "Los tres movimientos de la estupidez," *Gente de la Semana*, August 19, 1951, 41.

34 Emma Montenegro, "El gran teatro 'Esso,'" *Gente de la Semana*, April 27, 1952, 43.

35 Alberto Giró, "Carta abierta a todos los que trabajan en television," *Diario de la Marina*, October 31, 1952, 12; Alberto Giró, "Carta abierta y sincera a los artistas de video," *Diario de la Marina*, May 28, 1952, 15.

36 "La tensión estaba en el canal," *Bohemia*, February 4, 1951; and Alberto Giró, "Estudio 15," *Diario de la Marina*, April 6, 1951.

37 H. Espinet Borges, "Con artistas cubanos, ¿por qué no?," *Carteles*, April 29, 1951.

38 "Yo copio, tu copias, el copia," *Bohemia*, July 8, 1951.

39 Emma Pérez, "Más televerdades," *Gente de la Semana*, December 13, 1953, 43–44.

40 The unauthorized translation created a heated debate between Desi Arnaz and the author of the Cuban version, an event that was addressed in the Cuban press. H. Espinet Borges, "'Mi Esposo Favorito' 'I Love Lucy,'" *Carteles*, August 16, 1953; H. Espinet Borges, "'I Love Lucy'? . . . No!-dice Condall," *Carteles*, August 23, 1953.

41 Pérez, "Más televerdades."

42 Alberto Giró, "'Ante La Prensa,' por la CMQ-TV, esta noche, El Doctor Rafael Guas Inclán," *Diario de la Marina*, October 14, 1951, 39.

43 Castro, *Hasta el último aliento*.

44 As Jesús Martín Barbero observes, the historical circumstances that shaped Latin American nation-states and their political development (long periods under colonial rule, economic dependency, neocolonialism, and struggles to incorporate the popular classes into the political project) influenced their path toward modernization. Martín Barbero, *Communication, Culture and Hegemony*, 150–51. For information on media practices in the post-1990 period, see Venegas, *Digital Dilemmas*.

45 "Big TV Strides Seen in Latin America," *New York Times*, October 6, 1951.

46 Farber, *The Origins of the Cuban Revolution Reconsidered*, 21.

47 See, for example, "Televisión," *Bohemia*, April 9, 1950, 56; "Televisión en 1950," *Bohemia*, May 21, 1950, 92; "Goar Mestre hablará sobre televisión en el Aula Magna de La Universidad," *Diario de la Marina*, January 6, 1950, 37; "La Export Adv. Ass. concede un nuevo honor al Sr. Goar Mestre," *Diario de la Marina*, May 4, 1951, 38.

48 According to the critics, by mid-1951, Unión Radio-TV excelled in the technological aspects of television, while CMQ-TV had produced superb dramatic series and the best variety show (*Cabaret Regalias*). This disparity between technology and programming was a key aspect in Gaspar Pumarejo's inability to financially sustain his station. Due to the lack of sponsorship and Pumarejo's extensive debt, he sold Unión Radio-TV (channel 4) to movie producer

Manolo Alonzo in August 1951. In 1952, Manolo Alonzo sold the station to Radiotelevisora El Mundo S.A. See Alberto Giró, "Confirmó M. Alonso la compra de Unión Radio y U. Radio TV," *Diario de la Marina*, July 31, 1951; "Les presento al nuevo presidente de Unión Radio," *Bohemia*, August 5, 1951; Alberto Giró, "Vendidas Unión Radio y Unión Radio TV al Canal 2," *Diario de la Marina*, April 10, 1952, 15.

49 Radiocentro was first inaugurated in 1948, and the building was constructed for CMQ-Radio studios. Described as possessing the "most modern recording equipment," the new facilities were instrumental to the production of programming and exportation across the region. See González, *Llorar es un placer*, 119; and González, *El más humano de los autores*, 128–29.

50 "Anuario," *Circuito* CMQ, Industry Papers, March 1951, Centro de Investigaciones del Instituto Cubano de Radio y Televisión, Havana, Cuba.

51 CMQ-TV expanded to Santa Clara, Camaguey, and Santiago de Cuba. Alberto Giró, "La primera etapa de exhibiciones de UR-TV por la república ha constituído un emocionante éxito," *Diario de la Marina*, May 20, 1951, 49; H. Espinet Borges, "Un 'coup de chapeau' para Gaspar Pumarejo," *Carteles*, May 20, 1951, 23; "La carrera por la televisión," *Bohemia*, June 3, 1951, 37–38, 79.

52 Alberto Giró, "Primera cadena de televisión en la América Latina," *Diario de la Marina*, March 9, 1952, 38; Alberto Giró, "Quedo inaugurado ayer el servicio de CMQ-TV en toda la república," *Diario de la Marina*, March 9, 1952, 38.

53 "La TV en el Interior," *Bohemia*, June 15, 1952, 48; "La carta de la semana," *Bohemia*, October 25, 1953, 43; "La carta de la semana," *Bohemia*, November 22, 1953, 44, 110; "La carta de la semana," *Bohemia*, December 6, 1953, 46, 98.

54 Himpele, *Circuits of Culture*, 47.

55 "La carta de la semana," *Bohemia*, October 7, 1952, 52, 113; "La carta de la semana," *Bohemia*, October 12, 1952, 49, 111; "La carta de la semana," *Bohemia*, March 8, 1953, 44–83; "La carta de la semana," *Bohemia*, April 5, 1953.

56 The impact was measured via ratings. La Asociación de Anunciantes de Cuba (The Association of Cuban Advertisers) began to perform television surveys in 1953 and conducted the surveys four times per year: in February, May, August, and November. For shows longer than fifteen minutes, the sample included four hundred interviews. For thirty-minute shows or programs that were longer than thirty minutes, the sample included six hundred interviews. Rey, *A dónde va la televisión cubana?*, 29.

57 "Alarma en la emisora," *Bohemia*, June 17, 1951, 52–53; "Tarifas mínimas de televisión," *Bohemia*, April 29, 1951, 46; and H. Espinet Borges, "Noticulas," *Carteles*, January 6, 1952, 71. In 1954, a union devoted exclusively to radio and television actors was formed. See "El CRAC y la ACAT," *Bohemia*, June 13, 1954, 44–46. It is important to mention that prerevolutionary Cuba was characterized by strong labor organizations in all industries, including the arts. Actors,

circus performers, radio announcers, rumba dancers, and scriptwriters (to mention a few) had organizations such as the Cuban Association of Theater Artists; the Circle of Cuban Actors; the Association of Radio, Film, and Television Authors; and the Union of Radio and Television Operators. In 1959, when the revolutionary government initiated the takeover of broadcasting businesses tied to Fulgencio Batista's regime, theater and television labor leaders were in charge of reorganizing the confiscated television networks. For general information on union and creative talent, see López, *La radio en Cuba*.

58 The company obtained the exclusive television rights of 80 percent of the Mexican production of motion pictures for a period of ten years, and four years of TV rights for six hundred films already produced by Argentina's Sonofilm. Ames, "Snader Announces."

59 "La carta de la semana," *Bohemia*, October 25, 1953, 43; "La carta de la semana," *Bohemia*, November 22, 1953, 44, 110; "La carta de la semana," *Bohemia*, December 6, 1953, 46, 98.

60 "Análisis desde la lejanía," *Bohemia*, December 7, 1952.

61 Aldino Sanchez, "Cascabeles blindados," *Gente de la Semana*, March 23, 1952, 40.

62 "La carta de la semana," *Bohemia*, January 4, 1953, 38, 97; "La carta de la semana," *Bohemia*, January 18, 1953, 40, 81.

63 "La carta de la semana," *Bohemia*, December 2, 1952.

64 "La carta de la semana," *Bohemia*, December 2, 1952.

65 Here I am making a direct reference to Fernando Ortiz's *Contrapunteo cubano del tabaco y la azúcar*, in which the author establishes a distinction between the non-Western and communal elements of tobacco production and the Western, capitalist, and imperialist processes that defined the sugar economy. For an analysis of *Contrapunteo*, see Arroyo, *Travestismos culturales*.

66 A special thanks to Lillian Guerra and Vivian Martínez Tabares for their insightful comments about Pinar del Río.

67 For an analysis of the population distribution throughout Cuban rural and urban areas, see González Suárez, "La discriminación racial en el campo cubano."

68 "Mensaje a los pinareños," *Bohemia*, December 28, 1952.

69 "Mensaje a los pinareños."

70 H. Espinet Borges, "El 10 de marzo en radio y TV," *Carteles*, March 23, 1952, 22. Aware of radio's reach across the island, Batista used radio the day of the coup to communicate with the Cuban people.

71 Alberto Giró, "Quedo inaugurado ayer el servicio de CMQ-TV en toda la república," *Diario de la Marina*, March 9, 1952, 38.

72 For general information on Batista's censorship, see Gastón Baquero, "Derecho y revés de un incidente," *Diario de la Marina*, May 7, 1952, 4; Alberto Giró,

"Clausuran Unión Radio por 24 horas," *Diario de la Marina*, August 5, 1952, 14; Alberto Giró, "No televisaran mas los domingos 'Ante la Prensa,'" *Diario de la Marina*, October 1, 1952, 1; "Dispensa una calida acogida al Bloque de prensa para arribar a una solución cubana," *Diario de la Marina*, October 16, 1952, 1, 6; "Esperan los políticos la actitud e iniciativa del Bloque cubano de prensa," *Diario de la Marina*, October 21, 1952, 1, 25; "Responde el jefe del estado mayor, General Batista, a la exhortación patriótica del Bloque de prensa," *Diario de la Marina*, October 19, 1952, 1; "Bloque cubano de prensa: A la opinión pública," *Diario de la Marina*, November 8, 1952, 1, 14–15.

73 Salwen, *Radio and Television in Cuba*, 94.

74 Salwen, *Radio and Television in Cuba*, 93–107.

75 "Como protesta por la censura previa no exhibirán los cines mas noticiarios del extranjero," *Diario de la Marina*, May 13, 1953, 1, 18; Rodolfo Rodríguez Zaldivar, "La censura previa: Prensa, cine, radio y televisión unidos contra la impopular medida," *Bohemia*, May 17, 1953; "El 'rollo' de 'Audiencia pública,'" *Bohemia*, June 7, 1953, 43–44; H. Espinet Borges, "'Ante La Prensa': Fin de otra etapa," *Carteles*, June 7, 1953, 23.

76 Ameringer, "The Auténtico Party and the Political Opposition in Cuba, 1952–1957."

77 H. Espinet Borges, "Ley de Radio y TV," *Carteles*, January 17, 1954, 22.

78 "Aconseja Goar Mestre tener la radio y la TV alejadas del gbno," *Diario de la Marina*, March 23, 1954; "Expone progresos de radio y televisión en América Latina," *El Mundo*, March 23, 1954.

79 "Responde el jefe del estado mayor."

80 Fulgencio Batista, President, and Pablo Cabrera Jústiz, Minister of Communication, "Comunicaciones y Transportes," *Gaceta Oficial de la República de Cuba* (1953), 7.

81 "Sugerencia a La Ley Radial," *Diario de la Marina*, October 9, 1952, 4.

82 Cuban advertisers placed audiences into five categories. Class A was part of the upper crust of Cuban society. It had all the luxury and financial resources. Class B had comfort and some of the luxuries available to Class A, such as appliances, a maid, and a car. People in Class B, however, lacked the financial resources of those in Class A. The people who constituted Class C might have lived in a small house or apartment. They did not have any luxuries, although they had basic appliances such as a refrigerator, radio, and television. Class D had a very low level of comfort, with limited appliances and no car. This class was financially strapped. Finally, Class E represented the poorest sector of Cuban society. *Investigación de televisión verificada en poblaciones de 25,000 o más habitantes*, unpublished report (Havana: Asociación de Anunciantes de Cuba, 1959), Centro de Investigaciones del Instituto Cuban de Radio y Televisión, Havana, Cuba.

83 Batista and Cabrera Jústiz, "Comunicaciones y Transportes" (1953).

84 Batista and Cabrera Jústiz, "Comunicaciones y Transportes" (1953), 8.

85 Batista and Cabrera Jústiz, "Comunicaciones y Transportes" (1953), 6.

86 It should be noted that the plans for Telemundo were initiated in 1952. For information on Havana's television expansion, see "Se nutre por día el staff del Canal 2," *Diario de la Marina*, May 4, 1952, 38; "Cinco canales de un tiro," *Bohemia*, February 8, 1953, 42; H. Espinet Borges, "Canal 4: Ahora TV Nacional Canal 2: Ahora TV Panorama," *Carteles*, October 11, 1953, 23; "Otro canal: El 11," *Bohemia*, October 11, 1953, 44; "Cuba's 5th TV Station Opens," *New York Times*, November 12, 1953, 43; "La inauguración de 'TV Caribe,'" *Carteles*, November 22, 1953; Alberto Giró, "Canal 11, bienvenido," *Carteles*, November 8, 1953.

87 Estanislao Vega-Caballero, "En radiotelefonía, Cuba, ahora, es uno de los países más avanzados," *Diario de la Marina*, October 4, 1952, 8.

88 Pérez, *On Becoming Cuban*, 420.

89 "Panorama de nuestra TV," *Bohemia*, February 21, 1954, 46, 42–43.

90 Eduardo Mora-Basart, "Apuntes para una historia del Canal 2," *En Vivo: Revista Cubana de Radio y Televisión*, accessed June 2012, http://www.envivo.icrt.cu/memorias/206-apuntes-para-una-historia-del-canal-2.

91 For information on programming cancelations and the television crisis, see "Decisión firme," *Bohemia* 46, June 13, 1954, 44; "La mocha en el aire," *Bohemia* 46, December 17, 1954, 46–47. For information on the 1954 crisis, see also "Cartabón," *Ataja*, March 18, 1954; "Cartabón," *Ataja*, May 22 1954; "Confetis," *Carteles*, March 14, 1954, 52; "Liquidado El Canal 11," *Prensa Libre*, May 14, 1954; Roberto Baez-Miro, "Desaparecera la competencia en nuestro video?," *Cinema*, January 17, 1954; Roberto Baez-Miro, "Infausto cumplimiento de un augurio," *Cinema*, May 8, 1954; F. Meluza Otero, "La crisis y unos comentarios," *Alerta*, May 3, 1954.

92 Rivero, "Havana as a 1940s–1950s Latin American Media Capital."

93 *Television: A World Survey*, 50.

94 Kapcia, *Havana*; Rojas, *La máquina del olvido*; Scarpaci, Segre, and Coyula, *Havana*; Sublette, *Cuba and Its Music*.

CHAPTER THREE. Spectacles of Decency

1 Alberto Giró, *Diario de la Marina*, September 7, 1950.

2 Similar debates regarding high and low culture in relation to radio's and television's educational potential took place in the United States. See, for example, Douglas, *Inventing American Broadcasting 1899–1902*; Hilmes, *Radio Voices*; and Keeler, "'Sugar Coat the Educational Pill.'"

3 Bourdieu, *Distinction*, 483.

4 *Television: A World Survey*, 49–50.

5 *Television: A World Survey*, 49–50.

6 In both periods, many of the educational radio conferences were published in the magazine *Cuadernos de la Universidad de Aire*. Garcés, *Los dueños del aíre*; 73–74; López, *La radio en Cuba*, 333–36.

7 *Television: A World Survey*, 49.

8 Alberto Giró, "Un comentario justificado," *Diario de la Marina*, June 14, 1951, 2; Alberto Giró, "Mañana lunes ofrecerá UR-TV una hora completa de teatro con 'El pecado de ayer' de L. Blanco," *Diario de la Marina*, July 29, 1951, 59; Mayra Cue Sierra, "Las Zarzuelas de Ernesto Lecuona llegan a la televisión cubana," *Cubarte: El portal de la cultura cubana*, March 31, 2007; Mayra Cue Sierra, "Las puntas y los giros llegan a la pantalla cubana," *Cubarte: El portal de la cultura cubana*, December 1, 2004.

9 Alberto Giró, "Menciones de honor de la semana en televisión," *Diario de la Marina*, February 13, 1955, 2-C.

10 Rojas, *La máquina del olvido*, 48.

11 Stoler, *Carnal Knowledge and Imperial Power*, 54.

12 See Pérez, *Cuba*; Pérez-Stable, "La transición pacífica que no tuvo lugar (1954–1956)"; Sáenz Rovner, *The Cuban Connection*.

13 Alberto Giró, "Peligrosa perspectiva," *Diario de la Marina*, December 5, 1950.

14 Giró, "Peligrosa perspectiva."

15 See Foucault, *The History of Sexuality, Vol. 2: The Use of Pleasure*; and Taylor, *Modern Social Imaginaries*.

16 In the 1940s, the rumba performed in upper-class casino cabaret shows went through various transformations to restructure traditional, noncommercial rumba's sexual musical and dance expressions. Moore, *Nationalizing Blackness*, 169, 185, 187.

17 Stoler, *Race and the Education of Desire*, 97. While Stoler's reinterpretation of Michel Foucault's *The History of Sexuality, Vol. 2: The Use of Pleasure* centers on Europe and its colonies, her analysis of bourgeois sexuality and racialized sexuality pertains to Cuban modernity.

18 Stoler, *Race and the Education of Desire*, 97.

19 Alberto Giró, "Auge de la televisión en Cuba," *Diario de la Marina*, December 15, 1950.

20 Alberto Giró, "Más respeto," *Diario de la Marina*, January 26, 1951.

21 As several scholars and music critics note, variety shows became important venues for Afro-Cuban musicians and musical styles. See Moore, *Nationalizing Blackness*; and Sublette, *Cuba and Its Music*.

22 "Survey sobre TV," *Bohemia*, February 18, 1951.

23 H. Espinet Borges, "Otra vez el 'survey' de video," *Carteles*, April 1, 1951; "Revelaciones de un 'survey,'" *Bohemia*, April 6, 1952; and "Los mejores programas de TV," *Carteles*, August 9, 1953.

24 "Survey de televisión," *Bohemia*, March 14, 1954, 48; "Una prueba que poco prueba," *Bohemia*, September 26, 1954, 44.

25 During television's first year, the CRE remained practically silent. In a January 1951 article, the Commission's president indicated that the organization was in the process of developing rules specifically designed for television. "Actuación y nuevos objetivos de la 'Comisión de Etica Radial' y el comisionado Dr. Tarajano," *Diario de la Marina*, January 7, 1951.

26 "Momentos terribles en la vida de un productor," *Bohemia*, June 22, 1952. See also "Un propósito y dos noticias," *Bohemia*, June 26, 1952; and "Planes en cartelera," *Bohemia*, July 6, 1952.

27 For information on sexual norms and women's rights before and after 1959, see Hamilton, *Sexual Revolutions in Cuba*; Stoner, *From the House to the Streets*.

28 Hamilton, *Sexual Revolutions in Cuba*, 25. The quotation is in reference to Mirta de la Torre Mulhare's analysis of sexual practices prior to the Cuban Revolution. de la Torre Mulhare, "Sexual Ideology in Pre–Castro Cuba."

29 McClintock, *Imperial Leather*, 5.

30 "La TV sobre el tapete," *Bohemia*, May 3, 1953.

31 "La TV sobre el tapete."

32 "La TV sobre el tapete." See also "Dos suspensiones," *Bohemia*, May 24, 1953.

33 While the CRE had suspended male performers because of their use of "inappropriate language and gestures," none of the regulations and suspensions were related to men being presented as sensual-sexual objects. See "Dos suspensions."

34 Wade, *Music, Race, and Nation*, 23.

35 Kutzinski, *Sugar's Secrets*, 11.

36 Sommer, *Foundational Fictions*. As Alejandro de la Fuente writes, Fulgencio Batista's nonwhiteness was a contested issue for the U.S. government and the Cuban elite. See de la Fuente, *A Nation for All*, 208, 253.

37 Podalsky, "Guajiras, mulatas y puros cubanos."

38 Kinescope is "a film made of a live television broadcast." O'Dell, "Kinescope," 1263.

39 "La TV sobre el tapete."

40 "La carta de la semana," *Bohemia*, March 28, 1954, 46, 109.

41 "Acuerdo de la Comisión de Ética Radial," *Prensa Libre*, October 10, 1954; H. Espinet Borges, "El beso en televisión," *Carteles*, October 24, 1954, 53; Alberto Giró, "La Comisión de Ética y los espectáculos contrarios a la civilización," *Diario de la Marina*, October 18, 1954; Alberto Giró, "Coreografías sobre creencias o cultos contrarios a la civilización," *Diario de la Marina*, October 26, 1954; "Memoria para refrescar la memoria," *Bohemia*, April 17, 1955, 46.

42 "Memoria para refrescar la memoria," *Bohemia*, April 17, 1955.

43 Alberto Giró, "Coreografías sobre creencias o cultos contrarios a la civilización," *Diario de la Marina*, October 26, 1954.

44 Sublette, *Cuba and Its Music*, 205. For information about mainstream prejudice against Abakuá, see Moore, *Music and Revolution*; and Vélez, *Drumming for the Gods*.

45 Moore, *Music and Revolution*, 172.

46 Moore, *Music and Revolution*, 38.

47 Moore, *Music and Revolution*, 200.

48 A unique television venue for black singers was Sepia café, a prime-time music show that began to air in 1954. Broadcast on Telemundo (channel 2), Sepia café included renowned black musicians such as Celia Cruz, Benny Moré, and Bola de Nieve.

49 Alberto Giró, "Noticias de la Dirección de Radio," *Diario de la Marina*, July 20, 1947, 37; H. Espinet Borges, "Censurada," *Carteles*, November 14, 1954, 56.

50 Alberto Giró, "El beso en televisión," *Diario de la Marina*, February 16, 1955, 14-A; "Veto al beso," *Bohemia*, April 24, 1955, 40–43.

51 "El Ministro enjuicia y el comisionado responde," *Bohemia*, May 1, 1955, 46, 98.

52 It should be noted that the Ministry of Communication began a sporadic suspension of artists (mostly dancers) in 1954. See "Cartabón," *Ataja*, February 21, 1954; "Memoria para refrescar la memoria," *Bohemia*, April 17, 1955, 46, 95; "Verdades," *Carteles*, July 10, 1955, 52; "Verdades," *Carteles*, August 7, 1955, 52.

53 Alberto Giró, "Resumen de la semana en radio y video," *Diario de la Marina*, June 22, 1952.

54 Another strategy Giró used was to write articles about the work done by U.S. organizations (such as the National Association of Educational Broadcasters) to promote educational programs and the popularity of dramatic series (such as Studio One and Television Playhouse) for the U.S. audience. Alberto Giró, "Más programas dramatizados reclama la TV nacional," *Diario de la Marina*, June 29, 1952; "Los programas dramáticos en la televisión," *Diario de la Marina*, October 19, 1952; "Tres comentarios dominicales," *Diario de la Marina*, November 9, 1952; "La enseñanza de la historia mediante la radio y la TV," *Diario de la Marina*, August 9, 1952, 12; "Necesidad y conveniencia de programas patrióticos," *Diario de la Marina*, December 17, 1952; "En torno al programa del Ministerio de Educación," *Diario de la Marina*, January 13, 1953. Giró was also in favor of informative shows. See "En torno a la 'Mesa Redonda' de CMQ-Televisión," *Diario de la Marina*, October 22, 1952.

55 Emma Pérez, "Televerdades," *Gente de la Semana*, December 28, 1952. 40. See also "Una hora de arte y cultura," *Gente de la Semana*, July 20, 1952.

56 Emma Pérez, "TV y bomba atómica," *Bohemia*, July 24, 1955, 56, 90; Emma Pérez, "Boing Boing, Bla Bla, Cuá Cuá (Clac!)," *Bohemia*, August 21, 1955, 48–49. See also "¿Está usted a favor o en contra de la TV?," *Bohemia*, August 7, 1955, 62–75; "Cada 'camarilla intocable' es una conspiración contra la democracia," *Bohemia*, August 28, 1955, 48, 82; "De usted también diremos algo . . . ,"

Bohemia, September 18, 1955, 53, 93; "En Cuba no se ha librado una campaña contra la televisión," *Bohemia*, November 27, 1955, 56, 97; "Nuestra televisión no seguirá igual: Seguirá peor," *Bohemia*, September 25, 1955, 52.

57 Emma Pérez, "En Italia se exige a la televisión que contribuya a la cultura," *Bohemia*, July 24, 1955, 57; "Invasión de hormigas del trópico por TV!!!," *Bohemia*, September 4, 1955, 51–52; "Nuestra televisión no seguirá igual: Seguirá peor," *Bohemia*, September 25, 1955, 52; "En Cuba no se ha librado una campaña contra la televisión," *Bohemia*, November 27, 1955, 56, 97. See also "10,000 receptores en Francia," *Gente de la Semana*, July 23, 1953, 20–21.

58 Enrique Nuñez Rodríguez, "Verdades," *Carteles*, August 7, 1955, 52.

59 H. Espinet Borges, "Oyendo radio," *Carteles*, June 21, 1953.

60 "Memoria para refrescar la memoria," *Bohemia*, April 17, 1955, 46, 95.

61 Emma Pérez, "O la TV se democratiza, o será la primera víctima del totalitarismo 1955," *Bohemia*, December 4, 1955, 62, 92.

62 Emma Pérez, "Que puede mejorar nuestra TV?," *Bohemia*, August 14, 1955, 52. See also Emma Pérez, "Los errores de la democracia se curan con más democracia," *Bohemia*, November 13, 1955.

63 "Festejaron los Leones de modo brillante el 'Día de la publicidad,'" *Diario de la Marina*, June 29, 1955, front page, 22-A.

64 "Brillantísimo homenaje del Club Rotario al 'Día de la Publicidad,'" *Diario de la Marina*, June 24, 1955, front page, 14-A. See also "Dedica al Día de la Publicidad su editorial El Noticiero CMQ," *Diario de la Marina*, June 24, 1955, 3-A.

65 "Creada por decreto la oficina para reprimir en Cuba el comunismo," *Diario de la Marina*, May 5, 1955, front page, 10-B.

66 The topic of morality in entertainment programming took center stage in Cuba's public sphere when producer Gaspar Pumarejo questioned the methodology Cuba's Association of Advertisers used to conduct its surveys. Indirectly accusing the organization of favoring CMQ-TV's programming, Pumarejo described high-rated shows as immoral and as promoting social malaise. See Alfredo Pedraza, "Hablan los anunciantes sobre los surveys," *Diario de la Marina*, March 20, 1955, 1-C; Gaspar Pumarejo, "Los surveys de la Asociación de Anunciantes," *Diario de la Marina*, March 20, 1955, 1-C.

67 Enrique Nuñez Rodríguez, "Verdades," *Carteles*, April 24, 1955, 52.

68 Enrique Nuñez Rodríguez, "Un organismo Innecesario," *Carteles*, July 31, 1955, 52.

69 According to Louis A. Pérez, many citizens were worried about Cuba's "economic dislocation" due to the island's mono-economy. Pérez, *Cuba*, 295.

70 Pérez-Stable, "La transición pacífica que no tuvo lugar (1954–1956)."

71 Pérez-Stable, "La transición pacífica que no tuvo lugar (1954–1956)," 293.

72 Enrique Nuñez Rodríguez, "Verdades," *Carteles*, November 13, 1955, 52.

73 Instead of being confined only to television sections, the discussion about the

possibility of instituting the Comisión Revisora de los Programas Novelizados Radiales y Televisados took center stage in newspapers and magazines. See Emma Pérez's previously cited articles and "Terminó anoche la información sobre radio y televisión," *Diario de la Marina*, November 2, 1955, front page, 8-A.

74 For a description of what the CRE considered immoral and for a list of the types of acts suspended by the organization, see Juan José Tarrajano, "Cuidadosa labor que efectúa la Comisión de Ética Radial y TV," *Diario de la Marina*, April 28, 1955, 1-B.

75 "Cuida comunicaciones del nivel moral en los programas de TV," *Diario de la Marina*, March 25, 1955, 1-A.

76 "Cartabón," *Ataja*, February 21, 1954; "Memoria para refrescar la memoria," *Bohemia*, April 17, 1955, 46, 95; "Verdades," *Carteles*, July 10, 1955, 52; "Verdades," *Carteles*, August 7, 1955, 52.

77 Juan José Tarrajano, "Cuidadosa labor que efectúa la Comisión de Ética Radial y TV," *Diario de la Marina*, April 28, 1955, 1-B. According to Alberto Giró, the Afro-Cuban performances were indecent and lowered the cultural level of Cuban television. See "Bajó esta semana el nivel cultural de la televisión," *Diario de la Marina*, March 26, 1955, 16-A.

78 Alberto Giró, "Algunos programas infantiles y la salud moral de los niños," *Diario de la Marina*, January 4, 1955, 20-A.

79 "Más tela y menos malla," *Bohemia*, June 12, 1955, 44–45. As discussed earlier, rumbas and other Afro-Cuban rhythms were transformed before their commercialization; therefore, the adulteration mentioned by the *Bohemia* critic had already taken place before musicians and dancers appeared on television. Nonetheless, what is particularly interesting about the critic's comments is not only the denunciation of the Ministry of Communication and the CRE's racist ruling but also the way in which he saw the "African influence" as a key factor in Cuban music's popularity outside Cuba. However, in the case of the United States, the Afro-Cuban musical styles entered the mainstream through a performative racial cleansing. That is, many of the musicians and performers who popularized the rhythms—particularly in film and television—were white men (e.g., Desi Arnaz and Xavier Cugat). Thus, even as black and white Cuban musicians were part of the Cuban musical craze, only the commercialized Afro–Cuban musical and dance rhythms performed by white males entered U.S. mainstream culture. Consequently, though the performative racial cleansing processes were different, the adulteration mentioned by the *Bohemia* critic occurred in both countries. For information on Cuban music's popularity in U.S. mainstream and Latino communities, see Macias, *Mexican American Mojo*; Roberts, *The Latin Tinge*; and Abreu, "Authentic Assertions, Commercial Concessions."

80 Dianteill and Swearingern, "From Hierography to Ethnography and Back." See also the articles about Lydia Cabrera published in the Cuban magazine *Extramuros: De la ciudad, imagen, y palabra.*

81 See González Echevarría, *Cuban Fiestas*, chap. 4.

82 Alberto Giró, "Algunos programas infantiles y la salud moral de los niños," *Diario de la Marina*, January 4, 1955, 20-A.

83 Alberto Giró, "La intervención artística de los niños en la televisión cubana," *Diario de la Marina*, June 17, 1955.

84 "Nos dicen, decimos," *Bohemia*, January 22, 1956, 40; "Ni voces ni sonrisas infantiles," *Bohemia*, June 26, 1955, 42–43.

85 Pirula, Mamacusa, and Prematura were the three characters performed by men. Some reviewers believed that the focus on Pirula, the first character to be eliminated, resulted from the CRE's favoritism toward CMQ-TV, the network where the other two characters appeared.

86 Sifuentes-Jáuregui, *Transvestism, Masculinity and Latin American Literature*, 12.

87 "Fijes y Corridos," *Bohemia*, March 25, 1956, 50.

88 Sieg, *Ethnic Drag*, 85.

89 See Enrique Nuñez Rodríguez, "Verdades," *Carteles*, April 10, 1955, 52; "Resolución inesperada," *Bohemia*, April 22, 1956, 46–47; Enrique Nuñez Rodríguez, "Verdades," *Carteles*, May 6, 1956, 52; "Allá no es como aquí," *Bohemia*, June 10, 1956, 47; "Resumen de 1956," *Bohemia*, December 30, 1956, 52–56, 80.

90 "Expone la Legión de la Decencia el auge que toma el vicio en Cuba," *Diario de la Marina*, August 24, 1956, 3-A.

91 "Expone la Legión de la Decencia el auge que toma el vicio en Cuba," 3-A.

92 Scarpaci, Segre, and Coyula, *Havana*, 14.

93 "Reclaman otra legislación para la revisión cinematográfica," *Diario de la Marina*, October 11, 1955, 1-A, 10-B. For information about the Catholic Church's involvement in movie censorship and the government-run movie organization, see Mercedes Alemán, "'Prohibida para menores' como actúa la Comisión Revisora De Películas," *Vanidades*, February 3, 1955, 14, 129; Ramos, "Cine e Iglesia Católica en Cuba (1934–1950)," 106–24.

94 See the reproduction of *Leyes del Gobierno Provisional de la Revolución*, tomo XIII, Editorial Lex, La Habana, Octobre de 1959, 59–69, and notes in http://manuelzayas.wordpress.com/ley-no-589-comision-peliculas; Feeney, "Hollywood in Havana."

95 Feeney, "Hollywood in Havana," chap. 5.

96 Feeney, "Hollywood in Havana."

97 "El cine en los teatros y en la televisión," *Diario de la Marina*, August 1, 1956, 4-A; "Una peleita limpia," *Carteles*, June 24, 1956, 53; Enrique Nuñez Rodríguez, "Verdades," *Carteles*, October 28, 1956, 52.

98 The mayor of Havana began to "clean" the city in 1955 by closing several sex-

related places. "Clausurados por la alcaldía 6 nuevos antros de inmoralidad," *Diario de la Marina*, March 4, 1955, 1-A. "Una comisión coordinadora para fiscalizar la radio y televisión," *Diario de la Marina*, June 8, 1956, 1-A.

99 "Suspenden películas en el Canal 7 de TV," *El Crisol*, February 8, 1957; "Suspende Vasconcelos 2 programas de TV, por estimarlos inmorales," *Avance*, February 21, 1957; "Han prohibido el rock and roll en programa de TV," *Diario de la Marina*, February 14, 1957; "Miscelanias," *Información*, February 15, 1957; Alejandro Roque, "La guerra al rock and roll: Aldeanismo y arteriosclerosis contra optimismo y Juventud," *Bohemia*, March 5, 1957; "Suspende el ministro de comunicaciones un programa de televisión," *Diario de la Marina*, March 13, 1957; "Suspenden 15 transmisiones de una novela transmitida por CMQ-TV," *Avance*, March 15, 1957; "Suspenden en TV a una bailarina y una modelo," *El Mundo*, April 12, 1957; "No hay fuerza moral!," *Gente de la Semana*, April 7, 1957; "Suspende Vasconcelos 5 actuaciones por TV de la bailarina Ana Gloria," *Avance*, April 8, 1957; "Nos dicen," *Bohemia*, April 28, 1957, 56; "Suspendidos dos programas de TV," *El País*, May 12, 1957; "Suspende Vasconcelos programas televisados que ofenden a la moral," *Diario de la Marina*, May 23, 1957; Ramón Vasconcelos, "Revolución de micrófono," *Alerta*, July 6, 1957.

100 See Emma Pérez, "'A crecer, pueblos de America Latina!'" *Bohemia*, June 16, 1957, 36–37; Andrés Valdespino, "Cuba se nos llena de hampones y tahures," *Bohemia*, February 16, 1958, 63.

101 Stoler, *Carnal Knowledge and Imperial Power*, 44.

102 García-Pérez, *Insurrection and Revolution*, 78. For an analysis of students' political mobilization against Batista, see Bronfman, "'Batista Is Dead.'"

103 "La Federación De Radioemisores formula enérgica protesta," *Diario de la Marina*, January 24, 1956, 18-A; "Libres de revisión a partir de mañana diarios y revistas," *Diario de la Marina*, June 2, 1956, 1-A.

104 "Fidel Castro y seis cubanos más, arrestados en la capital Azteca," *Diario de la Marina*, June 23, 1956; "Querían atentar contra la vida de Batista los exilados en Mexico," *Diario de la Marina*, June 26, 1956.

105 "Por que se suspendió el 'Survey,'" *Carteles*, May 27, 1956, 12. See also García-Pérez, *Insurrection and Revolution*.

106 "Señales hermanadas," *Bohemia*, January 16, 1955, 38–39; "Competencia de señales," *Bohemia*, April 10, 1955, 38; "La carrera de los canales," *Bohemia*, May 29, 1955, 48, 85; Charlie Seiglie, "Tele-Impresiones," *El Mundo*, January 29, 1956, C-12; "Television directa para todos," *Bohemia*, February 12, 1956, 44, 110; "Tele-Mundo en oriente," *Bohemia*, July 15, 1956, 56; "Cambio de antenna," *Bohemia*, July 29, 1956, 46; "Baraúnda," *Bohemia*, July 1, 1956, 38. To learn about audience complaints, see "Cartas son cartas," *Carteles*, January 8, 1956, 53; Enrique Nuñez Rodríguez, "Verdades," *Carteles*, July 24, 1955, 52; "Nos dicen," *Bohemia*, September 9, 1956, 40.

107 "Cuba: Una de las 'cuatro grandes' en la televisión mundial," *Carteles*, April 1, 1956, 52; "Cuba, entre los grandes de la prensa, el radio y la televisión Latinas," *Carteles*, July 1, 1956, 52.

108 "El ballet llega al pueblo," *Bohemia*, February 20, 1955, 42–43; "Otro acontecimiento: Liberace," *Bohemia*, June 3, 1956, 40–41; "Atracciones internacionales," *Bohemia*, July 15, 1956, 52.

109 "La mocha en el aire," *Bohemia*, December 17, 1954, 46–47; "Cambios y mas cambios," *Bohemia*, February 20, 1955, 46, 107; "Baraúnda," *Bohemia*, February 12, 1956, 42; "Otro programa que se va," *Bohemia*, June 10, 1956, 46; "Baraúnda," *Bohemia*, July 1, 1956, 38.

110 "Demuestran la importancia de Cuba en el giro publicitario—destacada actuación de Mariano Guastella en una conferencia ofrecida en Nueva York," *El Mundo*, January 29, 1954; "Admiran en América del Sur el avance de la televisión en Cuba," *Pueblo*, April 14, 1954; "La televisión cubana ya es internacional," *Carteles*, April 24, 1955, 56; "Baraúnda," *Bohemia*, May 2, 1954, 46, 95; "Cubanos en la TV Colombiana," *Bohemia*, July 25, 1954, 48, 96; "Nuevos Mercados," *Bohemia*, May 16, 1954, 44; Cesar Pomar, "El 13," *Tiempo*, May 23, 1954; "'Cuba y Puerto Rico Son . . . ,'" *Bohemia*, August 22, 1954, 44–45; Alquimides Rivero, "Actor cubano que triunfa en Venezuela: Mario Santa Cruz," *Show*, March 1955, 40; Alquimides Rivero, "Caracas habla!," *Show*, March 1955, 36; Raúl Romero, "Los artistas cubanos, los primeros en Caracas," *Show*, April 1956, 20.

111 Emma Pérez, "De usted también diremos algo . . . ," *Bohemia*, January 15, 1956, 57; "Nos dicen," *Bohemia*, June 10, 1956, 50; "Nos dicen," *Bohemia*, July 1, 1956, 26; "Nos dicen," *Bohemia*, July 29, 1956, 46, 89; Emma Pérez, "De usted también diremos algo . . . ," *Bohemia*, November 11, 1956, 77.

112 Pérez, *On Becoming Cuban*, 471.

CHAPTER FOUR. Spectacles of Democracy and a Prelude
to the Spectacles of Revolution

1 The third network was CMBF-Cadena Nacional S.A. "Reinas por un día," *Bohemia*, April 17, 1957, 53; Alberto Giró, "'Reina por un día,' programa del momento en el video criollo," *Diario de la Marina*, April 25, 1957; Hart Phillips, "Give-Away Hits Cuba Like Storm," *New York Times*, May 5, 1957; Alberto Giró, "'Reina por un día' produce gran impacto emocional, Canal 2 TV," *Diario de la Marina*, May 9, 1957; "Se impone una rectificación," *Gente de la Semana*, May 18, 1958, 26; Enrique Nuñez Rodríguez, "A la contraofensiva," *Carteles*, May 24, 1957, 52; "Necesaria competencia," *Bohemia*, May 19, 1957, 54–55; "El que imita . . . ," *Carteles*, June 2, 1957, 53; Joaló, "Televisando," *El Crisol*, June 8, 1957.

2 Enrique Grau, "Cuba a la cabeza de las comunicaciones internacionales," *Diario de la Marina*, August 15, 1957.

3 "Televising to Cuba Approved by F.C.C.," *New York Times*, June 1, 1957, 37; "Phone-TV System with Cuba Set Up over the Horizon," *New York Times*, August 13, 1957, 28; "Telecast of Game Grips Cuba's Fans," *New York Times*, October 3, 1957, 35; Charlie Seiglie, "118 emisoras en Estados Unidos, transmitirán la inauguración del Canal 10, Televisión Habanera," *Pueblo*, August 10, 1958; Gilberto Blanch, "Se internacionaliza la TV," *Pueblo*, August 10, 1958; "Transmitirán a E.U. televisión de Cuba," *El Mundo*, August 13, 1957. While, in the *Television Factbook*, Amadeo Barletta (Telemundo's owner) appears as the owner of channel 10, Cuban-based news stories of the time described the channel as an NBC affiliate. NBC's original plans to buy a station in Cuba were reported in a 1956 *Variety* article. See "NBC May Buy Cuba TV Station" in the National Broadcasting Company Records, Part 8, Office Files, 1921–1969, box 281, folder 21, the State Historical Society of Wisconsin, Madison.

4 "Cuba, primer eslabón de una cadena de TV entre E.U. y América Central," *Diario de la Marina*, February 18, 1957.

5 Spellacy, "Mapping the Metaphor of the Good Neighbor."

6 "Pan American Day," *New York Times*, April 14, 1958, 24.

7 Curtin, *Redeeming the Wasteland*, 86.

8 "La Diosa fortuna y la televisión," *Carteles*, November 3, 1957, 69.

9 The Mestre brothers owned channel 7. The television sets costing almost $700 became part of the 315,000 apparatuses available in Cuba by the end of 1958. "Lo que allá dicen de aquí," *Bohemia*, June 22, 1958, 54; *Television Factbook*, vol. Fall–Winter (Washington, DC: Television Digest, 1958), 300. See also Joaló, "Televisión en colores en Cuba!," *El Crisol*, August 24, 1957; "Resumen semanal de la TV," *El Mundo*, March 23, 1958; Mike Alonso, "Mike Alonso on the Air," *Havana Post*, March 28, 1958.

10 Cesar Pomar, "El 13," *Tiempo*, May 23, 1954; "'Cuba y Puerto Rico Son . . . ,'" *Bohemia*, August 22, 1954, 44–45.

11 According to Mestre, Mexico charged between $950 and $1,200 for a half hour show, while Puerto Rico charged between $700 and $850 for the same product. The cheapest and "worst quality" dubbing came from Spain, which charged around $650. "Habla Goar Mestre sobre el doblaje," *Carteles*, October 12, 1958, 87, 114. See also "Los Mestre al negocio de los discos," *Diario Nacional*, June 1, 1958; Gilberto Blanch, "Se internacionaliza la TV," *Pueblo*, August 10, 1958; "Películas y doblaje," *Bohemia*, August 24, 1958, 56.

12 "La opinión pública," *Bohemia*, January 13, 1957, 52–53; Enrique Gutierrez, "La cuota sindical," *Carteles*, April 7, 1957; Enrique Nuñez Rodríguez, "Pequeñas verdades," *Carteles*, March 2, 1958; Lourdes Bertrand, "Demandas de los artistas," *El País*, March 4, 1958; "Discutirán salarios mínimos en la radio y televisión," *Avance*, March 28, 1958; "Investigarán planes de regalos por televisión," *El Crisol*, March 27, 1958.

13 See, for example, "Survey de T.V.," *Bohemia*, June 23, 1957, 52; "Survey," *Gente de la Semana*, June 30, 1957, 26; Enrique Nuñez Rodríguez, "Año nuevo, programas nuevos," *Carteles*, January 19, 1958, 55; "El survey de televisión," *Carteles*, July 20, 1958, 53; Alberto Giró, "El triunfo de los programas fílmicos por la CMBF-TV," *Diario de la Marina*, March 13, 1958; Gilberto Blanch, "Los surveys y la crisis," *Pueblo*, July 7, 1958; "Volvió 'El Casino' al primer lugar," *Carteles*, September 28, 1958, 87.

14 "La ofensiva del celuloide," *Carteles*, August 3, 1958, 53.

15 Roberto Baez-Miro, "Continúan bajando los ratings en TV," *Cinema*, June 23, 1957; Roberto Baez-Miro, "¿Crisis de autores en el video nacional?," *Cinema*, April 7, 1957. See also "Más programas vivos," *Carteles*, November 10, 1957, 68.

16 "Tiempos nuevos," *Carteles*, May 18, 1958, 87; Gilberto Blanch, "Los surveys y la crisis," *Pueblo*, July 7, 1958.

17 Roberto Baez-Miro, "¿Se impondrá en Cuba la televisión pagada?," *Cinema*, September 1, 1958.

18 "Opera en televisión," *Carteles*, September 8, 1957, 52; "Televisando," *El Crisol*, April 18, 1957; Esther Costales, "Cortando el aire en cinema," *Cinema*, March 8, 1958; Roberto Baez-Miro, "Continúan bajando los ratings en TV," *Cinema*, June 23, 1957.

19 Ramón Vasconcelos, Minister of Communication, "Comunicaciones," *Gaceta Oficial de la República de Cuba*, Decreto No. 78, January 24, 1957, 1719–20; Ramón Vasconcelos, Minister of Communication, "Comunicaciones," *Gaceta Oficial de la República de Cuba*, Decreto No. 2111, August 9, 1957, 15430; Fulgencio Batista, President, Andres Rivero-Aguero, Prime Minister, and Ramón Vasconcelos, Minister of Communication, "Comunicaciones," *Gaceta Oficial de la República de Cuba*, Decreto No. 2389, September 5, 1957, 17156–59. See also "Censura en radio y televisión se organizó hoy en el interior actúan miembros del ejercito," *Avance*, January 18, 1957; "Censura," *Carteles*, January 27, 1957, 40.

20 Salwen, *Radio and Television in Cuba*, 103.

21 Regino Martín, "Durante la censura sucedieron muchas cosas," *Carteles*, March 10, 1957, 20–23.

22 Martín, "Durante la censura sucedieron muchas cosas," 23.

23 "Anniversary in Cuba," *New York Times*, March 10, 1953, 28. See also Herbert L. Matthews, "Students in Cuba Opposing Batista," *New York Times*, April 5, 1952, 5; Herbert L. Matthews, "Batista Is Facing Fateful Decisions," *New York Times*, October 22, 1953, 15; Associated Press, "The Power in Cuba," *New York Times*, April 30, 1956, 4.

24 Herbert L. Matthews, "Cuban Rebel Is Visited in Hideout," *New York Times*, February 24, 1957, 1, 34; Herbert L. Matthews, "Rebel Strength Gaining in Cuba, but Batista Has the Upper Hand," *New York Times*, February 25, 1957, 1, 11; Her-

bert L. Matthews, "Old Order in Cuba Is Threatened by Forces of an Internal Revolt," *New York Times*, February 26, 1957, 13.

25 See Len Allen, "Police Brutality, Cuba: Castro Forces, Las Villas Province," March 26, 1958, in the National Broadcasting Company Records, Part 8, Office Files, 1921–1969, box 282, folder 52, State Historical Society of Wisconsin.

26 "Protestan los radioemisores por clausura," *El Mundo*, April 18, 1957; "Garantías como las de E.E.U.U. piden los radioemisores," *Información*, May 3, 1957; "Protesta la Federación de Radioemisores por la clausura de R. Mambí," *Avance*, May 23, 1957; "Protesta periodistica y radial por la ocupación," *El País*, May 24, 1957; Mike Alonso, "Piden los radioemisores libertad de información," *El Crisol*, June 13, 1957; "Revisión," *Información*, June 8, 1957; "Protesta de las radioemisores," *El País*, June 13, 1957.

27 "El estudio vacío," *Carteles*, July 14, 1957, 53.

28 Ramón Vasconcelos, "Respuesta a Don Abel Mestre," *Alerta*, May 6, 1957.

29 Ramón Vasconcelos, "Medidas legales y saludables," *Alerta*, June 17, 1957. See also "No puede cimentarse el futuro de Cuba con asesinos y terroristas," *Pueblo*, June 7, 1957.

30 "Del Mediodía," *Información*, July 6, 1957.

31 Ramón Vasconcelos, "Revolución de micrófono," *Alerta*, July 6, 1957. "In Mexico, where we enjoy all liberties, talking about politics or religion via the Hertzian waves is prohibited. . . . And then the [Cuban] State, which should have the most powerful stations for its official business, is resigned to depending on what is being said." Certainly, the Mexican situation was more complex than the quote implies. Whereas freedom of expression was legally protected, Mexico's Partido Revolucionario Independiente (PRI) controlled the media via business arrangements with owners as well as by bribing journalists. See Hughes, *Newsrooms in Conflict*.

32 Ramón Vasconcelos, Minister of Communication, "Comunicaciones," *Gaceta Oficial de la República de Cuba*, Decreto No. 2111, August 9, 1957, 15430; "Establecen censura en los noticieros de radio y televisión," *Avance*, August 3, 1957; "Cuba Censors Entry of News, TV Films," *New York Times*, August 27, 1957, 18; "Son restablecidas las garantías constitucionales y es abolida la censura de prensa, desde hoy," *Diario de la Marina*, January 25, 1958, 1-A, 14-A; "Restitución de garantías y abolición de la censura de la prensa," *Carteles*, February 2, 1958, 20.

33 Inglehart and Welzel, *Modernization, Cultural Change and Democracy*, 9.

34 The multiplicity of voices is hinted at in the first paragraph: "The sovereignty and the control of the State on the channels destined for broadcasting do not prevent the concession of their use to particular entities as long as they observe all the legal dispositions and rules destined for its operation." Fulgencio Batista, President, Andres Rivero-Aguero, Prime Minister, and Ramón Vasconcelos,

Minister of Communication, "Comunicaciones," *Gaceta Oficial de la República de Cuba*, Decreto No. 2389, September 5 (1957), 17156–59.

35 Batista, Rivero-Aguero, Vasconcelos, "Comunicaciones" (1957), 17157.

36 Batista, Rivero-Aguero, Vasconcelos, "Comunicaciones" (1957), 17158.

37 Batista, Rivero-Aguero, Vasconcelos, "Comunicaciones" (1957), 17158.

38 Batista, Rivero-Aguero, Vasconcelos, "Comunicaciones" (1957), 17158.

39 "Suspenden películas en el canal 7 de TV," *El Crisol*, February 8, 1957; "Suspenden programa de televisión por exhibición inmoral," *El País*, February 8, 1957.

40 Mraz, *Looking for Mexico*, 130–31.

41 "Suspenden programa de televisión por exhibición inmoral," *El País*, February 8, 1957.

42 "Suspende Vasconcelos programas televisados que ofenden a la moral," *Diario de la Marina*, May 23, 1957.

43 "Han prohibido el rock and roll en Programa de TV," *Diario de la Marina*, February 14, 1957, 1, 9-B.

44 Delmont, *The Nicest Kids in Town*.

45 Delmont, *The Nicest Kids in Town*, 138.

46 "Cuba Restores Rock 'n' Roll," *New York Times*, February 15, 1957.

47 For information on cine clubs in Havana, see Feeney, "Hollywood in Havana."

48 Medovoi, *Rebels*, 42.

49 Von Eschen, *Race against Empire*; Von Eschen, *Satchmo Blows Up the World*.

50 Medovoi, *Rebels*, 24, 30.

51 "Suspende Vasconcelos 2 programas de TV, por estimarlos inmorales," *Avance*, February 21, 1957; "Suspende el ministro de comunicaciones un programa de televisión," *Diario de la Marina*, March 13, 1957; "Suspenden 15 transmisiones de una novela transmitida por CMQ-TV," *Avance*, March 15, 1957; "Suspende Vasconcelos 5 actuaciones por TV de la bailarina Ana Gloria," *Avance*, April 8, 1957; "Suspendido el bingo por la TV," *Pueblo*, April 11, 1957; "Suspenden en TV a una bailarina y una modelo," *El Mundo*, April 12, 1957; "Suspendidos dos programas de TV," *El País*, May 12 1957.

52 "Misceláneas," *Información*, February 15, 1957; Alejandro Roque, "La guerra al rock and roll: Aldeanismo y arteriosclerosis contra optimismo y juventud," *Bohemia*, March 5, 1957.

53 "El proboscidio en la vidriera," *Carteles*, May 24, 1957, 53.

54 "No hay fuerza moral!," *Gente de la Semana*, April 7, 1957; "Nos dicen," *Bohemia*, April 28, 1957, 56; "Tarajano: Y si no, renuncie . . . ," *Gente de la Semana*, December 1, 1957.

55 Domínguez, "The Batista Regime in Cuba," 127.

56 Various dictatorial regimes in Latin America have used censorship and repression while concomitantly creating progressive legislation. See, for example, Htun, *Sex and the State*; Chehabi and Linz, *Sultanistic Regimes*.

57 "Firmó Bastista el reglamento," *El País*, June 1, 1958.

58 DePalma, *The Man Who Invented Fidel*.

59 My examination of the Cuban Revolution's iconography was influenced by José Quiroga's analysis of Castro's photographic images. See "A Cuban Love Affair with the Image," in Quiroga, *Cuban Palimpsests*, 81–113.

60 Herbert L. Matthews, "Cuban Rebel Is Visited in Hideout," *New York Times*, February 24, 1957.

61 Denning, *The Cultural Front*, 9.

62 For information on the use of documentary in broadcasting news during the late 1950s and early 1960s, see Curtin, *Redeeming the Wasteland*.

63 Nichols, *Representing Reality*.

64 Nichols, *Representing Reality*, 107.

65 Hewitt, "Rebels of Sierra Maestra."

66 Gosse, *Where the Boys Are*.

67 *Reading for Americans*, 176.

68 Unlike Joanne P. Sharp's analysis in *Condensing the Cold War*, the focus of the book was not the Soviet Union per se, though the title of each section in *Reading for Americans* ("Leaders Who Helped Make America," "Struggle toward Freedom for All," "America's Riches—Ours to Guard," "Challenge and Rewards of Citizenship," "Cherishing the American Spirit," and "Improving the You in the U.S.A.") clearly lays out the ideological spectrum of the book. Sharp, *Condensing the Cold War*; *Reading for Americans*.

69 Nichols, *Representing Reality*, 107.

70 Gosse, *Where the Boys Are*, 85.

71 Quiroga, *Cuban Palimpsests*, 95.

72 Hemion, *The Steve Allen Show*.

73 Jack Gould, "TV: Ethel Merman and Dinah Shore: Singers Make a Fine Team on N.B.C. Steve Allen Visits Havana," *New York Times*, January 20, 1958.

74 López, "Are All Latins from Manhattan?"

75 For information on news coverage, see Len Allen, "Police Brutality, Cuba: Castro Forces, Las Villas Province," in the National Broadcasting Company Records, Part 8, Office Files, 1921–1969, box 281, folder 52, State Historical Society of Wisconsin. See also Gosse, *Where the Boys Are*.

76 "Nuestra protesta," *Alerta*, June 1, 1958.

77 "Investigan una denuncia de un programa de TV," *Avance*, June 3, 1958; "Suprimirá malos programas de TV la D.N. de Radio," *Ataja*, June 3, 1958; Enrique Nuñez Rodríguez, "Verdades," *Carteles*, August 10, 1958, 86; "Resumen semanal," *Carteles*, August 17, 1958, 53, 68; "El único remedio," *Bohemia*, August 17, 1958, 62; "Suspendidos 2 programas de televisión," *El Mundo*, October 26, 1958; "Resumen semanal en TV," *El Mundo*, November 6, 1958; "Nueva política," *Carteles*, November 23, 1958, 87; Juan José Tarajano, "El caso Celeste Mendoza,"

Carteles, November 30, 1958, 53; Enrique Nuñez Rodríguez, "Verdades," *Carteles*, November 23, 1958. Surprisingly, despite the emphasis on morality, the new minister of communication allowed one of the characters portrayed by men in drag (Mamacusa) to return to television. There was no explanation of the motivation behind the decision. See Enrique Nuñez Rodríguez, "Verdades," *Carteles*, August 10, 1958, 86.

78 "El único remedio," *Bohemia*, August 17, 1958, 62; Enrique Nuñez Rodríguez, "Verdades," *Carteles*, November 23, 1958, 86.

79 "Firmó Bastista el reglamento," *El País*, June 1, 1958.

80 "Batista to Extend His Rule by Decree," *New York Times*, May 25, 1958, 11.

81 Luis Hernández Serrano, "El dictador de Valle Azul," *Juventud Rebelde*, December 25, 2012; López, *La Radio en Cuba*.

82 Delia Fiallo interview, video recording, September 29, 2012, the Luis J. Botifoll Oral History Project, Cuban Heritage Collection, University of Miami.

83 González-Castro, *Hasta el último aliento*.

CHAPTER FIVE. Spectacles of Revolution

1 For a detailed recounting and analysis of these transformations, see Guerra, *Visions of Power in Cuba*.

2 Pérez, *Cuba*, 321.

3 Salwen, *Radio and Television in Cuba*, 158–59.

4 For information about the first years of the ICAIC, see Burton, "Film and Revolution in Cuba"; and Chanan, *Cuban Cinema*.

5 Pedraza, *Political Disaffection in Cuba's Revolution and Exodus*, 60.

6 Matthews, "Cuban Rebel Is Visited in Hideout," *New York Times*, February 24, 1957, 1, 34.

7 See Guerra, *Visions of Power in Cuba*; and Pérez-Stable, *The Cuban Revolution*.

8 Guerra, *Visions of Power in Cuba*, 137.

9 For information about communists' conceptualization of modernity, see Arnason, "Communism and Modernity."

10 Williams, *Marxism and Literature*.

11 As Lillian Guerra writes, "As early as 1959, Fidel Castro, Raúl Castro and Che Guevara pursued the related goals of national sovereignty and economic independence through speech acts" that appropriated the basic premises present in "the writings of nineteenth-century nationalist ideologue José Martí." Guerra, *Visions of Power in Cuba*, 6–7.

12 Even the reviewer of the conservative newspaper *Diario de la Marina* praised and supported the focus on the revolution. See, for example, Alberto Giró, "Patriótico programa ofreció el 'Casino de la alegría,'" *Diario de la Marina*, January 10, 1959; "Gran transmisión de CMQ-TV desde el Coliseo Deportivo,"

Diario de la Marina, January 24, 1959; "Valioso servicio prestó CMQ a la causa del proceso revolucionario," *Diario de la Marina*, February 1, 1959; "'Tu vida y la mía,' una obra inspirada en la gesta cubana," *Diario de la Marina*, February 10, 1959, A18; "Noticias de televisión," *Diario de la Marina*, February 17, 1959, A16; "Noticias de televisión," *Diario de la Marina*, February 17, 1959, A16; "Magnífica demostración de solidaridad del radio y TV," *Diario de la Marina*, July 28, 1959.

13 "Facilidades a los periodistas en el M. de Comunicaciones," *Diario de la Marina*, January 19, 1959. A similar approach regarding the freedom of the press characterized the coverage of a rally in favor of public trials and assassinations of Fulgencio Batista's men. The Cuban government invited U.S. journalists to demonstrate the openness of the new regime and the citizens' support for the trials and executions. "Invitados 150 periodistas de la prensa, radio y TV de E.U.," *Diario de la Marina*, January 21, 1959, A1.

14 Schudson, *The Power of News*, 38.

15 "Gina Cabrera en 'Por quien doblan las campanas,' hoy, a las 9:00 pm en 'Sueños de mujer' por CMQ," *El País*, February 25, 1959; Alberto Giró, "Sueños de mujer de CMQ-TV se anotó un rotundo éxito," *Diario de la Marina*, March 3, 1959, A14; Alberto Giró, "Un mismo personaje en dos emotivas novelas cubanas," *Diario de la Marina*, November 11, 1959.

16 One could say that televised dramas had elements of what Alison Landsberg refers to as "prosthetic memory," a memory obtained via commodified cultures. According to Landsberg, while watching a film (or attending a museum), "the person does not simply apprehend a historical narrative but takes on a more personal, deeply felt memory of the past event through which he or she did not live." In the case of Cuban television dramas, the effect on the personal memory was stronger, since audiences were part of the revolution's present. Thus, what the televised dramas did, similar to Landsberg's prosthetic memory concept, was add some of the missing elements of the revolutionary experience. Landsberg, *Prosthetic Memory*, 2.

17 Guerra, *Visions of Power in Cuba*, 30.

18 Quiroga, *Cuban Palimpsests*, 93.

19 Alberto Giró, "Hizo Tito Hernández gran imitación de Fidel Castro," *Diario de la Marina*, January 20, 1959. See also Alberto Giró, "'La historia me absolverá,' hoy por CMQ y Canal 2, TV," *Diario de la Marina*, July 25, 1959, A17.

20 This change was a product of the closing of casinos and the decline in tourism. Viewed as symbols of corruption and economic exploitation, casinos were the target of citizens and the government. By the end of 1959, many had been closed or nationalized. See Moore, *Music and Revolution*, 61–63.

21 Alberto Giró, "Cubano y emotivo programa de 'Jueves' por CMQ-Televisión," *Diario de la Marina*, January 17, 1959; Alberto Giró, "Patriótico programa ofreció el 'Casino de la alegría,'" *Diario de la Marina*, January 10, 1959; Alberto

Giró, "'Noche cubana' un tributo de CMBF-TV a nuestro arte," *Diario de la Marina*, March 5, 1959; Alberto Giró, "'Como Lo Soñó Martí,' primer lugar en el hit parade de Radio Progreso," *Diario de la Marina*, March 28, 1959.

22 Enrique Nuñez Rodríguez, "Revolución en el éter," *Carteles*, March 15, 1959, 63. See also Alberto Giró, "Halló marco en la 'Noche cubana' la música guajira," *Diario de la Marina*, July 16, 1959; Alberto Giró, "Saluda la televisión cubana a la concentración guajira," *Diario de la Marina*, July 23, 1959, A12.

23 Alberto Giró, "Reeditó Carmina Benguría su anterior triunfo por CMQ-TV," *Diario de la Marina*, September 25, 1959, A8.

24 Nuñez Rodríguez, "Revolución en el éter."

25 Esther Costales, "Cortando el aire en Cinema," *Cinema*, February 15, 1959; see also Nuñez Rodríguez, "Revolución en el éter"; and "Los barbudos no son payasos," *Carteles*, January 25, 1959, 85.

26 "Grandioso homenaje esta noche a los 'barbudos,' en el Teatro Blanquita," *El País*, January 15, 1959; Alberto Giró, "Patriótico programa ofreció el 'Casino de la alegría,'" *Diario de la Marina*, January 10, 1959; Giró, "Cubano y emotivo programa de 'Jueves' por CMQ-Televisión"; Alberto Giró, "Gran transmisión de CMQ-TV desde el 'Coliseo Deportivo,'" *Diario de la Marina*, January 24, 1959; Enrique Nuñez Rodríguez, "La radio y la televisión en el movimiento revolucionario," *Carteles*, January 25, 1959; Alberto Giró, "Valioso servicio prestó CMQ a la causa del proceso revolucionario," *Diario de la Marina*, February 1, 1959; Alberto Giró, "Inician el 'Telemaratón' por el Canal 2 de TV el día 3 de abril," *Diario de la Marina*, March 20, 1959; Alberto Giró, "Saluda la televisión cubana a la concentración guajira," *Diario de la Marina*, July 23, 1959; Alberto Giró, "Rindieron un eficaz servicio las emisoras de radio y TV," *Diario de la Marina*, October 28, 1959.

27 de la Fuente, *A Nation for All*, 263–64.

28 de la Fuente, *A Nation for All*, 285–90. See also "Campaña contra la discriminación racial," *Revolución*, April 3, 1959; Enrique Nuñez Rodríguez, "Verdades," *Carteles*, April 12, 1959, 62.

29 Alberto Giró, "Noticias de televisión," *Diario de la Marina*, April 17, 1959, A15; Alberto Giró, "Una bella producción ofreció 'Noche cubana' CMBF-TV," *Diario de la Marina*, September 10, 1959, A10.

30 Alberto Giró, *Diario de la Marina*, April 8, 1959, A10; Giró, "Una bella producción ofreció 'Noche cubana' CMBF-TV."

31 "La nota del día," *Exelsior* (*El País*), June 12, 1959; "Baraúnda," *Bohemia*, September 13, 1959, 58.

32 "Una novela integracionista," *Bohemia*, November 29, 1959, 52.

33 Pedro Meluzá, "Radio y TV," *Revolución*, February 23, 1959. See also Alberto Giró, "La televisión como vehículo de cultura y de educación," *Diario de la Marina*, April 15, 1959.

34 Esther Costales, "Carta abierta al Sr. Goar Mestre," *Cinema*, January 25, 1959.

35 "Comisión para estudiar la nueva ley de radiodifusión," *Diario de la Marina*, March 24, 1959, A1; Olga Abreu, "La dirección de radio," *Cinema*, March 31, 1959; "Hay interés por la nueva ley de radio y televisión," *El País*, April 2, 1959; "Ley de radio," *Información*, April 3, 1959; Alberto Giró, "Radiovisión," *Diario de la Marina*, April 18, 1959, A12; "Ondas, doctrina, y cultura," *Carteles*, April 19, 1959; "Estudian nueva ley," *Diario Libre*, May 1, 1959; Alberto Giró, "Crea el Dr. Armando Hart un programa educacional, cmq," *Diario de la Marina*, May 7, 1959; "Instruirán a campesinos con una planta de televisión," *Prensa Libre*, June 6, 1959; Enrique Nuñez Rodríguez, "La nueva ley de radiodifusión," *Carteles*, June 7, 1959, 63; "Cadena nacional de radio creará el estado dentro de poco," *Información*, June 19, 1959; "Cadena oficial de TV," *Información*, July 4, 1959; Enrique Nuñez Rodríguez, "Verdades," *Carteles*, October 25, 1959.

36 Although the government did not intend to maintain the station financially, the loss of advertisers and the resignation of many managers and technical staff forced it to take charge of channel 12. "Cambios en el bull pen," *Carteles*, January 4, 1959, 53; Enrique Nuñez Rodríguez, "El ídolo caído," *Carteles*, May 10, 1959, 63; Enrique Nuñez Rodríguez, "Completando a docena," *Carteles*, June 21, 1959, 63; "No permitirán su destrucción," *Prensa Libre*, June 27, 1959.

37 Alberto Giró, "Otra audición del 'El pueblo pregunta,' hoy por el Canal 12," *Diario de la Marina*, April 3, 1959; "Revolución recomienda," *Revolución*, July 6, 1959; "Sigue ofreciendo el canal 12 de TV 'El forum nacional de la Reforma Agraria,'" *Diario de la Marina*, July 11, 1959. For a list of other public affairs programs and participants, see Cué Sierra, "El Canal 12 y sus programas de debate sobre el proyecto revolucionario."

38 Alberto Giró, "Radiovisión," *Diario de la Marina*, March 17, 1959; Alberto Giró, "¿Qué sabe usted de Cuba? Un interesante programa del Canal 12 de TV," *Diario de la Marina*, April 1, 1959; Alberto Giró, "Inicia 'Teatro del sábado' del Canal 12 ciclo de obras cubanas," *Diario de la Marina*, April 25, 1959; Alberto Giró, "Noticias de televisión," *Diario de la Marina*, June 6, 1959. For a list of *Así se escribió la historia* titles, see Cué Sierra, "1959."

39 Alberto Giró, "'Amor y orgullo' esta noche por el Canal 12 de televisión," *Diario de la Marina*, October 27, 1959; Alberto Giró, "'La Madrid 113' una comedia de Paco Alonso por el Canal 12," *Diario de la Marina*, October 27, 1959.

40 As Castro remarked during a 1976 speech, "In 1959 the radio and television monopoly, with the support of North American companies and national capital, maintained a solid foundation. The selling of scripts and programs to more than ten Latin American countries was already established. Cuba's capitalistic radio [and television] was a source of deformation and ideological penetration, not only for our country, but it extended to other countries as well." See Fidel

Castro citation in Nuñez-Machín, *Pensamiento revolucionario y medios de difusión masiva*, 54.

41 Alberto Giró, "Los veinte programas más vistos de la 'TV' cubana," *Diario de la Marina*, March 18, 1959, A14; "Survey de TV," *Bohemia*, March 29, 1959, 54; "Survey de televisión," *Carteles*, April 15, 1959; "El survey de televisión," *Revolución*, June 24, 1959; "Survey de TV y radio," *Bohemia*, July 5, 1959, 56; Heriberto Espinet Borges, "TV y radio," *Información*, July 19, 1959.

42 "Cuba," *Television Factbook 1959*, 284. The Cuban population in 1959 was approximately 6,300,000.

43 Enrique Nuñez Rodríguez, "Cámara y micrófono," *Carteles*, May 24, 1959.

44 Alberto Giró, "Adhesiones a una sugerencia nuestra," *Diario de la Marina*, January 15, 1959. See also Alberto Giró, "Concurrirá esta noche, 'Ante la prensa' de CMQ-TV, el jefe de la revolución, Dr. Castro," *Diario de la Marina*, February 19, 1959; Alberto Giró, "Fidel Castro, el miércoles, en el Canal 12: Conferencia de prensa," *Diario de la Marina*, March 22, 1959; Alberto Giró, "Fidel Castro concurrirá esta noche a 'Ante la prensa' de CMQ-TV," *Diario de la Marina*, April 2, 1959.

45 "4 Hour TV Appearance," Foreign Broadcast Information Service, February 20, 1959, in Castro Speech Data Base, Latin American Network Information Center, accessed July 30, 2009, http://www1.1anic.utexas.edu/la/cb/cuba/castro.html.

46 This quotation is included in Jorge Mañach's article that addresses Castro's powerful charisma. Mañach, "El ángel de Fidel," *Diario de la Marina*, April 4, 1959.

47 See A. Hernández, "Fidel y la televisión," *Diario Libre*, July 4, 1959.

48 Pérez-Stable, *The Cuban Revolution*. See also de la Fuente, *A Nation for All*.

49 One of the first transformations enacted by the revolutionary government was enforcing strict rules to end gender discrimination in the workplace. The right to remain on the job during and after pregnancy, hiring practices, and the installation of separate facilities were some of the legislative acts enacted by the Labor Ministry. Whereas the Cuban constitution of 1940 instituted laws to protect women, the revolutionary government's Labor Ministry rigorously enforced the law. Therefore, the gender distribution of the *Telemundo pregunta* audience might have been associated with the revolutionary government's efforts to achieve gender equality. Yet, besides this sociopolitical justification, one also needs to consider women's attraction to Castro, a man who, although highly respected, had celebrity status. For information about women's support for the revolutionary movement, see Pérez-Stable, *The Cuban Revolution*, 76–77.

50 Enrique Nuñez Rodríguez, "Verdades," *Carteles*, August 30, 1959, 62.

51 Quiroga, *Cuban Palimpsests*, 95.

52 See Guerra, *Visions of Power in Cuba*, chap. 10.

53 My analysis of Fidel Castro "live" has been influenced by Philip Auslander's theorization of live and mediatized performance and his examination of the similarities between early television and theater. As Auslander writes, "Unlike film, but like theatre, a television broadcast is characterized as a performance in the present." Auslander, *Liveness*, 15; see also the chart on page 61.

54 Guerra, *Visions of Power in Cuba*, 28.

55 I am drawing from Diana Taylor's concepts of the archive and the repertoire. According to Taylor, the archives are "enduring material," and the repertoire includes "performances, gestures, orality, movement, dance, [and] singing, . . . which require presence." Taylor, *The Archive and the Repertoire*, 19–20.

56 R. Hart Phillips, "Castro Assails Cuban President, Forcing Him Out," *New York Times*, July 18, 1959.

57 José Luis Massó, "En dramática comparecencia, Fidel Castro ejecuto una vez más la voluntad del pueblo de Cuba," *Bohemia*, July 26, 1959.

58 *Carteles*, July 12, 1959.

59 Mittell, *Genre and Television*, 36.

60 See, for example, Jorge Mañach's column "El ángel de Fidel."

61 Olga Abreu, "Fidel Castro en 'Comentarios Económicos,'" *Cinema*, October 4, 1959.

62 "Face the Nation," CBS News, Havana, Cuba, January 11, 1959.

63 Jack Gould, "TV: An Absorbing Close-Up of Castro," *New York Times*, January 12, 1959.

64 "Meet the Press: Fidel Castro," NBC News, Washington, DC, April 19, 1959.

65 Salwen, *Radio and Television in Cuba*, 132.

66 Marifeli Pérez-Stable, *The Cuban Revolution*, 9. See also de la Fuente, *A Nation for All*.

67 Here I am referring to John Corner's reworking of Erving Goffman's "presentation of the self" to theorize the performance of political figures. As Corner writes, "The self-presentation of politicians, however, is widely seen to be distinctive as a result of the scale of its projection (in political leaders this becomes national and possibly global), the degree of self-conscious strategy attending its planning and performance, the intensity of its interaction with media systems and the degree to which certain personal qualities are seen not merely to enhance but to *underwrite* political values." Corner, "Mediated Persona and Political Culture," 387.

68 For information about news coverage, see Heriberto Espinet Borges, "La televisión en acción," *Información*, January 7, 1959; Nuñez Rodríguez, "Revolución en el éter."

69 Williams, *Television*, 83.

70 In this regard, Cuba's commercial television disturbances between 1959 and

1960 differed from what Daniel Dayan and Elihu Katz refer to as interruptions to the schedules caused by "media events." During "media events," as Dayan and Katz observe, "regular broadcasting is suspended and preempted as we are guided by a series of special announcements and preludes that transform daily life into something special and, upon the conclusion of the event, are guided back again." Contrary to "media events," Castro's appearance on television was not planned; in fact, in many cases it was impromptu, especially for the producers of the show who did not anticipate his presence at the studio. Dayan and Katz, *Media Events*, 5.

71 Newcomb, "Reflections on TV."

72 Dayan and Katz, *Media Events*, 76.

73 See Escalante, *Sobre la propaganda revolucionaria*.

74 "Nos dicen," *Bohemia*, September 27, 1959.

75 As Lillian Guerra observes regarding the barbudos' reception in the country's capital, "*Habaneros* in particular found the combination of the men's appalling lack of education, ignorance of urban lifeways, disheveled beards, and bushy, Afro-style hair deeply disturbing." Guerra, *Visions of Power in Cuba*, 51.

76 Pérez, *On Becoming Cuban*, 482.

77 Hanchard, "Afro-Modernity," 253.

78 Escalante, *Sobre la propaganda revolucionaria*.

79 Bejel, *Gay Cuban Nation*, 101–2.

80 Bejel, *Gay Cuban Nation*, 99. As José Quiroga writes regarding gender norms and homosexuality in revolutionary Cuba, "Propaganda could produce female figures such as the exemplary female revolutionary, the platoon leader of the women's militia, or the architect of social engineering, but not, openly, the lesbian. The male homosexual, on the contrary, was always part of a baroque project, . . . a useful thing that is ultimately worthless, unless he is being tolerated as an exemplary cultural worker." Quiroga, *Cuban Palimpsests*, 124–25. For similar trends regarding masculinity and homophobia during times of revolutionary change, but in a different national context, see Irwin, *Mexican Masculinities*.

81 For an excellent theorization of Cuba's sexual politics after the adoption of communism and its connection to Stalinism, see Epps, "Proper Conduct."

82 Guerra, *Visions of Power in Cuba*, 96.

83 Fidel Castro cited in Pérez, *On Becoming Cuban*, 482. See also Guerra, *Visions of Power in Cuba*, 97–98.

84 A. Hernández, "Fidel y la televisión," *Diario Libre*, July 4, 1959; Heriberto Espinet Borges, "TV y radio," *Información*, July 19, 1959.

85 "Los artistas se defienden," *Bohemia*, March 22, 1959, 52–54; Enrique Nuñez Rodríguez, "Vivos vs muertos," *Carteles*, March 29, 1959; "Cosas," *Bohemia*, September 13, 1959, 56. For a percentage of foreign programming per network

and station in 1959 and a detailed account of the changes taking place between 1959 and 1962, see Quincoces-Quintana, "Estudio de la TV cubana."

86 Williams, *Marxism and Literature*, 122.

CHAPTER SIX. From Broadcasting Modernity to Constructing Modernity

1 Antonio Pequeño, "La exposición soviética en La Habana," *INRA*, February 1960, 24–29.

2 "Los actores opinan," *INRA*, February 1960, 74–75.

3 Jaime Saruski, "Los maestros en la Sierra," *INRA*, August 1960, 14–19.

4 Osvaldo Dórticos-Torrado, Fidel Castro-Ruz, and Faure Chomón-Mediavilla, "Ley No. 1030," *Gaceta Oficial de la República de Cuba* (1962), 6945–46.

5 "Weekly TV for Castro," *New York Times*, May 8, 1960, 123.

6 Both the confiscation of Telemundo and the banning of foreign-made advertising occurred in February 1960. In terms of advertising, all ads were eliminated in March 1961. "Lo que sea . . . sonara," *Bohemia*, February 14, 1960, 40; "Cuban TV Seizure," *Television Digest*, February 29, 1960, 6; "Castro Tightens Screws on TV Ads," *Television Digest*, February 29, 1960, 2; "Un experimento sensacional," *Bohemia*, March 5, 1961. For a detailed account of the nationalization of television industries, including personal interviews with people involved in the process, see Quincoces-Quintana, "Estudio de la TV cubana." For information on the disappearance of advertising, see "Un experimento sensacional."

7 "De nuevo los artistas," *Bohemia*, March 6, 1960, 42; Nivio López Pellon, "Hoy más que nunca, publicidad!" *Bohemia*, March 27, 1960, 36–39.

8 Goar Mestre cited in Salwen, *Radio and Television in Cuba*, 163; Renaldo Infante, member of the National Committee of Revolutionary Orientation, cited in Quincoces-Quintana, "Estudio de la TV cubana," 30.

9 A relevant exception was CMQ-TV, which was nationalized without any justification. Also, it is important to mention that Televisión Camaguey, which began operations in 1959, ceased to exist due to financial problems caused by a lack of sponsorship. See Salwen, *Radio and Television in Cuba*, 164; "TV en Camaguey," *Bohemia*, April 16, 1959, 56; Quincoces-Quintana, "Estudio de la TV cubana," 47.

10 This television campaign followed the structure of the highly successful 1959 campaign "Abrele tu puerta a un campesino," in which Havana residents provided homes for the peasants invited by the government to visit the capital for the first celebration of the 26th of July Movement. "Enseñando en TV," *Bohemia*, May 15, 1960, 46, 48, 50, 95, 96.

11 Through nationalization, the shrinking of advertising (particularly from foreign firms), and the gradual exodus of talent and media professionals (a

topic rarely discussed in newspaper and magazine articles), Cuban television endured a short-lived yet transformative crisis prior to the government's appropriation of CMQ-TV. "Una lágrima mas para nuestra TV," *Bohemia*, May 29, 1960, 38, 40; "'Economitis durañona,'" *Bohemia*, June 5, 1960, 36; the Luis J. Botifoll Oral History Project, Cuban Heritage Collection, University of Miami, Florida.

12 In July 1960, Miguel Angel Quevedo, owner and editor of *Bohemia* magazine and a strong supporter of Fidel Castro and the revolution throughout the 1950s, asked for political asylum at the Venezuelan embassy in Havana. Other publishers and people who worked for *Bohemia* as well as other magazines where Quevedo had investments (such as *Carteles* and *Vanidades*) followed his lead. By November 1960, all newspapers had either closed due to financial difficulties or been nationalized. See "The Press in Cuba," *New York Times*, July 21, 1960, 26; "The Cuban Defectors," *New York Times*, August 5, 1960, 22; "Havana Paper Closes," *New York Times*, September 8, 1960, 12; Charles Grutzner, "Magazine in Exile Opposing Castro," *New York Times*, November 4, 1960, 38; "Havana Paper Closes," *New York Times*, September 8, 1960, 12.

13 Tad Szulc, "Most Cubans Back Castro, but Discontent Is Rising," *New York Times*, August 1, 1960, 1–2.

14 "¡Ahora o nunca!," *Bohemia*, October 23, 1960, 29.

15 "La reforma hertziana," *Bohemia*, October 30, 1960, 46; "También el Canal 4," *Bohemia*, October 30, 1960, 46–47; "La utilidad del survey," *Bohemia*, November 20, 1960, 38; Luis Orticon, "Guía de arte, literatura, radio, televisión," *Bohemia*, December 11, 1960, 30.

16 Guerra, *Visions of Power in Cuba*, 9.

17 "Más entretenimiento, más alegría," *Bohemia*, November 20, 1960, 28.

18 "Más entretenimiento, más alegría," 28.

19 "También el Canal 4."

20 It is important to mention that some foreign artists visited the island. For example, one of the most famous Latin American figures on Cuban television in late 1960 was Mexican actor and director Alfonso Aráu, who, as a supporter of the Cuban Revolution, moved to the island and created the variety program *El show de Aráu*. Described as the "most imaginative, dynamic, modern, and consistent" program on Cuban television, *El Show de Aráu* was considered an oasis of entertainment in the midst of educational, propaganda, and high-culture programming. Based on an article published in 1962, *El show de Aráu* ended in 1962 when the actor-director left the island to fulfill other professional commitments. Another Latin American figure who visited the island and stayed for some time was Mario Suárez, a renowned singer from Venezuela. See "Punto: Un año de buena TV," *Bohemia*, July 30, 1961, 108;

Orlando Quiroga, "Aráu: 'No me retiro de La televisión, pero . . . ,'" *Bohemia*, April 6, 1962, 82; and "Mario Suárez, El más grande cantante de Venezuela ha sido arrebato en La Habana," *Show*, April–May 1961, 63–64.

21 Pedraza, *Political Disaffection in Cuba's Revolution and Exodus*, 78.

22 Dávila, *Latinos, Inc.*; Rivero, *Tuning Out Blackness*; Sinclair, "The Hollywood of Latin America"; Varela, *La televisión criolla*.

23 Another important aspect to consider in the deterioration of television was the intellectuals' prioritization of the ICAIC and its politically engaged documentary filmmaking. Even as the ICAIC documentaries were broadcast on television, the medium did not receive attention from intellectuals like the ICAIC did. For information on intellectuals' involvement with the ICAIC during the early years of the revolution, see Chanan, *Cuban Cinema*, chap. 6.

24 "Análisis de la televisión," *Bohemia*, March 19, 1961, 37–38.

25 "Punto: CMBF Televisión Revolución," *Bohemia*, June 25, 1961, 83.

26 "Punto: CMBF Televisión Revolución"; "La TV en función social," *Bohemia*, March 19, 1961, 38.

27 Luis López, "Cine debate en televisión," *Bohemia*, October 8, 1961; "Imagen y sonido," *Bohemia*, July 16, 1961, 88; "Más teatro que tele," *Bohemia*, September 17, 1961, 76.

28 Rojas, *Motivos de Anteo*, 35.

29 Rojas, *Motivos de Anteo*, 35. See also Rojas, *La máquina del olvido*.

30 Mickiewicz, *Changing Channels*, 25.

31 Escalante, *Sobre la propaganda revolucionaria*, 26.

32 Escalante, *Sobre la propaganda revolucionaria*, 20–21.

33 As Ellen Mickiewicz explains, the Soviet-Stalinist use of media included three main components: centralization of media and people, state control (which was interconnected to the Communist Party), and saturation. Mickiewicz, *Changing Channels*, 25–29.

34 Quincoces-Quintana, "Estudio de la TV cubana," 50; Paquita Armas-Fonseca, "La television: Una profesión de fe para Mirta Muñiz," Instituto Cubano de Radio y Televisión, http://www.tvcubana.icrt.cu/seccion-historia/46-historia/52 -la-television-una-profesion-de-fe-para-mirta-muniz.

35 Osvaldo Dórticos-Torrado, Fidel Castro-Ruz, and Faure Chomón-Mediavilla, "Ley No. 1030," *Gaceta Oficial de la República de Cuba* (1962), 6945–46.

36 Armas-Fonseca, "La televisión."

37 Armas-Fonseca, "La televisión."

38 Orlando Quiroga, "La Teve al servicio de la conciencia," *Bohemia*, June 8, 1962, 80; Orlando Quiroga, "Cámara Rápida," *Bohemia*, June 8, 1962, 82.

39 In terms of cultural performances, see Luis Reyes, "La Opera de Pekin," *INRA*, August 1960, 80–85; "Praga y su Noneto," *Bohemia*, June 25, 1961, 82; Alejo

Beltrán, "El ballet Moiseyev baila en toda Cuba," *INRA*, July 1961, 8–13. Other visitors were government officials from socialist countries who were shown participating in televised rallies and political events.

40 For an excellent analysis of the influence of Russian culture in Cuba, see Loss, *Dreaming in Russian*, 132.

41 The reference to technicians, businesspeople, and advisers traveling from the countries of the socialist bloc to Cuba was taken from the documentary program *Bell & Howell Close-UP!*, which devoted one segment to examining communism in Cuba. John H. Secondari, executive producer, "Ninety Miles to Communism," *Bell & Howell Close-UP!*, ABC Network, April 18, 1961, 30 min.

42 Arturo Acevedo-Avalos, "Exposición industrial: La RDA trabaja para el mundo," *INRA*, December 1961, 14–19. Also see "Checoslovaquia en La Habana: Exposición de un pueblo de amigos," *INRA*, July 1961, 54–61.

43 As Ariana Hernández-Reguant writes regarding inventions and the Marxist construction of mental and manual labor, "Under socialism, the official worship of these machine-artifacts—and the parallel disregard for the consumer commodity—signaled the displacement of the fetish effect from the commodity to the means of production." Hernández-Reguant, "The Inventor, the Machine, and the New Man," 204.

44 See, for example, Julian Goodman, producer, "Nixon-Kennedy Debate # 2," CBS Network, October 7, 1960, 60 min.; Michael J. Marlow, producer, *Face the Nation*, CBS Network, October 30, 1960, 30 min.; Secondari, "Ninety Miles to Communism"; Fred W. Friendly, producer, *CBS Reports: Walter Lippmann*, CBS Network, June 15, 1961, 60 min.

45 Gosse, *Where the Boys Are*, 149.

46 For an impressive analysis of the "Afro-Cuban-American solidarities" before and after the Cuban revolution, see Tyson, *Radio Free Dixie*; and Guridy, *Forging Diaspora*.

47 Curtin, *Redeeming the Wasteland*, 209.

48 Seondari, "Ninety Miles to Communism."

49 Eduardo Toledo Sainz, "Las elecciones yanquis: Espectáculo en decadencia," *INRA*, November 1960, 104–5.

50 Ernesto Medialdea, "La TV y la radio nacional en Oriente," *Bohemia*, August 3, 1962, 70–71.

51 For an excellent overview of the use of propaganda in socialist Cuba, see Hernández-Reguant, "Radio Taíno and the Globalization of the Cuban Culture Industries." For information on how advertising techniques were used to develop the socialist consciousness, see Ernesto Medialdea, "La publicidad se transforma," *Bohemia*, July 16, 1961, 80, 82; Orlando Quiroga, "Modigliani Publicitario?," *Bohemia*, April 20, 1962, 78.

52 Rojas, *La máquina del olvido*, 143–54.

53 Guerra, *Visions of Power in Cuba*, 222–23.

54 Moreno, "From Traditional to Modern Values," 494. Comparatively, in Russia after the 1930s, the availability of items and cultural practices formerly associated with the bourgeoisie helped "legitimate the new socialist order and symbolized its accomplishments." For an in-depth examination of modernity under Stalinism, see Hoffmann, *Stalinist Values*, 4.

55 Escalante, *Sobre la propaganda revolucionaria*, 10.

EPILOGUE

1 Pertierra, "Private Pleasures."

2 See Venegas, *Digital Dilemmas*.

3 Pertierra, "Private Pleasures," 116–17.

4 See Hernández-Reguant, *Cuba in the Special Period*.

5 Gordy, "Sales + Economy + Efficiency = Revolution."

6 Since 2014 a new type of underground media entrepreneurship has emerged in Cuba—the selling of *paquetes*. Paquetes (packages) are USB flash drives filled with movies, television series, sporting events, music, gossip shows, and magazine content. Priced between one and five dollars, paquetes are home delivered or picked up at casas particularles. Carlos Batista, "Sin internet o parabólica, cubanos se entretienen con el 'paquete'," *El Nuevo Herald*, April 21, 2014, accessed July 3, 2014. http://www.elnuevoherald.com/2014/04/21/1731178 /a-falta-de-internet-y-parabolicas.html.

7 Quiroga, *Cuban Palimpsests*, ix.

8 Appadurai, *Modernity at Large*, 178–83.

BIBLIOGRAPHY

Abreu, Christina. "Authentic Assertions, Commercial Concessions: Race, Nation, and Popular Culture in Cuban New York City and Miami, 1940–1960." PhD diss., University of Michigan, 2012.

Agusti, María Sol, and Guillermo Mastrini. "Radio, economía y política entre 1920 y 1945: De los pioneros a las cadenas." In *Mucho ruido, pocas leyes: Economía y políticas de comunicación en la Argentina (1920–2004)*, edited by Guillermo Mastrini, 29–51. Buenos Aires: La Crujia Ediciones, 2005.

Ameringer, Charles D. "The Auténtico Party and the Political Opposition in Cuba, 1952–1957." *Hispanic American Historical Review* 65, no. 2 (1985): 327–51.

Appadurai, Arjun. *Modernity at Large: Cultural Dimensions of Globalization*. Minneapolis: University of Minnesota Press, 1996.

Arnason, Johann P. "Communism and Modernity." *Deadalus* 129 (2000): 61–90.

Arnavat, Gustavo. "The Cuban Constitution and the Future Democratic Transition." In *Looking Forward: Comparative Perspectives on Cuba's Transition*," edited by Marifeli Pérez-Stable, 72–95. Notre Dame, IN: University of Notre Dame Press, 2007.

Arroyo, Jossianna. *Travestismos culturales: Literatura y etnografía en Cuba y Brazil*. Pittsburgh, PA: Nuevo Siglo, 2003.

Auslander, Philip. *Liveness: Performance in a Mediatized Culture*. 2nd ed. London: Routledge, 2008.

Ayres, Ted. *Face the Nation*. 30 min. U.S.: CBS News, Havana, Cuba, January 11, 1959. Paley Center for Media iCollection for Colleges.

Bejel, Emilio. *Gay Cuban Nation*. Chicago: University of Chicago Press, 2001.

Birkenmaier, Anke. *Alejo Carpentier y la cultura del surrealismo en América Latina*. Madrid: Iberoamericana, 2006.

Bourdieu, Pierre. *Distinction: A Social Critique of the Judgment of Taste*. Cambridge, MA: Harvard University Press, 1984.

Bronfman, Alejandra. "'Batista Is Dead': Media, Violence, and Politics in 1950s Cuba." *Caribbean Studies* 40, no. 1 (2012): 37–58.

Burke, Kenneth. *Language as Symbolic Action*. Berkeley: University of California Press, 1966.

Burton, Julianne. "Film and Revolution in Cuba: The First Twenty-Five Years." In

New Latin American Cinema, edited by Michael T. Martin, 2:123–42. Detroit: Wayne State University Press, 1997.

Chanan, Michael. *Cuban Cinema.* Minneapolis: University of Minnesota Press, 2004.

Chehabi, H. E., and Juan J. Linz. *Sultanistic Regimes.* Baltimore: Johns Hopkins University Press, 1998.

Classen, Steven D. *Watching Jim Crow: The Struggles over Mississippi TV, 1955–1969.* Durham, NC: Duke University Press, 2004.

Cohen, Lizabeth. *A Consumers' Republic: The Politics of Mass Consumption in Postwar America.* New York: Knopf, 2003.

Coontz, Stephanie. *The Way We Never Were: American Families and the Nostalgia Trap.* New York: Basic Books, 2000.

Corner, John. "Mediated Persona and Political Culture." *European Journal of Cultural Studies* 3, no. 3 (2000): 386–402.

Crary, Jonathan. *Suspensions of Perception: Attention, Spectacle, and Modern Culture.* Cambridge, MA: MIT Press, 2001.

Cruz, Jesús. "Patterns of Middle Class Conduct in Nineteenth-Century Spain and Latin America: The Role of Emulation." Paper presented at the Institute of Governmental Affairs Conference, University of California–Davis, November 2–5, 2006.

Cué Sierra, Mayra. "El Canal 12 y sus programas de debate sobre el proyecto revolucionario." *Cubarte,* August 15, 2005.

Cué Sierra, Mayra. "El periplo de la ética en la radiodifusión cubana." *Cubarte,* October 10, 2010.

Cué Sierra, Mayra. "1959: Telerebelde y los dramatizados históricos." *Cubarte,* August 7, 2005.

Curtin, Michael. "Media Capital: Toward the Study of Spatial Flows." *International Journal of Cultural Studies* 6, no. 2 (2003): 202–28.

Curtin, Michael. *Playing to the World's Biggest Audience: The Globalization of Chinese Film and TV.* Berkeley: University of California Press, 2007.

Curtin, Michael. *Redeeming the Wasteland: Television Documentary and Cold War Politics.* New Brunswick, NJ: Rutgers University Press, 1995.

Dávila, Arlene. *Latinos, Inc.: The Marketing and Making of a People.* Berkeley: University of California Press, 2001.

Dayan, Daniel, and Elihu Katz. *Media Events: The Live Broadcasting of History.* Cambridge, MA: Harvard University Press, 1994.

Debord, Guy. *Society of the Spectacle.* Rev. ed. Detroit: Black and Red, 1977.

de la Fuente, Alejandro. *A Nation for All: Race, Inequality, and Politics in Twentieth-Century Cuba.* Chapel Hill: University of North Carolina Press, 2001.

de la Torre Mulhare, Mirta. "Sexual Ideology in Pre-Castro Cuba: A Cultural Analysis." PhD diss., University of Pittsburgh, 1969.

de la Uz, Félix. *Los monopolios extranjeros en Cuba, 1898–1958.* Havana: Editorial Ciencias Sociales, 1984.

Delmont, Matthew F. *The Nicest Kids in Town: American Bandstand, Rock 'n' Roll, and the Struggle for Civil Rights in 1950s Philadelphia.* Berkeley: University of California Press, 2012.

Denning, Michael. *The Cultural Front: The Laboring of American Culture in the Twentieth Century.* London: Verso, 1996.

DePalma, Anthony. *The Man Who Invented Fidel: Cuba, Castro, and Herbert L. Matthews of the New York Times.* New York: Public Affairs, 2006.

Dianteill, Erwan, and Martha Swearingern, "From Hierography to Ethnography and Back: Lydia Cabrera's Text and the Written Tradition in Afro-Cuban Religions." *Journal of American Folklore* 116, no. 461 (2003): 273–92.

Díaz Ayala, Cristóbal. *Música Cubana: Del Areyto Al Rap Cubano.* 4th. ed. San Juan, Puerto Rico: Fundación Musicalia, 2003.

Domínguez, Jorge I. "The Batista Regime in Cuba." In *Sultanistic Regimes*, edited by H. E. Chehabi and Juan J. Linz, 113–31. Baltimore: Johns Hopkins University Press, 1998.

Douglas, Susan J. *Inventing American Broadcasting 1899–1902.* Baltimore: Johns Hopkins University Press, 1987.

Eisenstadt, Shmuel Noah. "Multiple Modernities." Special issue, *Daedalus* 129, no. 1 (Winter 2000): 1–29.

Epps, Brad. "Proper Conduct: Reinaldo Arenas, Fidel Castro, and the Politics of Homosexuality." *Journal of the History of Sexuality* 6, no. 2 (1995): 231–83.

Escalante, César. *Sobre la propaganda revolucionaria.* Havana: Departamento de Orientación Revolucionaria del Comité Central del Partido Comunista, 1976.

Extramuros de la ciudad, imagen, y palabra. Havana: Centro del Libro y la Literatura de la Ciudad de la Habana, 1999.

Farber, Samuel. *The Origins of the Cuban Revolution Reconsidered: Envisioning Cuba.* Chapel Hill: University of North Carolina Press, 2006.

Feeney, Megan J. "Hollywood in Havana: Film Reception and Revolutionary Nationalism in Cuba before 1959." PhD diss., University of Minnesota, 2008.

Foucault, Michel. *The History of Sexuality, Vol. 2: The Use of Pleasure.* Translated by Robert Hurley. New York: Vintage, 1986.

Fox, Claire F. *Making Art Panamerican: Cultural Policy and the Cold War.* Minneapolis: University of Minnesota Press, 2013.

Fox, Elizabeth. "Media Policies in Latin America: An Overview." In *Media and Politics in Latin America: The Struggle for Democracy*, edited by Elizabeth Fox, 6–35. London: Sage, 1988.

Friendly, Fred W. CBS *Reports: Walter Lippmann.* 60 min. U.S.: CBS Network. June 15, 1961. Paley Center for Media iCollection for Colleges.

Gaonkar, Dilip Parameshwar, ed. *Alter/Native Modernities.* Durham, NC: Duke University Press, 1999.

Gaonkar, Dilip Parameshwar. "On Alternative Modernities." In *Alter/Native Moder-*

nities, edited by Dilip Parameshwar Gaonkar, 1–23. Durham, NC: Duke University Press, 1999.

Garcés, Raúl. *Los dueños del aire*. Havana: Editorial Pablo de la Torriente, 2005.

García-Pérez, Gladys Marel. *Insurrection and Revolution: Armed Struggle in Cuba, 1952–1959*. Translated by Juan Ortega. Boulder, CO: Lynne Rienner, 1998.

Giddens, Anthony. *The Consequences of Modernity*. Stanford, CA: Stanford University Press, 1990.

González, Reynaldo. *Llorar es un placer*. Havana: Editorial Letras Cubanas, 1988.

González, Reynaldo. *El más humano de los autores*. Havana: Ediciones Unión, 2009.

González-Castro, Vicente. *Hasta el último aliento*. Havana: Instituto Cubano de Radio y Televisión, 1995.

González Echevarría, Roberto. *Cuban Fiestas*. New Haven, CT: Yale University Press, 2010.

González Suárez, Dominga. "La discriminación racial en el campo cubano." *Afro-Cuban Anthology Journal* 13 (Fall 2004): 1–12.

Goodman, David. *Radio's Civic Ambition: American Broadcasting and Democracy in the 1930s*. New York: Oxford University Press, 2011.

Goodman, Julian. "Nixon-Kennedy Debate # 2." 60 min. U.S.: CBS, October 7, 1960. Paley Center for Media iCollection for Colleges.

Gordy, Katherine. "Sales + Economy + Efficiency = Revolution: Dollarization, Consumer Capitalism, and Popular Responses in Special Period Cuba." *Public Culture* 18 (2006): 383–412.

Gosse, Van. *Where the Boys Are: Cuba, Cold War and the Making of a New Left*. London: Verso, 1993.

Guerra, Lillian. *Visions of Power in Cuba: Revolution, Redemption, and Resistance, 1959–1971*. Chapel Hill: University of North Carolina Press, 2012.

Guridy, Frank Andre. *Forging Diaspora: Afro-Cubans and African Americans in a World of Empire and Jim Crow*. Chapel Hill: University of North Carolina Press, 2010.

Hamilton, Carrie. *Sexual Revolutions in Cuba: Passion, Politics, and Memory*. Chapel Hill: University of North Carolina Press, 2012.

Hanchard, Michael. "Afro-Modernity: Temporality, Politics, and the African Diaspora." In *Alter/Native Modernities*, edited by Dilip Parameshwar Gaonkar, 245–68. Durham, NC: Duke University Press, 1999.

Hanchard, Michael. "Black Cinderella? Race and the Public Sphere in Brazil." *Public Culture* 7 (1994): 165–85.

Hansen, Miriam Bratu. "The Mass Production of the Senses: Classical Cinema as Vernacular Modernism." *Modernism/Modernity* 6, no. 2 (1999): 59–77.

Hemion, Dwight A. *The Steve Allen Show*. 59 min. U.S.: NBC, 1958. Paley Center for Media iCollection for Colleges.

Hernández-Reguant, Ariana, ed. *Cuba in the Special Period: Culture and Ideology in the 1990s*. New York: Palgrave Macmillan, 2009.

Hernández-Reguant, Ariana. "The Inventor, the Machine, and the New Man." In *Caviar with Rum: Cuba-USSR and the Post-Soviet Experience*, edited by Jacqueline Loss and José Manuel Prieto, 199–209. New York: Palgrave Macmillan, 2012.

Hernández-Reguant, Ariana. "Radio Taíno and the Globalization of the Cuban Culture Industries." PhD diss., University of Chicago, 2002.

Hewitt, Don. "Rebels of Sierra Maestra: The Story of Cuba's Jungle Fighters." CBS News Special Report. 30 mins. U.S.: CBS, 1957. Paley Center for Media iCollection for Colleges.

Hilmes, Michele. *Only Connect: A Cultural History of Broadcasting in the United States*. Belmont, CA: Thomson, 2007.

Hilmes, Michele. *Radio Voices: American Broadcasting, 1922–1952*. Minneapolis: University of Minnesota Press, 1997.

Himpele, Jeff D. *Circuits of Culture: Media, Politics, and Indigenous Identity in the Andes*. Minneapolis: University of Minnesota Press, 2008.

Hoffmann, David L. *Stalinist Values: The Cultural Norms of Soviet Modernity, 1917–1941*. Ithaca, NY: Cornell University Press, 2003.

Htun, Mala. *Sex and the State: Abortion, Divorce, and the Family under Latin American Dictatorships and Democracies*. Cambridge: Cambridge University Press, 2003.

Hughes, Sallie. *Newsrooms in Conflict: Journalism and the Democratization of Mexico*. Pittsburgh: University of Pittsburgh Press, 2006.

Hyde, Timothy. *Constitutional Modernism: Architecture and Civil Society in Cuba, 1933–1959*. Minneapolis: University of Minnesota Press, 2013.

Inglehart, Ronald, and Christian Welzel. *Modernization, Cultural Change and Democracy: The Human Development Sequence*. New York: Cambridge University Press, 2005.

Irwin, Robert McKee. *Mexican Masculinities*. Minneapolis: University of Minnesota Press, 2003.

Jenkins, Keith. *Re-thinking History*. London: Routledge, 2003.

Kapcia, Antoni. *Havana: The Making of Cuban Culture*. Oxford: Berg, 2005.

Keeler, Amanda. "'Sugar Coat the Educational Pill': The Early Educational Aspirations of Film, Radio, and Television." PhD diss., Indiana University, 2011.

Kutzinski, Vera M. *Sugar's Secrets: Race and the Erotics of Cuban Nationalism*. Charlottesville: University Press of Virginia, 1993.

Landsberg, Alison. *Prosthetic Memory: The Transformation of American Remembrance in the Age of Mass Culture*. New York: Columbia University Press, 2004.

Larkin, Brian. *Signal and Noise: Media, Infrastructure, and Urban Culture in Nigeria*. Durham, NC: Duke University Press, 2008.

Lemogodeuc, Jean-Marie. "Orígenes, Ciclón, Lunes: Una literatura en ebullición." In *La Habana 1952–1961: El final de un mundo, el principio de una ilusión*, edited by Jacobo Machover, 145–58. Madrid: Alianza Editorial, 1994.

López, Ana. "Are All Latins from Manhattan? Hollywood, Ethnography, and Cultural Colonialism." In *Mediating Two Worlds: Cinematic Encounters in the Americas*, edited by Ana López and Manuel Alvarado, 67–80. London: BFI Publishing, 1993.

López, Ana. "Greater Cuba." In *The Ethnic Eye: Latino Media Arts*, edited by Chon Noriega and Ana López, 38–58. Minneapolis: University of Minnesota Press, 1996.

López, Ana. "'A Train of Shadows': Early Cinema and Modernity in Latin America." In *Through the Kaleidoscope: The Experience of Modernity in Latin America*, edited by Vivian Schelling, 148–76. London: Verso, 2000.

López, Oscar Luis. *La radio en Cuba*. Havana: Editorial Letras Cubanas, 1988.

Loss, Jacqueline. *Dreaming in Russian: The Cuban Soviet Imaginary*. Austin: University of Texas Press, 2013.

Macias, Anthony F. *Mexican American Mojo: Popular Music, Dance, and Urban Culture in Los Angeles, 1935–1968*. Durham, NC: Duke University Press, 2008.

Mañach, Jorge. "Introducción al curso." In *Cuadernos de la Universidad del Aire del Circuito CMQ 1*. Talleres de la Revista Crónica, 1949.

Marlow, Michael J. *Face the Nation*. 30 min. U.S.: CBS, October 30, 1960. Paley Center for Media iCollection for Colleges.

Martín Barbero, Jesús. *Communication, Culture and Hegemony: From the Media to Mediations*. Translated by Elizabeth Fox and Robert A. White. London: Sage, 1993.

McCarthy, Anna. *The Citizen Machine: Governing by Television in 1950s America*. New York: New Press, 2010.

McChesney, Robert. *Telecommunications, Mass Media, and Democracy: The Battle for Control of U.S. Broadcasting: 1928–1935*. New York: Oxford University Press, 1994.

McClintock, Anne. *Imperial Leather: Race, Gender, and Sexuality in the Colonial Contest*. New York: Routledge, 1995.

Medovoi, Leerom. *Rebels: Youth and the Cold War Origins of Identity*. Durham, NC: Duke University Press, 2005.

"Meet the Press: Fidel Castro." 30 min. U.S.: NBC News, Washington, DC, April 19, 1959. Paley Center for Media iCollection for Colleges.

Mesa-Lago, Carmelo. *Market, Socialist and Mixed Economies: Comparative Policy and Performance*. Baltimore: Johns Hopkins University Press, 2000.

Mickiewicz, Ellen. *Changing Channels: Television and the Struggle for Power in Russia*. Rev. ed. Durham, NC: Duke University Press, 1999.

Mignolo, Walter D. "The Geopolitics of Knowledge and the Colonial Difference." In *Coloniality at Large: Latin America and the Postcolonial Debate*, edited by Mabel Moraña, Enrique Dussel, and Carlos A. Jáuregui, 225–58. Durham, NC: Duke University Press, 2008.

Miller, Nicola. "A Revolutionary Modernity: The Cultural Policy of the Cuban Revolution." *Journal of Latin American Studies* 4 (2008): 675–96.

Mittell, Jason. *Genre and Television: From Cop Shows to Cartoons in American Culture*. London: Routledge, 2004.

Moore, Robin D. *Music and Revolution: Cultural Change in Socialist Cuba*. Berkeley: University of California Press, 2006.

Moore, Robin D. *Nationalizing Blackness: Afrocubanismo and Artistic Revolution in Havana, 1920–1940*. Pittsburgh: University of Pittsburgh Press, 1997.

Moraña, Mabel, Enrique Dussel, and Carlos A. Jáuregui. "Colonialism and Its Replicants." In *Coloniality at Large, Latin America and the Postcolonial Debate*, edited by Mabel Moraña, Enrique Dussel, and Carlos A. Jáuregui, 1–22. Durham, NC: Duke University Press, 2008.

Moraña, Mabel, Enrique Dussel, and Carlos A. Jáuregui, eds. *Coloniality at Large, Latin America and the Postcolonial Debate*. Durham, NC: Duke University Press, 2008.

Moreno, José A. "From Traditional to Modern Values." In *Revolutionary Change in Cuba*, edited by Carmelo Mesa-Lago, 471–97. Pittsburgh: University of Pittsburgh Press, 1971.

Mraz, John. *Looking for Mexico: Modern Visual Culture and National Identity*. Durham, NC: Duke University Press, 2009.

Mrázek, Rudolf. *Engineers of Happy Land: Technology and Nationalism in a Colony*. Princeton, NJ: Princeton University Press, 2002.

Newcomb, Horace. "Reflections on TV: The Most Popular Art." In *Thinking Outside the Box: A Contemporary Television Genre Reader*, edited Gary R. Edgerton and Brian G. Rose, 17–35. Lexington: University Press of Kentucky, 2005.

Nichols, Bill. *Representing Reality: Issues and Concepts in Documentary*. Bloomington: Indiana University Press, 1991.

Nuñez-Machín, Ana, ed. *Pensamiento revolucionario y medios de difusión masiva*. Havana: Editora Política, 1983.

Nye, David E. *America as Second Creation: Technology and Narratives of New Beginnings*. Cambridge, MA: MIT Press, 2003.

Nye, David E. "Technological Prediction: A Promethean Problem." In *Technological Visions: The Hopes and Fears That Shape New Technologies*, edited by Marita Sturken, Douglas Thomas, and Sandra J. Ball-Rokeach, 158–76. Philadelphia: Temple University Press, 2004.

O'Dell, Cary. "Kinescope." In *Encyclopedia of Television*, edited by Horace Newcomb, 1263–64. Chicago: Fitzroy Dearborn, 2004.

Oren, Tasha G. *Demon in the Box: Jews, Arabs, Politics, and Culture in the Making of Israeli Television*. New Brunswick, NJ: Rutgers University Press, 2004.

Ortiz, Fernando. *Contrapunteo cubano del tabaco y la azúcar*. Caracas, Venezuela: Biblioteca Ayacucho, 1978.

Pedraza, Silvia. *Political Disaffection in Cuba's Revolution and Exodus*. New York: Cambridge University Press, 2007.

Pérez, Louis A. *Cuba: Between Reform and Revolution*. New York: Oxford University Press, 1995.

Pérez, Louis A. *On Becoming Cuban: Identity, Nationality, and Culture*. New York: Ecco Press, 1999.

Pérez Firmat, Gustavo. *Life on the Hyphen: The Cuban-American Way*. Austin: University of Texas Press, 1994.

Pérez-Stable, Marifeli. *The Cuban Revolution: Origins, Course, and Legacy*. New York: Oxford University Press, 1993.

Pérez-Stable, Marifeli. "Reflections on Political Possibilities: Cuba's Peaceful Transition That Wasn't (1954–1956)." Unpublished manuscript.

Pérez-Stable, Marifeli. "La transición pacífica que no tuvo lugar (1954–1956)." *Encuentro* 24 (2002): 283–305.

Pertierra, Anna Cristina. "Private Pleasures: Watching Videos in Post-Soviet Cuba." *International Journal of Cultural Studies* 12 (2009): 113–30.

Pertierra, Anna Cristina, and Graeme Turner, *Locating Television: Zones of Consumption*. London: Routledge, 2013.

Podalsky, Laura. "Guajiras, mulatas y puros cubanos: Identidades nacionales en el cine pre-revolucionario." *Archivos de la filmoteca* 31 (1999): 156–71.

Quijano, Aníbal. "The Colonial Nature of Power and Latin America's Cultural Experience." In *Sociology in Latin America*, edited by Roberto Briceño-León and Heinz Sonntag, 27–38. Colonia Tovar, Venezuela: ISA, 1997.

Quijano, Aníbal. "Coloniality of Power, Eurocentrism, and Social Classification." In *Coloniality at Large: Latin America and the Postcolonial Debate*, edited by Mabel Moraña, Enrique Dussel, and Carlos A. Jáuregui, 181–224. Durham, NC: Duke University Press, 2008.

Quincoces-Quintana, Melvyn Yoel. "Estudio de la TV cubana entre enero de 1959 y mayo de 1962." Master's Thesis, University of Havana, 1999.

Quiroga, José. *Cuban Palimpsests*. Minneapolis: University of Minnesota Press, 2005.

Ramos, Alberto. "Cine e Iglesia Católica en Cuba (1934–1950)." In *Huellas olvidadas del cine cubano: Memorias del XV Taller De Crítica Cinematográfica*, edited by Armando Pérez Padrón, 106–24. Havana: Editorial Oriente, 2010.

Reading for Americans. Pleasantville, NY: Reader's Digest, 1951.

Rey, Carmelina. *A dónde va la televisión cubana?* Havana, 1959.

Rivero, Yeidy M. "Havana as a 1940s–1950s Latin American Media Capital." *Critical Studies in Media Communication* 26, no. 3 (August 2009): 275–93.

Rivero, Yeidy M. *Tuning Out Blackness: Race and Nation in the History of Puerto Rican Television*. Durham, NC: Duke University Press, 2005.

Robert, Alexander J. *A History of Organized Labor in Cuba*. Westport, CT: Praeger, 2002.

Roberts, John Storm. *The Latin Tinge: The Impact of Latin American Music on the United States*. New York: Oxford University Press, 1999.

Rodríguez, Clemencia, and Patricia Tellez. *La telenovela en Colombia: Mucho más que amor y lágrimas*. Bogotá: CINEP, 1989.

Rodríguez, Eduardo Luis. *The Havana Guide: Modern Architecture, 1925–1965*. New York: Princeton Architectural Press, 2000.

Rojas, Rafael. *La máquina del olvido: Mito, historia y poder en Cuba*. Mexico City: Taurus, 2012.

Rojas, Rafael. *Motivos de Anteo: Patria y nación en la historia intelectual de Cuba*. Madrid: Editorial Colibrí, 2008.

Sáenz Rovner, Eduardo. *The Cuban Connection: Drug Trafficking, Smuggling, and Gambling in Cuba from the 1920s to the Revolution*. Chapel Hill: University of North Carolina Press, 2008.

Salwen, Michael B. "The Dark Side of Cuban Journalism: Press Freedom and Corruption before Castro." In *Communication in Latin America: Journalism, Mass Media, and Society*, edited by Richard R. Cole, 139–54. Wilmington, DE: Scholarly Resources, 1996.

Salwen, Michael B. *Radio and Television in Cuba: The Pre-Castro Years*. Ames: Iowa State University Press, 1994.

Scarpaci, Joseph L., Roberto Segre, and Mario Coyula. *Havana: Two Faces of the Antillean Metropolis*. Chapel Hill: University of North Carolina Press, 2002.

Schudson, Michael. *The Power of News*. Cambridge, MA: Harvard University Press, 1996.

Schwock, James. *Global TV: New Media and the Cold War, 1946–69*. Urbana: University of Illinois Press, 2009.

Secondari, John H. "Ninety Miles to Communism." *Bell & Howell Close-UP!* 30 min. U.S.: ABC, April 18, 1961. Paley Center for Media iCollection for Colleges.

Sharp, Joanne P. *Condensing the Cold War: Reader's Digest and American Identity*. Minneapolis: University of Minnesota Press, 2000.

Sieg, Katrin. *Ethnic Drag: Performing Race, Nation, Sexuality in West Germany*. Ann Arbor: University of Michigan Press, 2002.

Sifuentes-Jáuregui, Ben. *Transvestism, Masculinity and Latin American Literature*. New York: Palgrave Macmillan, 2002.

Sinclair, John. "The Hollywood of Latin America: Miami as Regional Center in Television Trade." *Television and New Media* 4, no. 3 (2003): 211–29.

Slotten, Hugh R. *Radio and Television Regulation: Broadcast Technology in the United States, 1920–1960*. Baltimore: Johns Hopkins University Press, 2000.

Sommer, Doris. *Foundational Fictions: The National Romances of Latin America*. Berkeley: University of California Press, 1991.

Spellacy, Amy. "Mapping the Metaphor of the Good Neighbor: Geography, Globalism, and Pan-Americanism during the 1940s." *American Studies* 47, no. 2 (2006): 39–66.

Spigel, Lynn. *Make Room for TV: Television and the Family Ideal in Postwar America*. Chicago: University of Chicago Press, 1992.

Stoler, Ann Laura. *Carnal Knowledge and Imperial Power: Race and the Intimate in Colonial Rule*. Berkeley: University of California Press, 2002.

Stoler, Ann Laura. *Race and the Education of Desire: Foucault's History of Sexuality and the Colonial Order of Things*. Durham, NC: Duke University Press, 1995.

Stoner, Lynn K. *From the House to the Streets: The Cuban Woman's Movement for Legal Reform, 1898–1940*. Durham, NC: Duke University Press, 1991.

Streeter, Thomas. *Selling the Air: A Critique of the Policy of Commercial Broadcasting in the United States*. Chicago: University of Chicago Press, 1996.

Sturken, Marita, and Douglas Thomas. "Introduction: Technological Visions and the Rhetoric of the New." In *Technological Visions: The Hopes and Fears That Shape New Technologies*, edited by Marita Sturken, Douglas Thomas, and Sandra J. Ball-Rokeach, 1–18. Philadelphia: Temple University Press, 2004.

Sturken, Marita, Douglas Thomas, and Sandra J. Ball-Rokeach, eds. *Technological Visions: The Hopes and Fears That Shape New Technologies*. Philadelphia: Temple University Press, 2004.

Sublette, Ned. *Cuba and Its Music: From the First Drums to the Mambo*. Chicago: Chicago Review Press, 2004.

Taylor, Charles. *Modern Social Imaginaries*. Durham, NC: Duke University Press, 2004.

Taylor, Charles. "Two Theories of Modernity." In *Alter/Native Modernities*, edited by Dilip Parameshwar Gaonkar, 153–74. Durham, NC: Duke University Press, 1999.

Taylor, Diana. *The Archive and the Repertoire: Performing Cultural Memory in the Americas*. Durham, NC: Duke University Press, 2004.

Television: A World Survey. Paris: UNESCO, 1953.

Trouillot, Michel-Rolph. "The Otherwise Modern: Caribbean Lessons from the Savage Slot." In *Critically Modern: Alternatives, Alterities, Anthropologies*, edited by Bruce M. Knauft, 220–40. Bloomington: Indiana University Press, 2002.

Tyson, Timothy B. *Radio Free Dixie: Robert F. Williams and the Roots of Black Power*. Chapel Hill: University of North Carolina Press, 1999.

Varela, Mirta. *La televisión criolla: Desde sus inicios hasta la llegada del hombre a la Luna, 1951–1969*. Buenos Aires: Edhasa, 2005.

Vélez, María Teresa. *Drumming for the Gods: The Life and Times of Felipe García Villamil, Santero, Palero, and Abakuá*. Philadelphia: Temple University Press, 2000.

Venegas, Cristina. *Digital Dilemmas: The State, the Individual, and Digital Media in Cuba*. New Brunswick, NJ: Rutgers University Press, 2010.

Von Eschen, Penny M. *Race against Empire: Black Americans and Anticolonialism, 1937–1957*. Ithaca, NY: Cornell University Press, 1997.

Von Eschen, Penny M. *Satchmo Blows Up the World: Jazz Ambassadors Play the Cold War*. Cambridge, MA: Harvard University Press, 2004.

Wade, Peter. *Music, Race, and Nation: Música Tropical in Colombia*. Chicago: University of Chicago Press, 2000.

Williams, Raymond. *Marxism and Literature*. Oxford: Oxford University Press, 1977.

Williams, Raymond. *Television: Technology and Cultural Form*. Middletown, CT: Wesleyan University Press, 1992.

Zelizer, Barbie. *Remembering to Forget: Holocaust Memory through the Camera's Eye*. Chicago: University of Chicago Press, 1998.

INDEX

Note: Italicized numbers indicate a figure; n indicates an endnote

Abakuá, 86, 197n44
advertising: adaptations of U.S. strategies to Cuban, 35, 48; Association of Cuban Advertisers, 99, 145, 191n56; as a tool for developing socialist consciousness in Cuba, 171, 218n51; attempts to control in pre-Castro Cuba, 30, 33, 34, 37, 77, 114, 183n8; in Castro's Cuba, 156, 165–66, 215n6, 215–16n11, 218n51; and the categorization of audiences, 62–63, 65, 68, 99, 145, 193n82; and censorship, 38, 88–90, 111, 186n61; and the consolidation of Cuban preeminence in Latin American broadcasting, 35, 38, 47–48, 169; Cuban and U.S. affiliations, 35, 37–38, 58–59, 103; Cuban expertise in, 35, 37–38, 47–48, 169; on Cuban radio, 27, 28, 76, 183n8; on Cuban television, 62–63, 68, 88, 89, 90; economic downturn as an impetus for, 28; the financial necessity of to sustain broadcasting, 28, 35, 71, 76, 211n36; and freedom of expression, 89, 90; the influence of advertisers on programming, 19, 77, 88, 134, 156; the influence of U.S. strategies on Cuban, 35, 40; the initial legal prohibition of from Cuban radio, 23, 26, 27; legal stipulations regarding radio, 23, 26–27, 30, 33–34, 37, 42; the opposition of advertisers to government intervention, 88, 89, 90, 111, 114; surveys of the Cuban broadcast audience, 18–19, 68, 76, 80, 99, 191n56, 198n66; versus propaganda, 171. *See also* television sponsors

Afro-Cubans: African influences on Cuba's culture, 82, 86, 93–94, 199n79; African religious practices among, 86, 93–94; biases against among some Cubans, 86, 96, 214n75; censorship of the public dance and music of as immoral, 92, 94, 199n77; the cultural importance of in Castro's Cuba, 138–39, 191n7; the folklore of, 86; the musical rhythms associated with, 29, 82, 85, 93, 199n79; organizational efforts to fight racial discrimination, 43, 187n72; racial equality for under Castro, 138–39, 159, 173; and "racial time" in Cuba, 159–60; the religious traditions of, 85; the response to the vernacular culture of among intellectuals, 93–94, 96; televised cultural performances by, 86, 92, 93–94, 195n21, 197n48. *See also* working class

Agrarian Reform, 131, 136–37, 140–41, 144, 157, 162

by, 106–7, 109–10, 123, 157, 182n26; the March 1952 military coup of, 3, 50, 65–66, 106, 192n70, 196n36; the television coverage of his escape from Cuba, 156

Bay of Pigs, 170, 174

Bell & Howell Close-Up! (ABC), 173–74, 218n41

blacks: biases against Afro-Cuban performances by, 79–81, 86, 93; biases against in Cuba, 4–5, 14, 28–29, 81; the folklore traditions of working-class, 86, 93–94; as the objectified Other in Cuba, 4–5; performers, 18, 138–39, 197n48, 199n79; the populace of in Cuba, 4, 28; the popularity of Afro-Cuban performances by, 80, 86, 93; racial discrimination against Cuban, 43, 139–40, 159; racial equity extended to Cuban by Castro, 138–40, 174, 181n7; and "racial time" in Cuba, 159–60

Bohemia: the 1952 exchange between Sobrino and Mestre in, 63–65; as a socialist magazine, 167, 169, 174; Castro's confiscation of, 167, 216n12; the columns in dedicated to radio and television, 60; commentaries in regarding censorship and politics, 84–85, 89–90, 105, 129, 158, 199n79; critics' reviews of programs in, 55, 56; the disagreements of its television critic with the CRE, 84–85, 89, 93; the sociocultural orientation of, 16, 165–66

Brazil, 40

broadcasting: Batista's 1957 amendment to the 1953 Broadcasting Law, 109–16; the changes in produced by Cuba's transition to socialism, 164–65; government regulation of under Castro, 140; public, 24, 25, 33–34, 37, 67, 68–69, 77

broadcasting model: adaptations of U.S. strategies to create a Cuban, 36, 48; the British, 27, 77, 142, 184n24; the Cuban indigenized, 36, 48; the Soviet, 170–71; the U.S., 23, 27, 38, 40

broadcasting of modernity: as a means of globally displaying Cuba's modernity, 2–4, 7–8, 18; as a response to colonialism and neocolonialism, 4–5, 9, 11; changes to the by socialist Cuba, 11–12, 128, 133–34, 161–62; Cuban socioeconomic contradictions to its, 2, 6–7, 9–10. *See also* modernity

capitalism: the association of racial discrimination with, 138; capitalist democracy in Cuba, 36, 49, 74, 90; Castro's dismantling of mores and values associated with, 159–61, 162, 172, 174, 175, 211–12n40; the influence of on the expansion of Cuban media, 26, 36, 49, 70, 71; the influence of U.S. ideas on Cuban modernization, 3, 4–5, 11, 132, 185n40

Carteles: the columns in dedicated to radio and television, 39, 60, 89; commentaries by Rodríguez in, 89–92, 105; commentaries in regarding censorship and politics, 65–66, 90–92, 105–7; coverage of Castro by, 143, 148; critics' reviews of programs in, 54, 55, 56; the sociocultural orientation of, 16, 80, 129

Casino de la alegría, 77, 129, 136

casinos: as attractions for American tourists, 125–26, 209n20; cabaret shows in, 82, 94, 184n23, 195n16; the expansion of in Cuba, 35; televisions as gaming devices for, 103; the U.S. Mafia control of Cuban, 35, 98

Castro, Fidel: broadcast programming disruptions by, 145–47, 149, 156, 159, 165, 171, 213–14n70; and brother Raúl, 15, 121, 131, 208n11; the conflict with Matos over democracy for Cuba, 132–33; the coverage and support of by commercial Cuban television, 17, 130, 134–36, 143–50, 153–56; as Cuba's "bad boy," 114, 116–18, 121, 124, 146; as Cuba's leader-educator, 147, 148, 149–50, 153–55, 157, 165; the educational achievements of, 116, 117, 120, 173; the fight against illiteracy by, 166; the fight against racial discrimination by, 138–39, 159, 173; as the hub of Cuba's spectacles of revolution, 116–24, 130–32, 132–33, 134–43, 143–56, 157–62; the *humanism* of, 130, 132; the interviews of, 116–18, 132, 144, 152–53, 165–66; labeled a communist by the Batista government, 98, 107; the leadership of the 26th July Movement by, 66, 105, 107, 116–17; the messianic persona of, 130, 132–33, 158, 212n46; "minute of humor," 148, 152; the panel show as his preferred medium of communication, 135, 143, 147, 149–50, 152–53, 155–58, 161; photographic coverage of as a celebrity, 135, 146–47, 148, 155, 207n59; photographic coverage of in Sierra Maestra, 101, 116–17, 120–24; the political reforms of, 130–32; the popularity of, 144, 146, 147, 148, 155, 161–62, 212n49; portrayals of by actors, 135–37; the private-public reactions of Cubans to, 15, 19, 216n12; as rebel leader fighting for democracy, 10, 21, 114, 117, 124, 143; as reformer, 170, 208n11, 211n40, 215n6; scripted moments of "intimacy" with, 135, 146, 149; the self-acknowledgement of as a Marxist, 130, 162, 170; the socialist-nationalist regime of, 132–36, 140–41, 146, 153, 157–58, 161, 165; the speeches of, 132–35, 144, 146, 149, 153–56, 158, 165; U.S. characterization of as a dictator, 173, 174; U.S. coverage of his Sierra Maestra period, 10–11, 100–101, 105–6, 116–18, 120–24; the use of live programming by, 143–48, 149, 155–56, 157, 162, 172, 213n53; the use of personal drama and spectacle by, 18, 21, 116–17, 120–21, 147–48; the U.S. post-revolution appearances of, 150–53

Catholicism, 2, 9, 77–78, 79, 96, 200n93

CBS: *CBS Reports*, 173; *Rebels of the Sierra Maestra*, 21, 100, 106, 116–24, 158

censorship: the 1957 legalization of, 10, 100, 105–6, 109–12; the 1958 legalization of, 10, 127; the conversion of into advertising by its victims, 86–87; the financial damage produced by, 114–15; of the media in 1953 by Batista, 66; of men in drag, 92, 94–96, 207–8n77; of rock and roll, 112–14; the temporary suspension of by Batista, 106–7, 109, 115–16. *See also* suspension

Channel 2 (CMBA-TV), 45, 70, 197n48

Channel 4 (Unión Radio-TV), 23, 45, 54, 190–91n48

Channel 6 (CMQ-TV), 45, 54, 56

Channel 7 (CMBF-TV), 45, 70, 103, 112, 203n9

Channel 11 (TV Caribe, S.A.), 45, 70

Channel 12: as Tele-Rebelde, 141–43, 166, 211n36; under Pumarejo, 103, 131

children: as audience members, 96, 97, 111, 145; the censorship of child performers, 92, 94, 96; as performers, 63, 92–94; programming for, 37, 42, 56, 67–68, 77, 93

Christianity, 77, 79, 96

Cinema, 16, 17, 136

cinema. *See* film

civilization: displays of European as a

critics: as advocates of nationalistic programming, 55–58, 125–26, 135–39, 144, 146, 208–9n12; the biases of against non-European culture in Cuba, 9, 57–58, 77–78, 79–81, 85–86, 92–94; challenges to from the Cuban audience, 20, 65, 100, 167–68; changes in perspective regarding the role of Cuban television, 73, 167; on commercial television, 89; criticisms of specific programs by, 57, 125–26, 189n93; criticisms of television station owners by, 27, 88–89, 189n25; the dislike of advertising and consumerism among, 23, 39–40, 77, 88, 104–5, 167–68; film, 97–98; on morality and immorality in broadcasting, 38–39, 76–80, 84–86, 92–97, 113–15, 186n61; the opposition of to government interference in the media, 65–67, 87–88, 89–92, 94, 114–15; the opposition of to imported programs, 56–57, 104, 126–27; the opposition to censorship among, 57, 66, 84–85, 89–90, 97, 115; the perceptions of television technology as reflective of Cuban modernity, 1, 3, 8–9, 40–41, 52–56, 60, 65–66, 99–100; the perceptions the Cuban audience among, 9, 18, 73, 75–76, 78, 104; as political commentators, 66, 90–92, 97, 105; the power of television reviewers, 19, 167–68; the preferences of for a public broadcasting model for Cuba, 77, 157, 166; as self-perceived arbiters in programming, 23, 54–56, 79–81, 102, 149, 167–68, 190n48; and the striving for excellence in broadcasting, 39, 41, 43, 54–56, 65, 104–5; the support of broadcasting as an educational tool among, 75–77, 88–89, 140, 157, 166; the support of censorship among, 79–80; the support of cultural

programming on television by, 9, 77, 88–89, 104–5, 190n79. See also radio critics

Cuba: rural access to radio and television, 49; rural illiteracy in, 59, 140; the rural-urban divide in the modernization of, 9, 166, 192n67

Cubanness (cubanidad): as an ideology, 4, 14; as a response to counteract racial discrimination, 28, 56; the influence of on television, 21, 56–58, 73, 125–26, 139, 141; the redefinition of in Castro's Cuba, 133, 138, 139, 141, 158, 159, 162

Cuban Revolution: depictions of the in telenovelas, 134–36, 155, 158, 171; photographic coverage of the, 146; the polarizing impact of the, 13–16, 182n33

Curtin, Michael, 34, 103, 120, 173–74, 185–86n43, 207n62

dance: ballet, 72, 75–77, 88, 167–75; children performing Afro-Cuban, 93–94; erotic, 79–82, 92, 114; mambo, 80–84, 93, 94; racialized performance, 82, 92, 113; rock and roll, 98, 113; rumba, 79–82, 86, 93, 184n23, 195n16, 199n79; the sexuality of as a concern of regulators and critics, 39, 79–84, 92, 114

debates: Castro's use of panel shows for public, 135, 149; concerning Cubanness, 6; concerning morality, 21; concerning the introduction of television in Cuba, 6, 7, 12, 18, 43; continuing concerning Cuban television, 61, 91, 94, 102; the Nixon-Kennedy, 173, 174; public sociopolitical in Cuba, 36, 43, 92, 94, 140, 194n2

democracy: the 1940 constitution, 34, 43, 50, 81, 91–92, 212n49; the anticipated return to under Castro,

education: and advocacy for public broadcasting, 27–30, 68, 76, 89, 157, 195n6, 197n54; among Cuba's elite, 1, 9; as an element of Cuban modernity, 6, 24, 32, 36, 40–41, 73; as a topic of media-related legislation, 23–24, 30–31, 36–37, 42, 67–68, 76–77, 109–10; the combination of with entertainment in programming, 30; documentaries as tools for, 17, 120, 173, 207n62; formal in advertising, 35; formal in drama, 34; nationalist indoctrination of individuals into the Cuban Revolution, 157, 164, 169, 174–75; the overlap of with discussions of cultural programming, 23, 37, 40, 67, 75–76, 88; the overlap of with discussions of morality in the media, 21, 36, 79–80; in socialist Cuba, 131, 133, 140–42, 164–67, 174–75, 216–17n20; technical study, 29; television and radio as tools for, 24, 29–31, 36, 40, 42, 44, 75–76; the uneven access to in Cuba, 58–59, 159–60, 214n75. *See also* working class

El Mundo, 16, 70, 190–91n48

employment: and Cuban modernity, 3, 160, 175, 212n49, 218n43; labor conditions, 28, 117; labor strikes, 28, 98; for media professionals, 33, 42, 104, 144, 178, 185n42; unions, 19, 27, 43, 61, 126, 166, 191–92n57

Escalante, César, 170–71

Eurocentrism: as a complement to nationalist ideas of Cuban modernity, 5, 9, 24, 67, 91, 94, 99, 158; as a defining element of socioeconomic relations in Cuba, 4, 7, 9, 77–78, 90, 158; as evidence of Cuba's high civilization, 33, 39, 58, 93, 110–11

exiles, 13–14, 15, 18, 131, 156, 183n40, 216n12

Federation of Cuba's Broadcasters, 107

Fiallo, Delia, 127

film: actors as workers in socialist Cuba, 163–64; censorship of in Cuba, 66, 97, 112–13, 200n93; children's films, 77; cinema newsreels, 66, 97, 105, 108, 132, 135, 155; criticism, 97–98; the Cuban industry, 103–4, 163, 191–92n57, 217n23; Cuban-made depictions of Cuba, 82; in Cuban movie theaters, 97–98, 105, 113–14, 169–70; dubbing, 71, 104, 203n11; exiled Cuban filmmakers, 13–14; films as political messages and tools, 97, 103, 112–14, 123, 125–26, 170, 209n16; government monitoring of content, 97–98, 105, 111–12, 126–27; Hollywood articulations of U.S. vernacular culture, 31, 114, 118; the ICAIC, 131–32, 135, 146, 155, 163, 208n4, 217n23; the inclusion of imported English-language on television, 56, 61, 71, 168; the inclusion of imported on television, 42, 45–46, 68, 70, 100, 161, 177; the inclusion of imported Spanish-language on television, 61–62, 112, 192n58; the inclusion of in Cuban programming, 42, 60, 68, 97, 111; the influence of colonialism on Latin American, 9; kinescope, 60, 62, 70, 84, 104, 196n38; Movie Review Commission, 97, 111; Nichols on documentary filmmaking, 17, 120; in *paquetes,* 2196; *Rebels of the Sierra Maestra,* 21, 100, 106, 116–24, 125, 158, 173; versus television, 54; Yara Cinema, 1

folklore: the biases against among some Cuban modernists, 85–86, 93–94; the popularity in rural and working-class areas, 86; the popularizing of under Castro, 136, 138–39, 140

Ministry for the Recovery of Ill-Gotten Goods, 131, 141, 157

Ministry of Communication: as an arbiter of morality on television, 78, 87, 92–98, 105, 197n52, 199n79; as a political tool of the Batista regime, 107–10, 116; as a political tool of the Castro regime, 129, 134–35; the banning of child performers by the, 94, 96; the biased treatment of imported versus local programs, 97; Enrique Oltuski, 129, 134, 140, 207–8n77; the racial and sociocultural biases of the ministers heading the, 92; Ramón Vasconcelos, 88, 108–9, 112–13, 112–15, 138, 205n31; the regulation of radio transmissions by, 33; the relationship of with the CRE, 38, 87, 89, 93, 111–12, 115, 126–27; under Castro, 126–27, 171; the vendetta of the against rock and roll, 112–14

modernity: the conflicting indicators of in 1950s Cuba, 44, 50; Cuban broadcasting of, 7–8, 9–10, 59–60, 94; Cuba's indigenization of U.S. practices to achieve, 35–36; Cuba's use of the United States as a basis for assessing its own, 4, 8–9, 20, 183n3; individual self-identity and, 5–6, 8, 41; national manifestations of, 5, 78, 182n24; the socialist concept of, 160–61, 165; technology as an indicator of, 1–2, 6, 8, 43, 44, 137. See also broadcasting of modernity

morality: racialized concepts of, 63, 77, 79–82; self-regulation by radio stations, 186n61; Vasconcelos's supervision of Cuban, 108, 112–14

movies. See film

movie theaters, 97–98, 113

mulatos and mestiza, 4–5, 28, 43, 80–82, 93, 159. See also working class

music: Abakuá, 86, 197n44; Afro-Cuban as a nationalist symbol under Castro, 136, 138–39, 155, 161; as a topic of Cuban critics, 77, 114; attempts to censor in Cuba, 82, 84, 92–94; censorship of sexual references in Cuban, 39, 85; classical in Cuba, 40; Cuban musicians, 34, 72, 86, 93, 185n42, 195n21, 197n48; on Cuban radio, 30, 35; on Cuban television, 42, 77; the globalized taste of post-communist bloc Cubans, 177, 219n6; the influence of Afro-Cuban culture on popular, 77, 86, 199n79; live musical shows, 30; rock and roll, 112–14; rumba, 79, 86, 184n23, 195n16; and sexuality in Cuba, 82; variety show performances, 34, 72, 77, 79–80, 82, 92, 136

nationalism: Batista's assertions regarding Cuban, 100, 107; and discourses of Cuban socioeconomic problems, 64; the exaltation of in television variety shows, 136–37; the influence of on Cuban broadcasting laws, 25; the interconnections of civilization and morality with Cuban, 110; and the representation of Cubanness, 4, 14, 55, 159; and revolution in Cuba, 117, 126, 130, 132–33, 139, 161, 208n11; television technology as a symbol of Cuban, 65

NBC: affiliations with Cuban networks, 203n3; the high-culture programming of, 40, 56; Meet the Press, 57, 152, 153; The Steve Allen Show, 124–26

neocolonialism, 4–5, 9, 11, 25, 168, 182n24, 190n44

newspapers: the coverage of Castro by, 121, 126, 147–48, 155; discussions concerning media-related legislation in, 23–24, 27; discussions concerning morality in entertainment programming in, 81, 108, 112–13; discussions concerning television in, 39, 52, 59, 126; government monitoring and censorship of, 66, 98, 105, 106, 108, 198–99n73; Matthews's *New York Times* articles on Castro, 10, 100–101, 105, 106, 116–17, 124, 132; *New York Times,* 48–49, 125, 165, 167; in post-revolutionary Cuba, 171, 208–9n12, 215–16nn11-12; the powers of critics, 19; the spectrum of in pre-Castro Cuba, 16–17, 183n36; and their audiences, 18; working class Cubans as topics but not participants of discussion, 18–19, 42

newsreels, 66, 97, 105, 108, 132, 135, 155

news shows: as basic to public and commercial programming, 30, 35, 42, 45, 67, 77, 103; Batista's censorship, monitoring, and suppression of, 66, 87, 98, 105–10, 114–15; as constructs of truth and reality, 134–35, 207n62; coverage of the Cuban Revolution on, 134–35, 148, 156, 213n68; the production of, 185n41; in socialist Cuba, 156, 168, 172, 177

Nixon-Kennedy debates, 173, 174, 218n44

Noticias de Hoy, 16, 17

Nye, David E., 12, 24

Oltuski, Enrique, 129, 134, 140, 207–8n77

opera, 30, 40, 75, 76, 88, 175

palimpsest, 178–79

panel shows: *Ante la prensa* (Meet the press), 57, 66, 144, 148, 149, 157; as a topic for Cuban television critics, 84; as Castro's preferred genre for communication, 133, 134–35, 143, 147, 149–53, 155–58, 161; *El estudio vacio* (The empty studio), 108, 115; *El pueblo pregunta* (The people ask), 141; *Face the Nation* (CBS), 150,

152; the inclusion of in prime time television, 45, 54, 171; *Meet the Press* (NBC), 57, 152, 153; *Mesa redonda* (Roundtable), 97, 157, 176, 177, 178; as sites for Cuban political commentary, 57, 149; *Telemundo pregunta* (Telemundo asks), 145, 157, 212n49; the use of low-budget as television filler, 71, 76

paquetes, 61, 219n6

Pérez, Emma, 56, 75, 88–90, 105, 198–99n73

Pérez, Louis A.: on the mobster influence in Cuba, 34–35; on Castro's reforms, 131, 158; on the Cuban national identity, 4, 5–6, 8, 35, 46, 48, 100

Pérez-Stable, Marifeli, 91, 155, 212n49

Pinar del Río Province, 63–65

Platt Amendment, 28, 32

poetry, 30, 42, 136, 167

popular culture: Cuban media oriented to, 16; Cuba's vernacular culture as an element of its, 9, 86, 93, 96; in Havana, 34, 48; the non-European elements of Cuba's, 9, 31, 76–77, 114, 136, 177; in television programming, 30

population: as a factor in the expansion of television, 3, 25, 31, 60, 73, 145; Cuba's rural, 59, 64; the distribution of in Cuba, 192n67, 212n42; and the distribution of socioeconomic resources in Cuba, 39, 160, 171

pornography, 96, 97

Prensa Libre, 16, 17

programming. *See* radio programming; television programming

propaganda: Cold War ideological, 114; commercial, 68, 165; socialist in Cuba, 12, 146, 169, 170–71, 214n80, 216–17n20, 218n51; uses of the imagery of the revolution as, 146, 174; versus advertising, 171

Puerto Rico, 19, 40, 103–4, 136, 203n11

Pumarejo, Gaspar, 45, 103, 131, 140–41, 169, 190–91n48, 198n66

Quevedo, Miguel Angel, 216n12
Quiroga, José: on Cuban television as a palimpsest, 178–79; on the revolutionary glamour of Castro and his army, 124, 146, 207n59, 214n80

racism, 28, 43, 93, 138–39, 199n79; discrimination, 25, 62, 187n72; "racial time" in Cuba, 159–60
radio: the 1934 radio law, 27–30; the 1939 radio law, 25, 31–34, 75, 110; the 1942 radio law, 36; the 1950 radio law, 41; audience, 23, 49; broadcasting frequencies, 26, 27, 29, 32, 41–42, 48–49, 185n37; broadcast licensing, 26, 27, 29, 32, 38, 41, 185n37, 187n70; broadcast stations in Cuba, 26; the Code of Radio Ethics, 38–39; Giró on the law of, 23; imported music, 26; ownership in Cuban households, 14, 26, 130; production, 25, 34, 35–36, 37–38; public, 26–27; radio listeners' rights, 23; radionovelas, 31, 127; Radio Rebelde, 127; signals, 32, 121, 185n37; the U.S. model of, 23
radio broadcasting: the regulation of, 32, 36, 38, 171; telegraphy and telephony laws applied to, 25, 26, 29
Radiocentro, 1–2, 59, 191n49
radio critics: discussions of legislation of radio by, 23, 27; discussions of radio production practices by, 38; discussions of the introduction of television by, 39–40, 43, 52, 75. See also critics
radio networks: advertising on, 23, 26–28, 30, 33–34, 37, 42, 76; the displacement of radio stations by, 35; as elements of Cuban media businesses, 58, 71; as elements of transnational businesses, 37; the growth of in Cuba, 35; legislation regulating, 37; the presence of government censors at, 109

radio programming: advertising-to-programming ratios, 34; the advocacy of educational by Cuba's critics, 23; the aficionado category, 42, 185n41; as a means of displaying Cuban modernity, 31; based on the public station model, 29–30; the categories of, 33, 37, 42; for children, 37; the Code of Radio Ethics, 38–39; CRE monitoring of entertainment, 38; daily, 35; the elements of the 1934 radio law concerning, 27–28, 29; the elements of the 1939 radio law concerning, 31, 33–34; the elements of the 1942 radio law concerning, 36–37; featuring Cuban talent and themes, 27, 30, 37; government monitoring of and intervention in, 36, 37; legal parameters for the cultural elements of, 30; legal parameters for the educational elements of, 30, 36; legal parameters for the entertainment elements of, 30, 38–39; legal parameters for the informative elements of, 36; live shows as an element of, 30; mechanical, 185n42; morality and decency as concerns in, 38; program production expenses, 30; public, 30; recorded music, 30, 185n42; scheduling during the infancy of Cuban, 27–28; station owners' responsibilities for, 33, 36, 37
radio programs, 31, 54–55
radio stations: the displacement of by radio networks, 35; the effects on of Batista's 1957 amendment to the 1953 Broadcasting Law, 109–16; owners of, 28, 33, 36, 37, 38, 49, 185n42; the presence of government censors at,

Spain, 1, 59, 61, 64, 104, 203n11

Special Period, 18, 58, 178

spectacles of decency: the absorption of by the spectacles of revolution, 11, 134, 161; the functions of as obscuring mechanisms, 91, 99; government regulation of censorship and morality, 20–21; the interconnections of with democracy, progress, and revolution in Cuba, 7–8, 11, 12, 72, 134, 161; the purpose of Cuba's, 9

spectacles of democracy: the absorption of by the spectacles of revolution, 11, 100–101, 105; as a political illusion created by Batista, 10, 11, 21, 105, 107, 109, 115–16; the interconnections of with decency, progress, and revolution, 7–8, 11, 12, 72, 134, 161; and the U.S. audience, 10, 21, 107, 115–16

spectacles of progress: as a narration of Cuban success, 99; contradictions to these representations, 20, 44, 50–51, 99; economic and technological modernization as the point of reference for, 8, 65, 100; the interconnections of with decency, democracy, and revolution in Cuba, 7–8, 11, 12, 72, 134, 161; television technology as integral to Cuba's, 8–9, 20, 72, 168; the U.S. as a point of reference for Cuban, 8–9, 100.

spectacles of revolution: the absorption of complementary Cuban spectacles by the, 11, 133–34; Castro's political manipulation of Cuba's, 10, 136, 143–56, 162; the interconnections of with democracy, progress, and decency, 7–8, 10–12, 21, 72, 134, 161; the January 1959 inceptions of Cuba's, 11; and the production of a new concept of modernity, 161, 164–65; and the redefinition of Cubanness, 11–12, 28,

31, 168–69, 171–72; the U.S. media as a facilitator of Cuba's, 10–11, 21, 100–101, 105–6, 116–17

sponsors. See advertising; radio networks; television sponsors

sports programming, 30, 42, 45, 105, 164

Steve Allen Show, The (NBC), 124–26

sugar industry, 28, 34, 41, 48, 63–64, 71, 192n65

surveys: conducted between 1956 and 1957 of literacy among Cubans, 59; of television viewing in Castro's Cuba, 143, 145, 167, 176–77; of television viewing patterns among Cubans, 18–19, 68, 76, 80, 99, 191n56, 198n66

suspension: CRE powers of, 38–39, 84, 126, 139, 196n33, 199n74; the government power of over artists and broadcasting stations, 33, 95–96, 98, 108–9, 112, 114, 197n52; the politically motivated of Batista's media critics, 105, 107–8, 112, 114–16. See also censorship

Taber, Robert, 116–24, 117

technology. See radio technology; television technology

telenovelas: the influence of on Cuban morals, 88, 98, 114; the influence of the Cuban Revolution on, 134–36, 155, 158; the popularity of in Cuba, 13, 167, 178, 189n30; soap operas, 13, 129, 158, 171

Tele-Rebelde (Channel 12), 141–43, 166

television: as a tool for Cuban cultural affirmation, 100, 134; audiences, 12, 65, 68, 76, 100, 147, 175; color, 8, 103, 140, 143, 203n9; commercial networks, 48, 134, 137, 142; Cuban as a palimpsest, 178–79; early participants in the development of Cuban, 15–16; the influence of political events on, 6, 66, 130, 140, 211n36;

the infrastructure requirements for,
60; the portrayal of commercial as a
capitalist tool, 11, 170; prime-time, 54,
88, 134, 153, 177, 189n30, 197n48; the
role of in facilitating the Cuban Revolution, 17, 21, 130, 146–47, 155–58,
161–62; technical staff, 11, 19, 38, 42,
45, 50, 55
television broadcasting, 12, 143, 196n38,
213n53
television networks: as Castro's preferred medium of communication,
143–50, 155–58, 161; the coverage of
Castro's takeover of Cuba, 158; the
effects on of Batista's 1957 amendment to the 1953 Broadcasting Law,
109–16; the influence and growth of
in Cuba, 1, 8, 48, 60, 63, 99, 102–3;
the influence of U.S. programs on
Cuban, 40, 71; the infrastructure
requirements to support, 58, 60; legislation regarding programming for,
42; the nationalization of Cuba's, 131,
160, 165–67, 191–92n57; the presence
of government censors at, 109; proposals for transnational Cuban-U.S.,
103–4; Tele-Rebelde, 141–43, 166
television productions: assessments
of by critics, 54, 56–58, 104, 168;
in Castro's Cuba, 58, 132–34, 137,
139, 142, 159, 165; censorship as an
impediment to, 66, 97; the coverage
of costs for by sponsors, 61; Cuban,
42, 46–48, 68, 76, 97, 104, 161; Cuban
mastery in, 47–48, 50, 99–100, 168,
191n49, 192n58; the Cubanness of
as a point of evaluation, 56–57, 73;
as evidence of Cuban technological
modernity, 2, 6, 8–9, 11, 50, 59–60;
the socialist influence on Cuban, 165,
169–70, 171, 175
television programming: the 1954
transformations in, 71–74, 76–77,

194n91; the 1957 legal amendments
and censorship of, 109–11, 115; the
aficionado category, 67–68; the
alterations to under the 1953 law, 20,
67–68, 71; as a means of displaying
Cuban modernity, 3, 6, 7, 52, 134, 165,
190–91nn48-49; audience criticisms
of, 60, 61–62, 65, 167–68; the audience profile as a consideration for,
68, 75–76, 104–5; Castro's disruption
of the flows of, 21, 143–50, 156, 165;
the categories of, 42, 67–68, 77; the
critics' role in assessing, 54, 56, 60,
88–89, 92–93; Cubanness as an issue
in, 56; culturally-oriented, 67, 76–77,
88–89, 105, 109–10, 142; disruptions
versus media events, 213–14n70;
distributors, 45–46; during Cuba's
Special Period, 18; educational, 68,
76–77, 109–10, 142, 165; the elements
of the 1950 television law concerning, 41–42; the enabling role of in
Cuba's spectacles of revolution, 10,
11; entertainment, 67, 84–85, 89–90,
111–15, 127; featuring Cuban talent
and themes, 42, 190n48; featuring
morally questionable personalities,
200n85; fictional and nonfictional
inspired by the Cuban Revolution,
21; following the nationalization of
Cuba's media industries, 22; globalization and Cuba's underground,
176–78; government monitoring and
intervention in, 20–21, 87–88, 89–92,
105, 108–15, 127; historic preservation of early Cuban, 18; the impact
of dubbing on, 104, 203n11; imports
from foreign countries included in,
42, 214–15n85; imports from the
U.S. included in, 70–71, 102, 104–5;
the inclusion of appearances by
world-famous performers, 99; the
limited funding available for, 61;

television programming (*continued*)
live, 26, 30, 37, 42, 68, 146, 185n42; locally-produced, 42, 45, 68, 71, 104, 161, 168; as the means for displaying spectacles of decency, 9; mechanical, 42, 68; morality as a concern in defining "appropriate," 2, 78–81, 89–90, 105, 111–15, 198n66; morning, 56; news-related, 105, 108–9, 114–15; packaged programming, 61; political interruptions of, 65–66; the popularity of variety shows, 76, 77, 79–81, 168, 190–91n48, 216–17n20; pretelevision discussions regarding, 23–25, 40–41, 52, 73, 75; *programas paquetes,* 61; the propaganda-oriented nature of commercial, 12, 171; of public broadcasting stations, 67, 89, 142, 166; recorded, 68, 70, 104; the reliance of early Cuban on old products, 61; revolution-oriented nationalistic in Castro's Cuba, 141–42, 161, 168, 173–74; the socialist influence on Cuba's, 140–42, 149, 166–68, 171, 216–17n20; sports broadcasts, 8, 52, 189n25; by Tele-Rebelde, 141–43, 166; U.S. influences on Cuban, 41, 48, 56–57, 168

television programs: adaptations of radio programs, 54–55; adaptations of U.S. television programs, 56–57, 100, 168; baseball game broadcasts, 8, 52–53, 72, 89n25, 102; the double standards for local versus imported, 111, 127; entertainment shows, 54, 88, 92, 111, 127, 134–35, 141; the focus on the Cuban Revolution of, 134, 137; game shows, 71, 168; giveaway programs, 102; imported programs and movies from the U.S., 70–71, 104, 126–27, 161, 177; legal allowances for imported movies and programs, 42, 45, 56, 68; literary adaptations,

135, 140, 142, 161, 172; live shows, 8, 37, 84, 93, 104, 146–47; music shows, 71, 197n48; old Spanish-language movies, 61; panel shows, 45, 54, 57, 62, 71, 76, 149–51; panel shows as Castro's preferred medium of communication, 133–35, 143, 147, 149–51, 152–53, 155–58, 161

television sets: baseball as an incentive for Cuban ownership of, 189n25; the ownership of in early 1950s Cuba, 46–57; the ownership of in late 1950s Cuba, 99, 143; provisions of for Cuban schools, 166

television sponsors: American, 106, 126; the elimination of in Cuba, 165; as factors needed for the existence of programs, 45, 61, 99, 139, 190–91n48, 215n9; the power of over program content, 40, 88, 89, 90, 144, 166–67. *See also* advertising

television stations: the effects on of Batista's 1957 amendment to the 1953 Broadcasting Law, 109–16; the first three years of growth, 8, 45–47, 76–77; the management of censorship by owners of, 66–67, 79, 84, 87–88; the nationalization of under Castro, 140, 160; the owners of, 8, 19, 54, 99, 102–4; the plight of owners under Castro, 144, 155, 166; the presence of government censors at, 109; protests by owners of against government interference, 90, 94; the susceptibility of to economic crisis, 71, 103

television technology: as a contradiction to Cuban socioeconomic realities, 6–7, 24–25, 50; as a factor of the Cuban Revolution, 10–11, 12, 24–25, 50; as a technology of both the present and the future, 44; as the basis for Cuba's broadcasting of its modernity, 1–2, 6–9, 20, 24, 41, 50, 73; critics' commentaries regarding production quality, 54, 55, 57, 60, 65; critics' commentaries regarding the applications of, 24, 39–40, 41–42, 52, 76, 84, 140; Cuban expertise in, 38, 47–48, 52, 72, 99–100, 168, 190–91n48; Cuban technical achievements in, 8, 11, 52, 102–3; the embrace of by the Cuban public, 47, 49, 52; its deteriorated state during the Special Period, 17–18; legislation concerning Cuban, 3, 7, 24–25, 41–44; in revolutionary and socialist Cuba, 137, 147, 156, 163–64, 172, 175; the unevenness of the spread of in Cuba, 63–65, 78; the U.S. as a point of reference for Cuban, 3, 8, 24–25, 39–40, 52, 183n3

theater: as a topic for Cuban television critics, 40, 54, 84; the culturally elevating aura of in Cuba, 40, 75–76, 140, 161, 167, 172, 175; live television as performance, 213n53; television adaptations of, 45, 142, 170

transmissions: as the broadcasting of Cuban modernity, 3, 6, 8, 60, 73, 126; Castro's exploitation of media, 137, 146, 147, 155–56, 170; Cuban radio, 26–27, 29, 30–31, 33; expansions of in Cuba, 63, 66, 71; improvements in Cuban technology, 45–46, 52–53, 60, 72, 102; kinescopes, 60, 62, 70, 84, 104, 196n38; legislation concerning, 36, 41–42, 68, 92; by Radio Rebelde, 127; retransmissions, 62; television, 45

26th of July Movement: American coverage of the, 10, 21, 105, 107, 117–18, 122–24; as a milestone in Cuban history, 116, 215n10; and the desire to reinstate democracy in Cuba, 131–32; media depictions and reenactments

of the, 120, 122, 134, 135, 142; the Radio Rebelde programs of the, 127

Unión Radio-TV (Channel 4), 23; as a business venture of Gaspar Pumarejo, 58–60, 80; the conversion of to TV Nacional, 70; critical reviews of programs broadcast on, 55–56; the technological innovations by, 39, 43, 52, 54, 190–91n48

unions, 19, 27, 43, 61, 126, 166, 191–92n57

United States, the support of Castro's revolution among African American militants, 173–74, 218n46

Uruguay, 39, 48

USSR, 14–15, 130, 132, 152, 162–63, 172, 178

variety shows: as a topic for Cuban television critics, 54, 56, 75–76, 79, 102, 167–68; the attempts by authorities to regulate, 88, 92, 95, 112; on Cuban radio, 185n41; the inclusion of Afro-Cuban culture performances on, 82, 86, 93, 195n21; the inclusion of high-culture performances on, 18; the inclusion of in prime time television, 45; the popularity of in Cuba, 76, 77, 79–81, 190–91n48, 216–17n20; as the primary medium for exalting Cuban culture under Castro, 136–37, 138–39; references to the Cuban Revolution in, 134, 135, 136, 142, 155, 158; *The Steve Allen Show* (NBC), 124–26; the use of low-budget as television filler, 71

Vasconcelos, Ramón: the oversight of morality in the Cuban media by, 88, 112–13, 114, 115, 138; the self-justifications of for his acts of censorship, 108–9, 205n31

Venezuela, 40, 48, 179, 216n12, 216–17n20